Structured
Programming
in APL

WINTHROP COMPUTER SYSTEMS SERIES

Gerald M. Weinberg, *editor*

Future Titles

Structured Programming in APL

Dennis P. Geller

Daniel P. Freedman

School of Advanced Technology
State University of New York at Binghamton

Winthrop Publishers, Inc.

Cambridge, Massachusetts

Library of Congress Cataloging in Publication Data

Geller, Dennis P.
    Structured programming in APL.

    (Winthrop computer systems series)
    Includes index.
    1. APL (Computer program language) I. Freedman,
Daniel P.,   joint author.   II. Title.
QA76.A27G44   001.6'424   75-41472
ISBN 0-87626-859-9

TO

NAOMI

NORIE

AND THE BELLMAN

"Just the place for a Snark!" the Bellman cried,
    As he landed his crew with care;
Supporting each man on the top of the tide
    By a finger entwined in his hair.

From *The Hunting of the Snark* by Lewis Carroll, originally published in 1876 by Macmillan Publishing Co., Inc.

Contents

Foreword

APL has earned such a reputation for disorderly conduct that "structured APL" rings as off-key as "immaculate pigsty" or "honest politician." Yet we must not blame the language for the disorderly conduct of its users—or misusers. In the hands of responsible and properly educated programmers, APL becomes a marvelously disciplined tool, a tool unlike any other programming language in common use.

The problem, of course, lies in the phrase "properly educated." For too long, in too many places, APL users have learned their language "in the streets," as any examination of their programs would show. Their textbooks are little more than reference manuals, and offer no corrective to the worst effects of oral tradition. Users trained in the "traditional" APL manner may be unaware of many useful APL features, misuse features they know, underuse features they believe they have mastered, waste mind-boggling amounts of time and space and energy, and generally fail to achieve the satisfaction that such a refined tool as APL can offer.

Dennis Geller and Daniel Freedman, having watched hundreds of APLemmings follow one another to a fate worse than death, have decided to offer something different. What they offer is a sensible, well-considered, experience-based method of capturing APL's problem-solving power. Through a step-by-step development which all can follow—yet which is not offensive to the potential programming genius—

they show how APL can once more be the servant, and stop being the master.

Structured Programming in APL represents precisely the mixture of theory and experience, excellence of presentation, and recognition of the human aspects of programming that we hope will characterize the Winthrop Computer Systems Series. To an increasing extent, our future society is being created by the people who design and build our computer system—in agriculture and airlines, in banking and building, in communications and colleges. What facet of life remains untouched by their creations? If their job is well done, human life can attain quality beyond dreaming; if poorly done, human life can become an inferno. For these programmers, project leaders, analysts, and designers, the Winthrop Computer Systems Series will provide tools and techniques, emphasizing:

1. *Practicality*, including the recognition that *good* theory is the most pragmatic of tools.
2. *Excellence of presentation*—writing, organization, examples, and supplementary aids.
3. *The complex role of human beings*, both as creators and as users of computer systems.

Structured Programming in APL is a marvelous example of the combination of these three points of view. Indeed, *because* of the authors' appreciation of the complex role of human beings as creators of computer systems, anyone using APL will find this book immensely *practical*. Experience with this material in the authors' courses for professional and nonprofessional programmers has shown that their method *works*:

1. Students reach a given point of competence much faster than under previous methods.
2. Students progress beyond the limits of what was feasible under less disciplined approaches.
3. The cost of instruction, both in machine time and instructor time, is lowered.

I have witnessed the results this approach can yield, results which I believe are in the *true* spirit of APL. I myself learned APL at the feet of Ken Iverson in 1960, long before any implementation existed. At that time, we saw "Iverson notation" as one more tool to aid the thinking of the professional programmer, never dreaming that it would attain the wide range of uses it enjoys today. We could never, at that time, imagine the kind of abuse that APL sometimes gets today, and even now I cringe at some of the amateurish practices committed in the name of "the spirit of APL." What Geller and Freedman have done is to combine the *fun* of APL with the more mature *enjoyment* of the trained mind focussing a sharp tool on a real problem. That is what we are trying to achieve in this Series, and that is what any concerned instructor is trying to do in his/her life's work.

Gerald M. Weinberg

Series Editor

Preface

This is an introductory book on programming and on the computer language, APL. We have developed and tested it in classes, at various levels, for three years: it is suitable for beginning programming students from junior college to graduate school, for in-house education in industry, or for self-study by experienced programmers who wish to learn APL. This book embodies an approach which is quite different from the other books now available. Our aim is to bring the student very early to the point of writing working programs: further details on our approach and how to use the book most effectively are presented in the following paragraphs.

The book falls naturally into three sections of three chapters each. The first section deals with the basic concepts of programming and of APL: we introduce structure charts for describing algorithms, and then examine the data structures and operators of APL. The chapters in the second section teach the student to write programs from algorithms which have been expressed as structure charts. The third section deals with the design and development of programs, and of systems of programs. Also, sprinkled throughout the book, are Interludes which discuss important mechanical aspects of APL: signing on, creating and saving workspaces, using APL as an aid to debugging.

The book has been designed to be flexible, to be adaptable to the requirements of different teaching and learning situations. This flexibility manifests itself in a number of ways. The Interludes are not closely tied to the chapters they follow and may be taken up at any time. Since APL is often taught in half courses, or in combination with other languages, the last three chapters are independent of each other; although they do present different material, if time is limited any one or two can be chosen to complete the course. Conversely, there would be little conflict if the instructor desired to present additional material on collateral topics, such as computer organization or analysis of algorithms.

A *Teacher's Manual* is available as a companion to the book, containing suggestions for teaching from the text, and for additional material which might be presented. The *Manual* also contains a large number of classroom tested "visuals"—these can be detached and copied on transparencies for overhead projection.

AN APPROACH TO APL

The typical approach to teaching APL has focused on the versatility of the language while essentially ignoring programming concepts. Most of the written material on APL likewise concentrates on APL's powerful operators, with discussion of programming virtually limited to the mechanics of entering programs into the system. We know of a course in APL in which students were not required to write a single program!

This book is based on quite a different approach, one to which we were led by our experience teaching APL and other languages. Students do not (and there is no reason why they should) have innate talents for designing algorithms; thus, most of their trouble comes not from learning the language but from using it to write programs which do what they are supposed to do.

The basis of programming is the design of correct algorithms: much of what this involves is language independent, and while APL may be a richer language than many others, using it effectively still involves programming. Thus, our approach is to emphasize programming in APL; this approach has been used by others, with equally satisfactory results (see: T. Plum and G. M. Weinberg, "Teaching structured programming attitudes, even in APL, by example," *SIGSCE Bulletin*, February, 1974).

Our approach to programming begins in Chapter 1. We introduce structure charts (developed by I. Nassi and B. Schneiderman, in "Flowchart techniques for structured programming," *SIGPLAN Notices*, August, 1973) as a vehicle for expressing algorithms. Later, when students begin programming in APL they first learn to express their structure charts as APL programs.

Chapters 2 and 3 discuss the data structures and operators of APL. Our approach here, especially as regards the operators, capitalizes on the interactive nature of the language. We do not discuss each operator in detail: rather than teach the operators, we teach how to learn about the operators. Naturally, students need guidance when approaching any programming language, but they also need to develop the confidence and skills to learn (and review) by themselves. Chapter 3 discusses a number of operators, but also presents general principles which provide a framework for learning about the others. This learning is encouraged by the exercises, in which students are led to find out about operators not covered in the text.

Chapters 4 through 6 deal with the fundamentals of programming in APL. First, in Chapter 4, we present the concept of a program. Here, too, we cover the mechanics of entering and modifying programs. Chapter 5 introduces program structures for making choices, and Chapter 6 presents the concept of looping. We rely heavily on a set of three small utility programs which are listed in Appendix Four. Two are used to help strengthen the correspondence between the structure chart and the APL program: they contribute significantly to the readability of the programs, and help the students differentiate between statements which "do" something and statements which alter the flow of control. The third utility program is equally simple, and is used by the programmer to stop program execution when certain conditions are detected. From the very first program, verifying the validity of the input and of certain internal conditions, and programming for soft failures when these errors are detected, are essential features of all our programs. These utility programs should be placed in a workspace and introduced to the students when called for by the text.

Chapters 7, 8, and 9 build upon the basic skills presented thus far to illustrate the processes of program design and development. Each presents essentially the same process of moving from a design to a working program, and then refining the program to meet additional constraints. The emphases are slightly different, though: Chapter 7 concentrates on the construction of a program package, while Chapters 8 and 9 go further in emphasizing additional features of design and development. The three chapters provide a gradual introduction to producing large systems of programs, but if time is limited any one can be used as an example of the process.

The exercises are used to reinforce and extend the material presented in the chapters. They also present alternatives, either of approach or of detail. While such alternatives should probably not be emphasized too heavily in a first programming course, it is important that students get an early appreciation of the fact that there is more than one way to approach a problem, and that different approaches have different advantages and drawbacks.

The Interludes discuss the mechanical aspects: signing on, workspaces, system commands, debugging. All of our programming was done in APL/360, and it would be unrealistic to expect this not to be reflected in the text. However, we have collected almost all of the system dependent material into the Interludes, and explain more than once that the student may very likely be using a different system, with slightly difference features. The experiential approach to learning helps here, encouraging the student to actively discover those features which are different.

Overall, our approach is to present the fundamentals of programming in APL. Students may go on from here to learn to write faster programs, or more compact programs, or more aesthetic programs: this, we hope, is where they will learn to write *working* programs.

Acknowledgements

The book has benefited, in all stages of its development, from the able assistance of a number of good friends. Many people helped produce usable drafts from illegible scribblings: they include Debby King, Debby West, Jessica Brown, Charlotte McElfresh, and Andrea Birnbaum. Cheryl Plum and Helen Tarbell kept track of the various pieces as they floated around and introduced some organization to our chaos. Steven Schustack provided some valuable classroom testing, and many students suffered through the early drafts. We were lucky indeed to have editorial advice which helped us make significant improvements in the style and organization of the material. Naomi Geller and Gerald Weinberg helped point out the ten percent more work which was needed to make the book one hundred percent better.

Special thanks are also due to Al McBride of the IBM Endicott Sales office for making the production of the final copies of the figures possible, and to both Norie Yasukawa of SUNY Binghamton and Sister Miriam Teresa O'Donnell, R.S.M., of College Misericordia for their superior proofreading.

But most of all, we are grateful to B. Huntington Snark, without whom this book would have been written bottom up.

Structured
Programming
in APL

1

Algorithms and Structure Charts

He had bought a large map representing the sea,
  Without the least vestige of land:
And the crew were much pleased when they found it to be
  A map they could all understand.

"What's the good of Mercator's North Poles and Equators,
  Tropics, Zones, and Meridian Lines?"
So the Bellman would cry: and the crew would reply
  "They are merely conventional signs!

"Other maps are such shapes, with their islands and capes!
  But we've got our brave Captain to thank"
(So the crew would protest) "that he's bought us the best—
  A perfect and absolute blank!"

There is more to programming a digital computer than writing instructions for it in one of the many arcane "computer languages," such as APL. To program a digital computer is to ask it to perform some task and, quite obviously, we should decide what we want the computer to do before we give it any instructions.

However, it is not enough even to know what we want done! We must know *how* we want it done. If we want to have the computer print a large picture of Snoopy, for example, someone must first tell the computer which of the symbols in the picture goes where. This involves two distinct, but related, tasks. The programmer must first decide where each symbol goes and must then communicate this information to the computer.

Before we begin our study of how to communicate with the computer, we will investigate the process of setting up a problem; we will, in fact, develop certain standard forms for expressing the solution to a problem, and later will see that these forms enable us to communicate our solution method to the computer, often with very little trouble. Unfortunately, despite our best efforts and those of our colleagues, there is no technique which will guarantee that we will have absolutely no trouble communicating with a computer. Computers are sometimes unreliable, and occasionally unstable, but most of all they are picky. They will do *exactly* what you tell them to do. Unfortunately, what you tell them and what you *think* you are telling them are often very different. Much of the job of getting a program written and running is like communicating with a grammarian in a language that you don't know very well. Eventually, you will phrase your request just so, and you'll be told where the toilet is.

ALGORITHMS

Our dictionary defines *algorithm* as:

algorithm   al-go-rithm   *n*, in *mathematics*, any special method of solving a certain kind of problem; specifically, the repetitive calculations used in finding the greatest common divisor of two numbers (Euclid's Algorithm).

These days it is common to define an algorithm more informally, as a recipe for doing some job. Algorithms are not at all constrained to mathematical problems. Any set of directions is an algorithm for getting from one place to another. When a teacher tells you, "You will have to write two 10 page papers and one 25 page paper, and score above 89 percent on the final exam," that is an algorithm for passing the course. And as our informal definition suggests, a recipe for baking a loaf of bread is also an algorithm.

For example, consider the following recipe:

Helen's Irish Cake (like a bread)

3 cups flour	1 tbsp. shortening
1 or 2 eggs	1 to 1¼ cups milk
4 tsp. baking powder	1 tsp. cinnamon
½ tsp. salt	1 tsp. nutmeg
caraway seeds, as desired	½ pkg. (approx.) raisins

Beat all ingredients together, adding raisins last (add nuts if desired). Pour into greased loaf pan, and bake in slow, 325 degree oven about 1 hour.

Recipes, like knitting instructions, are sometimes written in a specialized language, and simple words often contain a great deal of meaning. While "beat all ingredients together" may seem to be a fairly clear instruction, the novice cook may be unsure as to exactly what is meant by "1 to 1¼ cups milk." We can set this same recipe down in a step by step fashion, as it might be explained to a novice.

Helen's Irish Cake (like a bread)

1. Sift 3 cups of flour with 4 tsp. baking powder and 1 tsp. salt.
2. Beat 1 or 2 eggs slightly with ½ cup sugar and add to flour mixture.
3. Add 1 tbsp. shortening and the spices (1 tsp. each of cinnamon and nutmeg).
4. If one egg was used, add 1¼ cups milk; if 2 eggs were used, add 1 cup milk.
5. Stir until fairly smooth. This is the *batter*.
6. Add caraway seeds and raisins and chopped nuts (optional).
7. Grease a loaf pan; pour batter into pan.
8. Bake in 325 degree oven. Test after 50 minutes by inserting a wooden pick into the middle. If it comes out clean, remove loaf from oven; if not, continue baking another 5–10 mins. until wooden pick comes out clean.
9. Let cool on wire rack for 10 mins. before turning pan to inverted position.
10. Remove from pan when almost cool.

We didn't go through all this so that you could try the recipe (although you should!) but because even so simple a thing as a recipe exhibits the same properties and structure as more complicated algorithms.

For example, a property which is basic to almost all algorithms is that it takes fewer steps to express a task than it does to execute it! In this example, which is rather simple as algorithms go, what we have listed as step 5 actually may require many minutes of stirring. Also, it is very rare to find an algorithm that specifies every action to the minutest detail. Step 8 does not begin:

> Open oven door. Lift baking pan off counter with two hands. Place on middle rack of oven. Close oven door gently. Set timer for 50 minutes.

However, anyone who is going to make this cake had better know how to do all these things when it comes time to execute step 8. Algorithms are usually expressed in steps "one level lower" than the task they are designed for. If this recipe were being made out for someone who didn't know how to open the oven door, there would probably be a separate algorithm written up to explain that step in more detail. That way, the basic plan of the recipe would be clear, and the specialized instructions would be accessible without cluttering things up.

For another example of an algorithm, suppose that you have the job of instructing a rather simpleminded robot as to how to find the door in a room. The basic plan you wish to give it is:

> Walk straight to a wall and then walk along the wall until you get to a door.

However, the robot, being sufficiently simpleminded, cannot act on instructions phrased so loosely (in this, it is much like the computers we will be working with later). Thus, you might present it with an algorithm more like the following:

1. Extend left hand straight ahead.
2. Until your left hand touches the wall or door, do the following:
   take one step with the left foot;
   take one step with the right foot.
3. If you are not yet touching the door, do the following:
   3.1. Turn your body so that the wall is to your left, and your hand is touching it.
   3.2. Until you reach the door, do the following:
   take one step with the left foot;
   take one step with the right foot.
4. Use the other algorithm I gave you to open the door and go through it.

EXERCISE

1-1. What does "take one step" mean? Could it be interpreted differently? Does it make a difference in the algorithm?

STRUCTURE CHARTS

Looking at this algorithm, we see some things in common with the previous one. Each is ultimately made up of a set of simple instructions ("pour the batter into a baking pan," "extend left hand straight ahead") and the simple instructions are grouped in a number of different ways. First of all, they are grouped physically on the page, one after another. Second, they are grouped chronologically, in the order they are to be performed. Third, they are grouped into certain conditional groups; for example, one group of statements is to be done continually until the left hand touches the wall, another group of statements is to be done only if the cake is not yet brown.

Were it not for these conditional groupings the physical listing of the steps of an algorithm would be exactly the same as the order in which they are to be performed, and it would be very easy to look at the algorithm and decide what must be done. Because of the conditional groupings, the way that we have been displaying our algorithms—one step below the next—can become somewhat confusing, since it does not really show us the order in which steps are to be done and how they interrelate. This may not be a serious problem for these simple algorithms, but when we start doing more complex things we will want to be able to get as much information as possible in the shortest amount of time when we look at the algorithm.

Thus, we are going to introduce a different method of writing the steps of an algorithm: a *structure chart*. As the name implies, this will show not only the simple steps of the algorithm, but also the way that they fit together.

A structure chart is always in the shape of a large rectangle, and is built up of smaller rectangles called *process blocks*. The simplest process block is the one for a simple statement and might look like Figure 1.1. Process blocks fit on top of one another, as in Figure 1.2. So far, this is just like what we were doing before: we read down a stack of process blocks. The differences come with the process blocks for the conditional statements. The process block for the "do until" statement, called a DO block, looks like Figure 1.3. This is not merely a rectangle; instead, it is a large rectangle with a small rectangle cut out of it. The small rectangle will contain the statements that are to be done until the robot reaches the door, and the leg of the box shows its *scope*; that is, it shows graphically which statements are the ones which are to be executed until the door is reached. Thus, the first two steps of our algorithm are expressed in Figure 1.4. What happens if the robot reaches the wall after stepping with its left foot? It might seem reasonable to say that as soon as it reaches the wall or door it will stop doing the statements in the scope of the DO block. While this would indeed be reasonable now, it would create many problems for us later on. We will thus adopt the opposite convention: If the condition in the DO block does not yet hold, all the

structure chart

process blocks

DO block

```
┌─────────────────────────┐
│ Take one step with      │
│ the left foot           │
└─────────────────────────┘
```

FIGURE 1.1. A simple process block.

```
┌─────────────────────────────────┐
│ Take one step with the left foot │
├─────────────────────────────────┤
│ Take one step with the right foot│
└─────────────────────────────────┘
```

FIGURE 1.2. A stack of process blocks.

```
┌─────────────────────────────────┐
│ DO until you reach the door      │
│   ┌─────────────────────────────
│   │
│   │
│   │
└───┘
```

FIGURE 1.3. A DO block.

```
┌─────────────────────────────────────┐
│ Extend left hand straight ahead      │
├─────────────────────────────────────┤
│    DO until door or wall is reached  │
│       ┌──────────────────────────────┤
│       │ Take one step with left foot  │
│       ├──────────────────────────────┤
│       │ Take one step with right foot │
└───────┴──────────────────────────────┘
```

FIGURE 1.4. Two steps of the robot algorithm.

statements within the scope are executed before the condition is checked again. Unless we know that the walls in the room are strong, this may result in the robot walking right through one of them. However, we will assume that they are sufficiently strong.

IF-THEN block

The last process block that we will introduce now is the IF-THEN block. The IF-THEN block looks like Figure 1.5. The upper triangle gives a condition to be checked. If the condition is true, the statements in the column marked "yes" are done; if it is false, then those in the "no" column are executed. If we look at step 3 of the algorithm, which is reproduced in Figure 1.6, we see that it specifies what to do if the robot has not reached the door. But does it specify what to do it if has reached the door? Not really! The *algorithm* specifies what to do when the door is reached, but that is to be done whether or not the steps 3.1 and 3.2 are executed first. To see the difference, consider the instructions which you might give to the robot to make it break a vase and then sweep the pieces under the rug:

1. If the vase is on the floor, pick it up and then drop it. Otherwise, push it off of whatever it is standing on.
2. Sweep the pieces under the rug.

In this case, there are explicit instructions for when the condition is true and also for when it is false, and then there is a step to be executed in either case. In the example above, there is no explicit instruction if the robot is touching the door, only the implicit instruction, go on to the next step. For this implicit instruction we introduce a special form of the simple statement process block, shown in Figure 1.7.

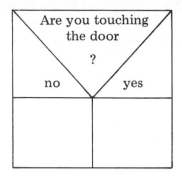

FIGURE 1.5. An IF-THEN process block.

3. If you are not yet touching the door, do the following:

    3.1. Turn your body so that the wall is to your left, and your hand is touching it.

    3.2. Until you reach the door, do the following:

        take one step with the left foot;

        take one step with the right foot.

FIGURE 1.6. The third step of the robot algorithm.

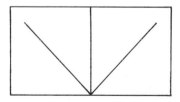

FIGURE 1.7. The process block for "go to the next step."

Step 3 can now be structure charted as shown in Figure 1.8. Notice that the block under the "no" column has been replaced with a whole structure chart, containing a DO group. In general we will find this nesting of conditional expressions within other conditional expressions to be a common feature of algorithms.

We can now stack together the structure charts for the different steps of our algorithm to produce the structure chart for the task: get to the door (see Figure 1.9).

Of course, the algorithm for opening and getting through the door can also be expressed as a structure chart, and placed in the last box or given separately. In general, one structure chart shouldn't be too crowded, however, and since all structure charts are rectangular, it is preferable to make a separate chart for a complicated operation, such as opening and getting through the door, and then just refer to it as we have done here.

EXERCISES

1-2. Rewrite Figure 1.9 for the robot so that it will not push through the wall.

1-3. Write a structure chart which will tell the robot how to open the door and go through it. Remember that depending on which path the robot takes through the structure chart above, it may or may not be facing the door.

1-4. Rewrite Figure 1.9 to take into account the fact that the robot may not be facing the wall containing the door when it starts out, so that it may have to turn corners.

1-5. Assume that the robot will fall on its face if it takes two steps with the same foot and rewrite Figure 1.9 to prevent this from happening.

1-6. Write the structure chart for Helen's Irish Cake.

1-7. Write a structure chart for Chicken Almondine.

1-8. Use the chart prepared in the previous exercise to make Chicken Almondine.

TWO NUMERICAL ALGORITHMS

It is a common misconception, obviously shared by our dictionary, that algorithms must have something to do with mathematics. While, as we have already seen, this is far from true, nevertheless many mathematical concepts are algorithmic in nature. Although we will not concentrate on mathematical problems in our study of programming, neither do we wish to completely ignore them.

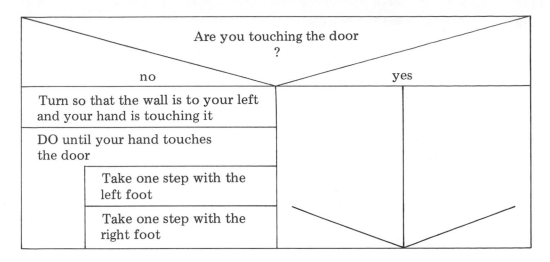

FIGURE 1.8. Structure chart for step three of the robot algorithm.

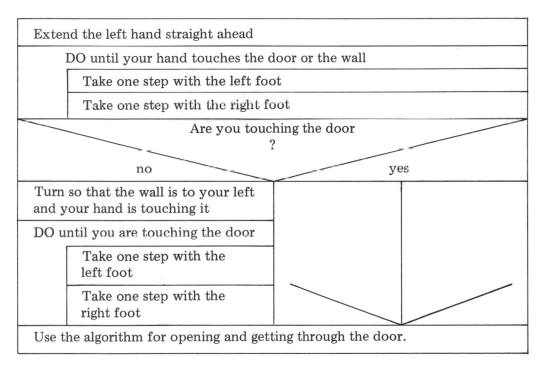

FIGURE 1.9. Structure chart for the robot algorithm.

11

Suppose that we are given two cups, one which can hold five ounces and one which can hold seven ounces, which have no markings on them. The task is to get exactly one ounce of water from a nearby stream.

One way to solve the problem is given in Figure 1.10. If we examine the procedure there carefully, we see that the seven ounce jar is filled three times and the five ounce jar is filled four times. Since $(3 \times 7) - (4 \times 5) = 1$, after filling the five ounce jar from the seven ounce jar in this way we are left with exactly one ounce in the seven ounce jar.

comments   The new symbol which appears in Figure 1.10 is a *comment* symbol, and the process box which contains it is a *comment* box. Comment boxes are used to make structure charts more readable by providing some information about what the algorithm is supposed to be doing; nothing is ever *done* as a result of a comment box.

Notice that while Figure 1.10 is perfectly correct, it is not very general. It would do us no good if, instead, we had a six ounce jar and a seven ounce jar and wanted to get exactly four ounces of water. However, the procedure which we used to generate this algorithm is somewhat more general. It suggests that we look for two numbers A and B such that $(7 \times A) - (6 \times B) = 4$. One set of values is A = 4, B = 4, since

	Fill the 7 ounce cup, and then fill the 5 ounce cup from it.
	Empty the 5 ounce cup, and then pour the rest of the water from the 7 ounce cup into it.

	There are now:
	
	       2 ounces in the 5 ounce cup
	
	       0 ounces in the 7 ounce cup

	Fill the 7 ounce cup, and then fill the 5 ounce cup from it.
	Empty the 5 ounce cup, and then pour the rest of the water from the 7 ounce cup into it.

	There are now:
	
	       4 ounces in the 5 ounce cup
	
	       0 ounces in the 7 ounce cup

	Fill the 7 ounce cup, and then fill the 5 ounce cup from it.
	Empty the 5 ounce cup, and then fill it from the 7 ounce cup.

	There are now:
	
	       5 ounces in the 5 ounce cup
	
	       1 ounce in the 7 ounce cup
	
	so we are done.

FIGURE 1.10. Measuring one ounce with five and seven ounce cups.

$(7 \times 4) - (6 \times 4) = 4$. Figure 1.11 shows an algorithm for getting four ounces of water based on this equation.

It is not too hard to verify that this technique works for any similar situation: if we have one cup which holds X ounces and one cup which holds Y ounces, and we want to end up with Z ounces, then we need only find integers A and B such that the equation $(A \times X) - (B \times Y) = Z$ is true. From this, we can start filling one cup from the stream, and then filling the second cup from the first; when we have filled the first cup exactly A times and the second exactly B times we will have the number of ounces (Z) that we want.

There are some hidden assumptions in this technique. First of all, Z cannot be too large for one of the cups to hold; i.e., unless we have another cup, we can never measure out 50 ounces from a ten ounce cup and a five ounce cup, even though we can write such an equation. We are also assuming that the two cups hold integer amounts of water.

	Fill the 7 ounce cup, and then fill the 6 ounce cup from it.
	Empty the 6 ounce cup, and then pour the rest of the water from the 7 ounce cup into it.
	There are now:
	1 ounce in the 6 ounce cup
	0 ounces in the 7 ounce cup
	Fill the 7 ounce cup, and then fill the 6 ounce cup from it.
	Empty the 6 ounce cup, and then pour the rest of the water from the 7 ounce cup into it.
	There are now:
	2 ounces in the 6 ounce cup
	0 ounces in the 7 ounce cup
	Fill the 7 ounce cup, and then fill the 6 ounce cup from it.
	Empty the 6 ounce cup, and then pour the rest of the water from the 7 ounce cup into it.
	There are now:
	3 ounces in the 6 ounce cup
	0 ounces in the 7 ounce cup
	Fill the 7 ounce cup, and then fill the 6 ounce cup from it.
	There are now:
	6 ounces in the 6 ounce cup
	4 ounces in the 7 ounce cup
	so we are done.

FIGURE 1.11. Measuring four ounces with six and seven ounce cups.

On the other hand, there is one thing which we are not assuming. It is not necessary that we fill the smaller cup from the larger. For example, Figure 1.12 shows another way to measure four ounces with six and seven ounce cups, this time based on the equation $(6 \times 3) - (7 \times 2) = 4$.

The difference between Figures 1.11 and 1.12 is a good illustration of the fact that a little more analysis can simplify any problem. Accepting this maxim, we should analyze our general problem a little more before we try to produce a general algorithm.

We might ask a slightly different question: what is the smallest amount that we can measure with two given cups? Of course, we can always measure zero ounces, but can we always measure one ounce? Consider a two ounce cup and a six ounce cup. We can fill the six ounce cup, and then fill the two ounce cup from it, leaving four ounces in the six ounce cup. If we empty the two ounce cup and then fill it again, we can have two ounces in the six ounce cup. It is easy to see that we can never end up with one ounce or three ounces or five ounces. In terms of our equation, this is because of the fact that, for any choice of integers A and B, $(6 \times A) - (2 \times B)$ is always an even number.

Delving a little deeper we should ask, Why is this always an even number? Clearly, it is always even because both six and two are even. This suggests a hypothesis: if the number of ounces that each cup can hold is divisible by two, then so is the smallest (nonzero) amount that they can measure. That this hypothesis is true can be proved mathematically or verified easily by trying a number of cases.

Suppose, however, that we had cups which could hold six and fifteen ounces, respectively. Since both numbers are not even, the previous analysis gives us no information, so we must experiment. If we fill the fifteen ounce cup, and then fill the six ounce cup from it, we are left with nine ounces in the larger cup. If we fill the six ounce cup again, we are left with three ounces in the fifteen ounce cup. Thus, we can measure three, six, nine or fifteen ounces; we can, of course, also measure twelve ounces by filling the fifteen ounce cup twice from the six ounce cup.

Again, it is easy to see that these are the only amounts which we can measure, so we are led to a second hypothesis: if the number of ounces that each cup can hold is divisible by three, then so is the smallest amount that they can measure.

It may be obvious where this is leading: if there is some integer N which is a divisor of the number of ounces that each cup can hold, then N must be a divisor of the smallest amount that they can measure. While this is useful, it does not really answer our question; it tells us a property of the smallest amount which two cups can measure, but it doesn't tell what that amount is.

Fill the 6 ounce cup, and then empty it into the 7 ounce cup.
Fill the 6 ounce cup, and then fill the 7 ounce cup from it.
There are now: 5 ounces in the 6 ounce cup / 7 ounces in the 7 ounce cup
Empty the 7 ounce cup, and then pour the water from the 6 ounce cup into it.
Fill the 6 ounce cup, and then fill the 7 ounce cup from it.
There are now: 4 ounces in the 6 ounce cup / 7 ounces in the 7 ounce cup so we are done.

FIGURE 1.12. Another way to measure four ounces.

We only have to go a little further to settle the problem. There are usually many numbers which will divide both of the numbers representing the cup capacities. For example, the number one divides any integer. But as we have seen, this does not mean that we can always measure one ounce. Suppose that we have a six ounce cup and a twelve ounce cup: each of one, two, three and six divides both six and twelve. However, it is surely obvious that with these two cups we can only measure six or twelve ounces.

In every example that we have looked at, the smallest amount that we could measure was the *largest* of the numbers which could divide both cup capacities. This is the general rule that we have been looking for! We have not, of course, proved this; the proof, though simple, is outside the scope of this book.

Now we have an exact description of the smallest number of ounces which can be measured with two cups, one holding X ounces and one holding Y ounces: it is the largest number which is a divisor of both X and Y. What we now need is an algorithm to find this number.

One algorithm to do this is shown in Figure 1.13. It starts with the smaller of the cup capacities and asks if it is a divisor of the larger. If it is, then this must be the number we want. (An example of this case is the situation where we have a six ounce cup and a twelve ounce cup.)

Otherwise, we take this number, called Z in the algorithm, subtract one from it, and try to see if it divides both X and Y. If it does we are done; otherwise we repeat this step. (An example here might be a six ounce cup and a fifteen ounce cup. We would start with Z = 6, and stop when Z = 3.) Eventually, if we do not stop beforehand, we will end up with Z = 1, in which case the smallest amount which can be measured is one ounce. (Here, a six ounce cup and a seven ounce cup are an example.)

This is a rather surprising structure chart. It looks like all we are doing is repeatedly subtracting one from Z. We are also performing many divisions, but there is no need to show algorithms for division since it is such a basic and familiar operation.

Notice one important feature of this algorithm which is not shared by the algorithm for the robot given in Figure 1.9. This algorithm has to stop! If the robot tried to follow the algorithm we wrote and was inside a room with an open door, it might just walk out through the door, out on to the street and then off into the distance, until it wore out. In Figure 1.13, on the other hand, we have an algorithm which must stop. If no number larger than one is a common divisor of X and Y, then the algorithm will stop with Z = 1. In fact, the first part of the "until condition," Z = 1, is actually redundant—since one is a divisor of every number, the second part of the condition alone is sufficient to ensure that the algorithm stops. However, including this redundancy is a good reminder of what is happening.

| Let Z be the minimum of X and Y |
| DO until Z = 1   OR   Z divides both X and Y evenly |
| Subtract 1 from Z |

FIGURE 1.13. Finding the greatest common divisor of X and Y.

Just writing a structure chart does not ensure its correctness. To be even reasonably sure that your algorithm really expresses what you intend it to, you should at least try it out for a number of different cases. For example, if we take X = 6 and Y = 8, Z starts out at six, which does not divide eight evenly, so it becomes five, and then four, then three and eventually two. One test case does not prove the algorithm, however. We should not choose our other test cases at random; each test case should be chosen to expose some possible flaw. Here we would probably want to test some of the more extreme cases, such as when X = Y, or when X = 1, or when the greatest common divisor of X and Y is one.

Although the algorithm works, it is rather inefficient. To find the greatest common divisor of 657 and 963, for example, we have to run through the algorithm 649 times, which means doing 1298 divisions.

In fact, the algorithm of Figure 1.13 is so slow that we should really consider doing more analysis. You may recall that for any integers X and Y we can always write the expression

$$X = (Q \times Y) + R$$

where Q is the quotient when X is divided by Y and R is the remainder: $0 \leq R < Y$.

Now, consider the fact that if Z divides both X and Y it must also divide R; this is essentially the same principle we stated earlier. Furthermore, if Z divides both Y and R, it must also divide X. Thus, once we find the remainder R we can then look for a number which divides both Y and R, ignoring X. As R cannot be larger than X, we will be dealing with smaller numbers; this modification will therefore yield a more efficient algorithm.

As an example, take the case X = 18 and Y = 12. If we divide eighteen by twelve the remainder is six, so we need only apply the algorithm in Figure 1.13 to the case X = 12 and Y = 6. Better yet, we can apply this simplification to the case X = 12 and Y = 6. When we divide twelve by six the remainder is zero; since six divides both six and twelve, it also divides both twelve and eighteen; thus, six is the number which we sought.

An algorithm incorporating this new idea is shown in Figure 1.14. For another example of how it works, take X = 963 and Y = 657:

1. X = 963   Y = 657   R = 306
2. X = 657   Y = 306   R = 45
3. X = 306   Y = 45   R = 36
4. X = 45   Y = 36   R = 9
5. X = 36   Y = 9   R = 0

	This algorithm finds the greatest common divisor of X and Y.
	DO until R, the remainder of X ÷ Y, is 0.
	Replace the value of X by Y
	Replace the value of Y by R
	When the algorithm is done, the value of Y is the greatest common divisor.

FIGURE 1.14. A faster algorithm for finding the greatest common divisor.

We arrive at the result that the greatest common divisor of 963 and 657 is nine after only five divisions, as compared with the 1298 required by Figure 1.13.

The analysis which we have done was first performed 2000 years ago: Figure 1.14 is known as Euclid's Algorithm and is the very example which our dictionary gave to illustrate the definition of algorithm.

EXERCISES

1-9. Find a faster procedure for arriving at one ounce of water with a five ounce cup and a seven ounce cup based on the fact $(5 \times 3) - (7 \times 2) = 1$.

1-10. Verify that Figure 1.14 gives the same result for $X = 657$, $Y = 963$.

1-11. Does the algorithm work if X or Y is zero?

1-12. One unfortunate feature of the algorithm is that as we proceed through it we lose the original values of X and Y. Fix up the structure chart so that the values of the variables X and Y do not change and the value of the greatest common divisor when the algorithm is over is held in a variable called G.

1-13. What is the smallest positive number of ounces which can be achieved with each of the following pairs of cups:
   a. 4 oz. and 1 oz.
   b. 11 oz. and 9 oz.
   c. 12 oz. and 4 oz.
   d. 12 oz. and 6 oz.
   e. 12 oz. and 10 oz.
   f. 963 oz. and 654 oz.

1-14. Find the greatest common divisor of each pair:
   a. 4 and 1
   b. 11 and 9
   c. 12 and 4
   d. 12 and 6
   e. 12 and 10

1-15. An integer is called *prime* if the only smaller number which divides it evenly is one. Draw the structure chart for an algorithm which, given the number N, terminates with the value of a variable Z being the Nth prime number.

1-16. If you are currently attending school, what would be involved in writing the structure chart which describes your school's registration process?

1-17. Write a structure chart which gives the algorithm for a change-making machine which breaks a quarter to two dimes and a nickel, a dime to two nickels, and two nickels to a dime.

1-18. A real change machine does not have an infinite reservoir of money. Modify the previous exercise by assuming that the machine starts out with five of each kind of coin and returns the customer's money if it can't make the proper change.

1-19. Modify the preceding structure chart by letting the machine keep the customer's money if it can't make the proper change.

1-20. While we found the smallest number of ounces which we can measure with two given cups, we have still not found a way to achieve it. Try to find an algorithm which, given cups holding X and Y ounces respectively, first uses Euclid's Algorithm to find the greatest common divisor G of X and Y, and then produces numbers A and B such that $(A \times X) - (B \times Y) = G$. (*Note*: This technique can be found in the book *Mathematics: The Man-Made Universe* by Sherman Stein [San Francisco: W. H. Freeman and Co., 1964], on page 67.)

2

The Nouns of APL —
Data Structures

"You may charge me with murder—or want of sense—
    (We are all of us weak at times):
But the slightest approach to a false pretence
    Was never among my crimes!

"I said it in Hebrew—I said it in Dutch—
    I said it in German and Greek:
But I wholly forgot (and it vexes me much)
    That English is what you speak!"

APL is a language. Anything that is said in a language is about something, and before we can properly begin to learn the APL language we have to understand something about the objects that the language can discuss. Among the things which can be discussed in APL are numbers and letters.

Of course, we tend to discuss numbers and letters somewhat differently. We can't, for example, ask, "What is the result of dividing the letter 'F' by the letter 'Q'?" A question which we might ask about letters is, "How many times does the letter 'i' follow the letter 'e' in the sentence:

'I believe that I can conceive that your neighbor might require relief from their deities.' "

Unlike numbers, letters have no intrinsic value or meaning as far as APL is concerned—they are just symbols. In the comic strip *Peanuts* one of the characters is named 555 95472; everyone calls him '5' for short. Clearly this is not a number which is meant to be added to other numbers. It is just a string of characters, all of which happen to come from the characters '1', '2', '3', '4', '5', '6', '7', '8', '9', '0'. We tend to think of such a string as a number, but it has no more numeric value than the letters in a license plate have meaning. We could just as easily have asked the question, "How many times does the character '5' follow the character '3' in:

'5 6385393 1298 5 872 0863583 7780 9121 83509782 75862 6390573 739537 8962 49356 4358532'?"

and gotten the same answer. There was no numeric meaning to those numeric characters.

NAMES AND EXPRESSIONS

character   If we wish to communicate a numeric character to APL we put it in quote marks, as

'5'

APL will understand that this is the character for five and that it has no numeric value. Notice that APL uses a single quote mark, or apostrophe, rather than the double quote marks normally used in English writing. Despite this, the concept is similar. If Reginald said "two plus two is five," then we use the quotation marks to indicate that what is between them is to be taken as is. When we write '5' it indicates in the same way that what is between the quote marks is not to be evaluated.

In APL we can use quote marks around alphabetic characters as well. We can thus write

'A'

names

to indicate the character A. If we write A without the quotes it may or may not have meaning. Without the quote marks characters and words are used in APL as *names*.

Not every word is a name, however. A word becomes a name when we write a sentence which tells what it names. An example of such a sentence is given in Figure 2.1.

This sentence can be read "TWO is assigned by zero," or as "zero is assigned to TWO." Do *not* read it as "TWO equals zero," a phraseology which is likely to be confusing. We need not fix the value of TWO at zero for all time; we can write the sentence in Figure 2.2 at some later time, and change the value of TWO. It should be clear from this example that no matter what a name may seem to mean in English, that meaning need have nothing to do with its meaning in APL, but there is no virtue in using intentionally confusing names either.

Another example of assignment is given in Figure 2.3. There, the value 'Y' is being assigned to the name INITIAL.

When we write a name, it is as if we had written the current value of that name. Suppose that we make the assignment shown in Figure 2.4A. Then the three assignments in Figure 2.4B each have the same effect—assigning the value 10 to the name SUM.

variables

We can see that names behave just like variables in mathematics, so we will call them *variables* from now on.

We know that we can change the value of a variable. In fact, we can even change the type of thing that a variable represents. Figure 2.4C shows this by repeating the previous assignments of the variable TWO, and then assigning to TWO the value 'X'. When we assign a value to a variable it makes no difference what the previous value was.

We can not, however, mix numbers and characters when we do arithmetic operations. Consider the assignments shown in Figure 2.4D. We can add SALARY to BALANCE, and get the result 5. We can *not* add IDENTIFICATION to BALANCE; IDENTIFICATION names a character, not a number.

We have seen that we can combine variables using the arithmetic *operator* + (if it makes sense to add their values).

Using the various APL operators, we can continue to build more and more complicated *expressions*. We will learn more about these operators later in the book. For now, we will just use the simple arithmetic operators + (plus), − (minus) and × (times) to illustrate the rules for finding the values of expressions. Since we will be looking at arithmetic operations, we will only be dealing with numbers for the moment.

TWO ← 0

FIGURE 2.1. Assigning a value to the name TWO.

TWO ← 17.5

FIGURE 2.2. Assigning another value to TWO.

INITIAL ← 'Y'

FIGURE 2.3. A character-valued assignment.

A)

    TALLY ← 5

B)

    SUM ← 5+5
    SUM ← 5+*TALLY*
    SUM ← *TALLY*+*TALLY*

C)

    TWO ← 0
    TWO ← 17.5
    TWO ← 'X'

D)

    BALANCE ← 0
    IDENTIFICATION ← '5'
    SALARY ← 5

FIGURE 2.4. Examples of assignments.

Don't be misled into believing that APL is just for working with numbers; later we will find out that APL has many powerful operators for dealing with characters.

Although you may not realize it, you were taught certain rules for dealing with arithmetic expressions. One of the rules tells you that the value of $10 - 2 \times 4$ is 2 and not 32. That is, the expression means $10 - (2 \times 4)$ and not $(10 - 2) \times 4$. Sometimes the rules are unclear, as in the case $8 - 8 - 8$. Here we would always use parentheses, to distinguish between $8 - (8 - 8)$ and $(8 - 8) - 8$. The familiar rules tell you that in the absence of parentheses multiplication and division are "more important" than addition and subtraction and should be done first. When there are only a few operations, it is simple to establish such rules of precedence. In APL this would be a serious problem as there are many, many operators and if we had to learn different rules of precedence for evaluating expressions we would probably never get done memorizing.

Instead, the designers of APL decided to use a rule different from the one we are used to. This way, instead of learning many new rules to fit with the ones we already know, we have only to learn a single rule which takes care of everything. This single rule is the *right-to-left rule*, and it says just about what its name implies: *In the absence of parentheses, expressions are evaluated from the right to the left.*

right-to-left rule

Some examples of the way that the rule operates are given in Figure 2.5. Each part of the figure shows an expression and its value, and then shows how that expression is evaluated according to the right-to-left rule. Thus, in Figure 2.5A, the rightmost part of the expression is picked off and evaluated, and then the value is effectively substituted back into the place of this part of the expression. You may wish to read this figure in conjunction with Figure 2.6, which is an algorithm for part of the right-to-left rule.

Parts A, B, and C of the figure are evaluated in a strict right-to-left manner. Part D, however, includes a parenthesized subexpression. When parentheses appear in an expression, the part which lies between them is evaluated first, still using the right-to-left rule.

In Figure 2.5E a new symbol appears. APL makes a distinction between the subtraction sign and the *unary minus sign*; the latter is used to indicate that a number is negative and is a part of the number in the same way that a decimal point is part of a number. You can not do operations with this symbol: it makes no sense to write ‾B or 2‾3.

unary minus sign

Part F of Figure 2.5 shows that we can do assignments within expressions. The expression in parenthesis results in a value being given to the variable SIZE.

EXPRESSION	VALUE	PART OF EXPRESSION	VALUE OF PART
A)			
8×5−3	16		
		5−3	2
		8×2	16
B)			
6×8−3	30		
		8−3	5
		6×5	30
C)			
5−4−3−2−1	3		
		2−1	1
		3−1	2
		4−2	2
		5−2	3
D)			
5−4−(3−2)−1	1		
		(3−2)	1
		1−1	0
		4−0	4
		5−4	1
E)			
4−3+11	⁻10		
		3+11	14
		4−14	⁻10
F)			
9+(SIZE←4)−8	5		
		(SIZE←4)	4
		SIZE−8	⁻4
		9+⁻4	5

FIGURE 2.5. Examples of the right-to-left rule.

	This is an algorithm for a skeletal version of the right-to-left rule. Input to this algorithm is a legal arithmetic expression containing only numbers and the operations +, −, and ×.
	DO until the expression is a single number
	Find the last three elements of the expression
	They should be a number, an operation and a number
	Perform the indicated operation to get a value
	Replace the last three elements by the value
	When the algorithm is done, the expression has been replaced by its value

FIGURE 2.6. An algorithm for part of the right-to-left rule.

EXERCISES

2–1. Try to improve the structure chart in Figure 2.6. Pick some feature which it does not have, such as the ability to evaluate expressions with parentheses or the ability to recognize errors in expressions, and try to add that feature.

2–2. Write a structure chart similar to Figure 2.6 for the algorithm which evaluates expressions involving only +, — and × according to the "usual" rules.

2–3. For each expression or sequence of expressions shown in Figure 2.7, explain why the indicated value is correct.

SCALARS AND VECTORS

Numbers and characters rarely exist in isolation. They are usually grouped in some way: a list of social security numbers, or a table of courses and grades, or the order that the horses ran in the fourth race at Hialeah. Perhaps the one most important feature of APL is the ease with which it lets us group data and use it. Here we will briefly touch upon the different ways that we can group data; in Chapter 3 we will see how we can use these groupings.

The simplest way to group data is to list it. An English sentence, such as "the horse is blue," is a list of letters of the alphabet plus the special character *blank* (the spaces between the letters). (Of course, as an English sentence, it is more than that since its component parts have meanings.) We can create a list of characters in APL by simply writing it down, as in Figure 2.8A.

vector

vector length

rho

This assignment statement makes the variable FABLE a *list*, or *string*; or *vector* of characters. Since it has 17 characters (the quote marks are *not* part of the vector, although the blanks are) we say that it has *length* or *size* 17. In APL we use the Greek letter rho (pronounced "row") to stand for the size of a vector.

Figure 2.8B shows what the symbol rho looks like. When we apply the operator rho to a vector the result is a number which we can use just like any other number; Figure 2.8C gives some examples of expressions involving rho.

indexing

The vector FABLE has 17 *elements* and APL lets us refer to each of them by a name: the fifth character, 'H', is named FABLE[5] (read "FABLE sub five"), and the sixteenth is FABLE[16], 'U'. Five and 16 are *subscripts*; they are the *indices* of 'H' and 'U', respectively, and the operation of naming elements of a vector is called *indexing*. We can use these names just like variables: in Figure 2.8D we give the fourteenth element of FABLE a new value, which changes the value of FABLE to

THE HORSE IS GLUE

```
A )
     5-3×8-1                        VALUE IS ¯16

B )
     COST ← 3×8
     5 - COST - 1                   VALUE IS ¯18

C )
     (1+2)×(2-3)+(3+4)              VALUE IS 18

D )
     (3-3-(3-3-3)-3-3)-3            VALUE IS 0

E )
     0-5-3×NET×8-NET←1              VALUE IS 16

F )
     (NET←5)+(3×(NET+1)-(NET←2))
                                    VALUE IS 8

G )
     TIMER←1
     TIMER←2×TIMER
     TIMER←3×TIMER
     TIMER←(2×TIMER)+(2×TIMER)
     TIMER←TIMER×3+1+1              VALUE IS 120
```

FIGURE 2.7. Exercises on the right-to-left rule.

```
A )
     FABLE ← 'THE HORSE IS BLUE'

B )
     ρ

C )
          EXPRESSION              VALUE
          ρFABLE                  17
          3.5+ρFABLE              20.5
          2×ρFABLE                34

D )
     FABLE[14] ← 'G'

E )
     A←'THE'
     B←'HORSE'
     C←'IS'
     D←'GLUE'

F )
          EXPRESSION              VALUE
          A,B,C,D                 THEHORSEISGLUE

G )
     SPC ← ' '

H )
          EXPRESSION              VALUE
          A,SPC,B,SPC,C,SPC,D     THE HORSE IS GLUE
          'IT',SPC,C,' BLUE'      IT IS BLUE
```

FIGURE 2.8. Some examples with character vectors.

We can also combine vectors to create other vectors. Consider the assignments in Figure 2.8E. We can string the separate parts together using the operation of *concatenation*, which is represented by a comma. Part F of the figure shows what happens when we concatenate the variables from part E. The resulting value is probably not what we intended, since there are no spaces in it. However we can assign to some variable the character *blank*, as in Figure 2.8G. Using this, we can concatenate the vectors of part E together so as to get the desired result, as the first example of part H shows.

There is no reason to treat the blank any differently from any other character. It can be included in any character vector, as indicated in the second example in Figure 2.8H.

Just as we can have vectors of characters, we can have vectors of numbers. For example, the daily balance of a checking account in the first seven days of a month might be kept in a variable called BALANCE (see Figure 2.9A).

On the first day the balance was BALANCE[1], or 500.23, while by the seventh it had dropped to an overdraft of $23. If on the eighth day a deposit of $800 is made, the new vector (now having size 8) will be created by the expression given in Figure 2.9B. That is, we concatenate the deposit plus the last balance to obtain the updated history of balances.

While we are permitted to have vectors of numbers or vectors of characters, it is not possible to have a vector in which numbers and characters are mixed. Figure 2.10 shows some valid and invalid examples of concatenations.

One other complication should be mentioned here. Usually single numbers and characters are not vectors, but *scalars*. They are *not* vectors of length 1—they have no length. To make matters worse, however, there are such things as vectors of length 1. We can distinguish between them by writing ,6 for the vector of length 1 whose first (and only) element is 6. Usually we will see no difference between the scalar and the vector; 5 + 6 and 5 + ,6 have the same value, although the second one is a vector. You can expect this to be troublesome on occasion.

A)
    BALANCE ← 500.23   445.36   223.87   132.66   101.03   54.20   ¯23.00

B)
    BALANCE ← *BALANCE*,(800+*BALANCE*[7])

FIGURE 2.9. Modifying a numeric vector.

EXPRESSION   *DISCUSSION*

'ABC','123'   *VALID CONCATENATION OF*
                                      CHARACTER STRINGS

'ABC',123   *INVALID ATTEMPT TO CONCATENATE*
                                      NUMBER 123 ONTO CHARACTER STRING

(1 2 3),(4 5)   *VALID CONCATENATION OF NUMERIC VECTORS*

(1 2 3),'4 5 6'   *INVALID ATTEMPT TO CONCATENATE*
                                      CHARACTER STRING ONTO NUMERIC VECTOR

'5','+','THREE','=8'   *VALID CONCATENATION OF CHARACTERS*

5,'+',3,'=',8   *INVALID MIXTURE OF NUMBERS*
                                      AND CHARACTERS

FIGURE 2.10. Valid and invalid concatenations.

EXERCISES

2–4. Explain why each expression in Figure 2.11A has the indicated value.

2–5. We can use a vector as an index of another vector. For example if we write 'ABCDE'[4 1 4] we are saying, "First take the fourth element of 'ABCDE', then the first and then the fourth." The result is therefore the vector 'DAD'. Explain why each expression in Figure 2.11B has the indicated value.

ARRAYS

array

row

column

In APL you are not limited to vectors. Numbers and characters can also be grouped into tables, or *arrays*. For example, in a certain bicycle race there were five contestants and four laps. The times can be placed, as in Figure 2.12, into a table with five *rows*, each representing a contestant, and four *columns*, each representing a lap. Thus, the number in the fourth row and second column is the time taken by the fourth contestant in the second lap.

APL has an efficient way of describing such arrays. We must, of course, show all the elements, but we do not need to arrange them in the form of a table. For example, the table

$$\begin{array}{ccc} 1 & 2 & 3 \\ 4 & 5 & 6 \end{array}$$

size

is described by the expression in Figure 2.13A. The symbol rho is being used to separate the vector (2 3) on the left, giving the numbers of rows and columns, from the vector 1 2 3 4 5 6 on the right, giving the elements. The numbers on the left determine the *shape* or *size* of the array—in this case there are two rows and three columns. The numbers on the right are the actual elements of the array, and they are read into the array row by row and column by column.

We can create a variable whose value is this array, as shown in Figure 2.13B.

As with vectors, we can reference any element by giving its location. For an array, we must give the row and the column of the element we want, and separate these by a semicolon.

```
        EXPRESSION                        VALUE
A)

   4,(3+7)                              4 10

   (3+7),4                              10 4

   ('THE'[2]),('ICE'[1])               HI

   T ← 3  5  7  9
   T[2] ← T[3]-T[1]
   T[1]+T[2]+T[3]+T[4]                  23

   L ← 'ABCLMN'
   L[2],'E',L[4],L[4]                   BELL
   L[5],L[1],L[ρL]                      MAN


B)

   (1 2 3 4 5 1 2 3)[7 1 6]    2 1 1

   'CAPITAL'[6  3  7]          APL

   LET ← 'ABCLMN'
   LET[2],'E',LET[4 4 5 1 6]   BELLMAN

   TEXT ← 'ABCDEFGHIJKLMNOPQRSTUVWXYZ'
   VOWEL ← 1  5  9  15  21
   TEXT[VOWEL]                 AEIOU
   TEXT[VOWEL[1  5  2  4  3]]  AUEOI
```

FIGURE 2.11. Some expressions to explain.

```
13.3          19.3           18.4          21.4
16.8          23             16.2          16.2
26.4          15.4           20.8          22.3
20.4          21.2           21.2          15.9
19.4          15.4           21.7          16.7
```

FIGURE 2.12. A bicycle race with four laps.

A)
   (2 3)ρ1 2 3 4 5 6

B)
   TABLE ← (2 3)ρ1 2 3 4 5 6

FIGURE 2.13. Describing an array.

Thus, suppose we make the assignment shown in Figure 2.14A. The variable HOMILY will have the value shown in Figure 2.14B. Notice that with character arrays the blank spaces are faithfully reproduced.

If we wish to change the fourth row, to make it line up with the second, third and fifth as shown in part C of the figure, we can proceed in (at least) three different ways.

One way is to change the fourth row element by element. This will require five assignments, as shown in Figure 2.14D. A second way is to treat the fourth row as a vector. Its name is HOMILY[4;] and, as shown in part E of the figure, we can assign a value to it all at once. Finally, the third method is similar to the second. Again referring to the entire fourth row, we can specify those elements which we wish to modify—in this case we are, of course, modifying all the elements.

In a similar way, we can refer to columns of the array. The fifth column is named HOMILY[;5] (refer to part C of the figure), and has value 'YD SE'. We write this horizontally because even though it is a column of the matrix, when we examine it separately it is just a vector.

If, for example, we want to change just a few elements in a row or column, we can do so. Figure 2.14G shows how we might change the third and fourth elements in the second column of the array. The new value of the array will be as shown in Figure 2.14H.

A)

    HOMILY ← (5 5)ρ'EVERY GOOD BOY DOES FINE'

B)
EVERY
 GOOD
 BOY
DOES
 FINE

C)
EVERY
 GOOD
 BOY
 DOES
 FINE

D)
    HOMILY[4;1] ← ' '
    HOMILY[4;2] ← 'D'
    HOMILY[4;3] ← 'O'
    HOMILY[4;4] ← 'E'
    HOMILY[4;5] ← 'S'

E)
    HOMILY[4;] ← ' DOES'

F)
    HOMILY[4;1 2 3 4 5] ← ' DOES'

G)
    HOMILY[3 4;2] ← 'JH'

H)
EVERY
 GOOD
 JOY
 HOES
 FINE

FIGURE 2.14. Changing parts of an array.

We should take note of the difference between the way a variable is assigned, the way it appears and its actual structure. Consider Figure 2.15. Part A shows how four variables might be assigned, and the rest of the figure shows how these variables would be printed. Note that while the first three are printed the same, only the first two have the same structure. It might be worthwhile to examine each of the assignments in more detail.

dimension　First, we can define the *dimension* of a variable or expression to be the "size of its size." The size of a variable (or expression) is *always* a vector; the number of elements in this vector (the "size of the size") depends on the type of thing that the variable is. The size of a vector has one element, the number of elements of the vector. For the vector INCOME in Figure 2.15 the size is the vector of length 1 whose single element is 3. So, the dimension of a vector is always 1.

For an array, the size is a vector with two elements, the first being the number of rows and the second being the number of columns. Thus, in Figure 2.15 EXPENSES is an array with one row and three columns, so its size is the vector 1 3. Its dimension, therefore, is 2. Actually, we will soon see that arrays can have any dimension—there are arrays of dimension 3, dimension 4 and so on. The arrays of the type we have been looking at so far are best referred to as "arrays of dimension 2."

empty　Finally, the size of a scalar is also a vector, a vector with no ele-
vector　ments. This is an artificial construct called the *empty vector* (or the *null* vector) and is a very useful part of APL. Since the size of a scalar has zero elements, the dimension of a scalar is zero.

Let us return now to Figure 2.15. Clearly, the variable INCOME is a vector of size 3, with elements 6, 4 and 9. The variable SALARY is the same, except that we have explicitly given its size before listing its elements. Once these variables are defined, there is no difference between their values. Other ways to get the same result are shown in Figure 2.16.

The variable EXPENSES is different: it is an array with one row and three columns. It *prints* exactly the same as INCOME or SALARY, but has a different structure. We can't ask for its first element; we can, however, ask for the first element in the first row. As we can see from its definition, it is two-dimensional.

The fourth variable, MILEAGE, also has two dimensions, but it has a different structure. It has three rows and one column and prints in exactly that way.

The similarity in the way that SALARY, EXPENSES and MILE-AGE were defined should be clear. In each case we gave the size, then the symbol rho and then listed the elements. For a vector we do not *need* to use this form, as the definition of INCOME showed. Using it gives us some advantages, however. If the list of values to the right of the rho is not long enough to yield all the elements needed, as indicated by the size, then the values are used over and over again, as necessary:

A)
```
    INCOME ← 6  4  9
    SALARY ← 3ρ6  4  9
    EXPENSES ← (1,3)ρ6  4  9
    MILEAGE ← (3,1)ρ6  4  9
```

B)
```
    INCOME
6    4    9


    SALARY
6    4    9


    EXPENSES
6    4    9


    MILEAGE
6
4
9
```

FIGURE 2.15. Some assignments and their values.


```
BONUS ← 6,4,9
GIFT  ← 3 ρ 6,4,9
RAISE ← 3 ρ(6  4  9)
```

FIGURE 2.16. Some assignments with the same value.

the elements on the right are taken from the left to the right, and when the end of the list is reached, if not enough elements have been given, values are again taken from the beginning. Figure 2.17 shows some examples. Note that if too many elements are given on the right then the superfluous ones are ignored.

Before we go on to consider higher dimensional arrays we should point out two unfortunate features of APL. If we wish to write down a vector each of whose elements is numeric we can just list the elements, as: 6 4 9. But if we have variables, even if they have numeric values, we must separate them by commas. The assignment to W in the fourth line of Figure 2.18A is *erroneous*—it is meaningless in APL, despite the fact that we may understand what was intended. The variables X, Y and Z should have been separated by commas, as

X,Y,Z

Of course, with numbers the commas are optional, and can be used if desired.

A related problem is illustrated in Figure 2.18B, a line which shows how we might try to define an array using the values of X and Y from part A. This is also erroneous. What happens here is that, because the expression is interpreted from right to left, the phrase "Y rho 0" is taken as one unit, to be concatenated onto X. Thus, the statement means the number 6 (value of X) followed by the vector with four (value of Y) elements, each of which is zero.

The solution is to enclose the "X,Y" in parentheses, as shown in Figure 2.19. Parentheses are not needed if the size being given is a numeric vector without commas, but it is a good idea to use them anyway. Figure 2.19 also shows some valid array definitions using numeric vectors.

EXPRESSION	VALUE
5ρ1 2 3	1 2 3 1 2
3ρ1 2 3 4 5	1 2 3
6ρ'ABCD'	ABCDAB
5ρ0	0 0 0 0 0
0ρ5	(EMPTY VECTOR)
(2,3)ρ'AEFG'	AEF
	GAE
(4,1)ρ'HO'	H
	O
	H
	O

FIGURE 2.17. Explicit assignments.

A)

```
    X ← 6
    Y ← 4
    Z ← 9
    W ← X Y Z
```

B)

```
    X,Y ρ 0
```

FIGURE 2.18. Examples of how not to do it.

```
(X,Y)ρ0

(6,4)ρ0
(6 4)ρ0
6 4 ρ 0
```

FIGURE 2.19. Correct array definitions.

EXERCISE

2-6. Explain why each expression in Figure 2.20 has the indicated value.

HIGHER DIMENSIONAL ARRAYS

When we left the bicycle race they had completed one day's riding, and we summarized the times per lap in Figure 2.12. If they decide to continue the race for two more days, then the results for the additional days will also be summarized in five-by-four arrays.

plane If we imagine stacking the three arrays one on top of the other, we get a structure with three *planes*, each of which is a five-by-four array representing one day of the race. This structure is a three-dimensional array; it has three planes, each of which has five rows, each of which has four columns, and so it has size 3 5 4. This array is shown in Figure 2.21.

```
EXPRESSION                      VALUE

(2,4)ρ'BELL MAN'                BELL
                                 MAN

(2,4)ρ'BELLMAN'                 BELL
                                MANB

TIMES←(4,4)ρ 1 2 3 4 5
TIMES                           1 2 3 4
                                5 1 2 3
                                4 5 1 2
                                3 4 5 1

TIMES[;3]                       3 2 1 5

TIMES[2;]                       5 1 2 3

TIMES[2;3]                      2

TIMES[2;3 1]                    2 5

TIMES[;3 1]                     3 1
                                2 5
                                1 4
                                5 3

0ρ0                             (EMPTY VECTOR)

XWORD←(4,4)ρ'LHEM A I TYT    T'
XWORD[1;1]←'T'
XWORD[3;3]←'ZOT'[2]
XWORD                           THEM
                                 A I
                                 TOT
                                   T

XWORD[1;1 3 3],XWORD[1 3;2]  TEETH

WHY←2
NOT←3
WHY,NOTρ1 4 9 16 25 36          2 1 4 9
WHY,NOTρ'CORRECT'               (ERRONIOUS)
```

FIGURE 2.20. Some expressions to explain.

```
13.3      19.3      18.4      21.4
16.8      23        16.2      16.2
26.4      15.4      20.8      22.3
20.4      21.2      21.2      15.9
19.4      15.4      21.7      16.7

16.5      12.6      26.3      22.9
21.1      23        15.2      16.7
17.1      25.5      19.5      18.5
20.9      18.5      21.2      14.4
19.3      28.7      22.7      17.9

28.4      18        19.2      15.1
22        14.3      24.4      19
17.5      19.7      19.2      17.6
19        22.4      14.7      19.5
25        25.4      21.5      25.2
```

FIGURE 2.21. A three day bicycle race.

We create such an array just as we created two-dimensional arrays and vectors: first give the size, then the symbol rho and then list the elements. For an example, see Figure 2.22. The variable GIFT which is defined there is an array with three planes, each of which has one row and three columns.

The first plane is GIFT[1;;] with value

THE

and so on. Although the plane by plane, row by row, column by column rule is the one used by APL in assigning elements into an array, we can take other "slices" as we wish. If we want all elements which lie in the second column (and in any row or plane) we can ask for GIFT[;;2], which is

HIO

Or we can ask for all elements in the third plane and the first row, which is GIFT[3;1;] with value

TOY

Notice that this looks the same as GIFT[3;;] since each plane has only one row. There is a difference, although we can't see it directly. The third plane of GIFT is an array with one row and three columns, while the first row of the third plane (GIFT[3;1;]) is a vector with three elements. The difference is similar to that between a one element vector and a scalar, inflated by one dimension.

Of course, each array and each slice of an array also has a size. Figure 2.23 shows an array and the sizes of some of its parts.

Notice that the number of elements in any array can be found by multiplying together all of the elements of its size vector. For example, a four-dimensional array with size 2 5 3 4 has $2 \times 5 \times 3 \times 4 = 120$ elements.

EXERCISES

2-7. Write the description of some arrays of different size, each having five dimensions and 32 elements.

2-8. How many differently sized arrays can you write with four dimensions and 120 elements; with four dimensions and 119 elements?

2-9. Write the description of an array with five dimensions and one element; with 25 dimensions and no elements.

EXPRESSION	VALUE
GIFT←(3,1,3)ρ'THEBIGTOY'	
GIFT	THE
	BIG
	TOY

FIGURE 2.22. A three-dimensional character array.

ARRAY←(2,4,3)ρ1 2 3 4 5 6 7 8 9 10

EXPRESSION	VALUE				SIZE
ARRAY	1	2	3		2 4 3
	4	5	6		
	7	8	9		
	10	1	2		
	3	4	5		
	6	7	8		
	9	10	1		
	2	3	4		
ARRAY[2;;]	3	4	5		4 3
	6	7	8		
	9	10	1		
	2	3	4		
ARRAY[;1;]	1	2	3		2 3
	3	4	5		
ARRAY[;;3]	3	6	9	2	2 4
	5	8	1	4	
ARRAY[1;;3]	3	6	9	2	4
ARRAY[2;1;3]	5				0ρ0

FIGURE 2.23. Some sections of an array.

Interlude One

Communicating with the Computer

Before we begin studying APL, we have to learn to make contact with the computer. There are many different computer systems offering APL and there is no one way for entering into dialogue with the computer which will work on all systems. While there are certain general principles common to (almost) all such systems, which will be enumerated here, it will be up to you to find out the fine points for yourself. There is probably a manual which describes your particular APL system. If possible, you should obtain a copy—often the important information can be summarized on a few pages and is supplied at low cost (or even free!) by the computer center.

SIGNING ON AND OFF

The first step is to locate the on-off switch of your particular terminal. It may be in plain view, underneath or behind. Turning the terminal on does *not* get you ready to use APL. In fact, you may not even be in contact with the computer yet, as many terminals have a switch which lets a user turn off the communication link to the main computer and use the terminal *locally*, as a typewriter. Of course, to communicate with the computer you should not be in *local mode*, but in *remote* (or *transmission*) *mode*. If you are using a *dial-up* terminal, you will have to dial the proper number and place the telephone receiver in the designated holder. There are so many different computer systems that we cannot possibly give detailed instructions for each one: you should have someone show you how to set up a connection with the computer.

To work with the APL system, you probably need some kind of sign-on code which identifies you to the system. For our purpose we will assume that the sign-on code is a number, say 123456789. Having turned on the machine, enter the sign-on number as follows

)123456789

and then press the RETURN key.

At this point there are at least six different things which can go wrong. Five of these result in the error messages shown in Figure I1.1 (for a discussion of error messages see Appendix One). You may find out that your particular system always gives one of the first two messages the very first time you sign on. In this case, simply try again. Otherwise, there is a problem. The error messages in APL are usually quite informative and precise. If one of these errors should occur, check its exact meaning in Appendix One and take the specified action.

On the other hand, even if you are able to sign on, there is still the possibility of a sixth error. When the system responds to you, it will probably print your name. If you entered the wrong sign-on code, then you can see that you are signed on to someone else's number and you should sign off immediately.

INCORRECT SIGN-ON

NUMBER NOT IN SYSTEM

ALREADY SIGNED-ON

NUMBER IN USE

NUMBER LOCKED

FIGURE I1.1. Some sign-on error messages.

To sign off it is only necessary to enter the system command

)OFF

(see Appendix Two for a discussion of system commands). This will terminate the session, and the computer will respond by giving you information about how long you were signed on and, possibly, how much your session cost. Typing this command does not turn the terminal off however: you must use the on-off switch for that.

It is possible to ensure that other users cannot sign on with your number (accidentally, of course). You can add to your number a password or *lock*. To lock your number, say with a lock like A372XR, sign off with the modified command

)OFF:A372XR

It is not necessary to do this every time you sign off; once you have locked your number it remains locked until you change the lock in the same way or remove it by ending a session with the command

)OFF:

As long as you end sessions with)OFF the current lock remains in force.

The effect of the lock is that your sign-on number is now changed, to 123456789:A372XR, and any attempt to sign on with just 123456789 results in the error message NUMBER NOT IN SYSTEM. Of course, a lock provides security only to the extent that you keep it secure, and you may wonder why all the bother. Why not just keep the sign-on number secret?

There are a few answers. First, sign-on numbers are often supplied systematically, so that the person coming in ahead of you would get 123456788 and the person coming after you would get 123456790. It is thus easy for someone who wants to sign on under another person's number to make an intelligent guess as to what a legal number might be; in a system where you are only allocated a certain amount of computer time, or in one where it costs real money to use the computer, it is quite important that no one else be able to use your number. Second, you may want to let someone else "borrow" some of the work that you are doing. To do this you have to give them a few pieces of information, including your sign-on number but *not* including your lock. Thus, if you have a lock you can release things in this way without at the same time giving anyone carte blanche to your sign-on.

EXERCISES

I1-1. Draw a structure chart for the procedure outlined here for signing on, locking your number and signing off.

I1-2. Draw a structure chart for the actual procedure which must be followed with your system for signing on, locking your number and signing off.

I1-3. When you sign on with a locked number, you have to type your lock. Invent at least three different ways to circumvent this breach of security. Use one. (*Note*: If it is important that others not be able to use your number, as in the case where you are only allotted a fixed amount of computer time, then you should be serious about security precautions. At one university, a professor was very careful about his lock, changing it regularly so that, even if it became known, only limited damage could be done. However, a group of [luckily honest] students found out that the lock was always the name of some character from a certain comic strip and so could usually sign on to the number after only a few tries.)

I1-4. It will sometimes be necessary to contact the computer center when problems arise. There is often an operator designated just to watch over APL and handle such problems. You should find out the operator's phone number and look up the system commands—)OPR and)OPRN—which allow you to communicate with the operator directly from the terminal. Sign on and then, using one of these commands, ask the operator how long APL will be available today. How long does it take to get a response? An answer?

I1-5. What do you have to do if you forget your lock?

I1-6. How can you tell if someone has been using your number?

I1-7. In many installations that use APL it takes a phone call to make the connection with the computer. When you type)OFF you break this connection, so the next user of the terminal has to redial. A way around this is provided by the command

)OFF HOLD

which tells the computer that you are done but that the line shouldn't be disconnected. Find out where you must place the lock if you want to lock your number and use)OFF HOLD to sign off.

I1-8. How long will the line be kept open for a new user when you sign off with)OFF HOLD?

TYPING

Figure I1.2 shows the APL keyboard as it should look. Unfortunately, most keyboards do not look like this. Often the APL symbols are produced by the keys shown in the figure, but the keys themselves are either labeled as conventional typewriter keys or have the APL symbols stuck on the front face, rather than the top. Some systems are not even able to print the APL symbols, and instead provide you with some sort of conversion chart. Since, as some of the originators of APL remark, "the visual interpretation of complex APL expressions is, of course, awkward with any but an APL printing element," we will assume that the full range of APL characters is available.

If we take a brief tour of the keyboard we will find 52 characters, other than letters and numbers, as well as some control keys. The names and uses of these characters will be discussed in the succeeding chapters; here we will just discuss the most important control keys. However, in Figure I1.3 we show a chart giving the names of the special symbols—for some symbols we give more than one name in order to show the mnemonics which may help you locate the symbols on the keyboard.

Some of the symbols shown in the figure are called *overstruck characters*: type one part of the symbol, and then backspace and type the other part.

When you type anything at all to APL you must follow by pressing the RETURN key. This combines the functions of line feed and carriage return, as well as actually sending the line that you typed to the computer. (In some systems it may take two or even three keys to effect all this.) Actually, the line that you type is accessible to the computer before you hit RETURN, but hitting RETURN is the signal that you are satisfied with the line and are ready for the computer to process it. It follows, then, that before you hit RETURN you can modify the line.

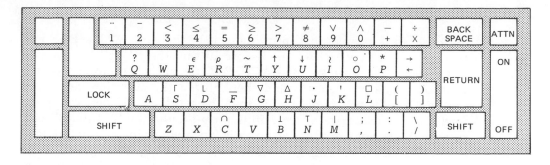

FIGURE I1.2. An APL keyboard.

SOME OVERSTRUCK CHARACTERS

FIGURE I1.3. Symbols and their names.

Suppose, for example, that in trying to type the word VARIABLE you actually produce VAREABLE. Before hitting the RETURN key, you can correct the mistake by BACKSPACing until the current typing position is the erroneous E and then hitting the attention key. What you will see (as in Figure I1.4) is that the terminal will perform a line feed (but not a carriage return), print a caret under the E, BACKSPACE so that the current printing position is again under the E, and line feed again. The effect is to wipe out the E and everything after it, while leaving everything in front of it. It will be as if you had typed VAR and then you can continue with IABLE.

EXERCISES

I1-9. Sit down at the terminal, sign on and experiment.

I1-10. Verify that the expressions given in Chapter 2 are correct by typing them in at the terminal (pressing RETURN after each one) and seeing what APL responds.

```
VAREABLE
    v
 IABLE ← 0
```

FIGURE I1.4. Correcting a typing mistake.

3
The Verbs of APL —
Operators

"To seek it with thimbles, to seek it with care;
   To pursue it with forks and hope;
To threaten its life with a railway-share;
   To charm it with smiles and soap!"

APL is a language—*A Programming Language*. As with any language, there are many ways to learn it. One way would be to begin by memorizing lists of vocabulary, and then rules of grammar, and to begin to make sentences and hold conversations only much later. At the other extreme is a technique used by linguists and anthropologists—find a native speaker of the language to use as an informant while you teach yourself. The native speaker may not know English, but can still be helpful by giving the name for things you point at and correcting the mistakes that you make.

Our approach to APL will be more like the linguist's. The terminal is a readily available native speaker of APL. There is also, in Appendix Three, a dictionary of the language. Some of the grammar (the right-to-left rule) has already been presented in Chapter 2 and the rest will be introduced when we begin programming. For now, rather than painstakingly going through the dictionary, explaining the meaning of every word in excruciating detail, we will spend some time investigating how to use the dictionary and the terminal to learn APL.

THE COMPUTER AS ECHO

The first thing to learn about APL is that it is very willing to help. If you say anything to the terminal it repeats that thing right back to you. For example, if (after signing on, of course) you type

    17

the terminal responds by typing

17

Note that what you type is indented while the response is flush left. The indentation is done by APL by spacing in from the edge of the line whenever it expects you to type something. This serves as a cue for you, and also lets you look back at your dialogue and sort out the speakers.

You may wish to try this again. Type

    .333

and the response is

.333

Type

    'THE TERMINAL IS TALKING TO ME'

and the response is

THE TERMINAL IS TALKING TO ME

Notice that the quote marks are not typed back. As explained in Chapter 2, they are not part of the message. Suppose we want to include a quote mark in a message. Try typing

'THE TERMINAL ISN'T TALKING TO ME'

and there will be no response. While it is easy for us to see by context that the quote mark in ISN'T is different from the others, APL has no way to make such a distinction. In general, the same symbol will not be assigned different meanings if there is likely to be confusion as to which meaning holds. In this case, APL assumes that you have typed the message 'THE TERMINAL ISN' followed by the symbols T TALKING TO ME and that you then began another message with '. In other words, as far as APL is concerned, anything you type now until you type another ' is part of the second message, and every time you hit RETURN it will wait patiently for more. If you try this at the terminal, you will see that the terminal does *not* indent for you at the beginning of a line when you are "inside" quotes. When you finally enter the ending quote, you will get an error message,

SYNTAX ERROR

and part of the message will be retyped. "Syntax error" means that APL recognized that the line you entered was not grammatically meaningful.

syntax error

How then do we get a quote mark in a message? Partly for historical reasons, APL uses the rule that two *successive* quote marks *within a message* stand for the character quote. Thus if we type

'THE TERMINAL ISN''T SPEAKING TO ME'

the message which APL receives and returns is

THE TERMINAL ISN'T SPEAKING TO ME

EXERCISES

3-1. What happens if you type four successive quote marks? Six? Seven?

3-2. What happens if you type only two successive quote marks?

3-3. Try to formulate, in the form of a structure chart, the rules for handling quote marks. That is, once a quote mark is encountered, successive symbols are looked at until another quote mark is found. Then the very next symbol must be looked at to see if it too is a quote mark, etc.

3-4. What is the size of a string which is entered as four successive quote marks?

3-5. When might you wish to include a RETURN as part of a character string?

CALCULATOR MODE

As we have seen, the terminal will not always type back *exactly* what you enter; it evaluates your entry before responding. This evaluation process is what makes the terminal so valuable in learning APL. For example, if you type the expression

3.5 + 6.5

the terminal prints back *not* this expression, but its value:

10

Each of the special symbols, which we called "vocabulary words" earlier, is an *operator*, like +. It performs some operation on its *arguments*, just as typing 3.5 + 6.5 causes the operation of addition to be performed on the arguments 3.5 and 6.5. For another example, type the line shown in Figure 3.1. This is an expression, consisting of the operator rho and one argument. The response will be

63

the number of characters in the argument. Some operators take two arguments and some take one—in fact, most can take either one or two, in which case the same operator is being used for two different (although usually related) meanings. The grammar at all times makes it clear which meaning is intended. Let's take a look at an operator. Figure 3.2 shows the definition of division as it appears in the dictionary (Appendix Three).

monadic
dyadic

As you can see, this operator has a form with one argument (the *monadic* form) and a form with two arguments (the *dyadic* form). The definition for the dyadic form says that the value of the expression $A \div B$ is the result of dividing A by B. Let's try some examples in Figure 3.3.

ρ'*THIS MESSAGE HAS 63 CHARACTERS, INCLUDING BLANKS BUT NOT QUOTES*'

FIGURE 3.1. An expression to be evaluated.

÷	÷
DIVISION	**RECIPROCAL**
Scalar, dyadic, numeric	Scalar, monadic, numeric
A ÷ B is A divided by B.	(÷B) is the same as (1÷B).
(0 ÷ 0) is 1.	The argument cannot be 0.
Any other division by 0 is an error.	

FIGURE 3.2. The definition of division.

```
      8÷4
2


      4÷8
0.5


      3÷2
1.5


      0÷7
0


      9÷1
9
```

FIGURE 3.3. Some divisions.

What happens if we try some extreme cases? Look first at Figure 3.4A. For each operator only certain types of arguments are allowed. It certainly makes no sense to talk of dividing a character by a number; if you try to do this the message says that at least one of the arguments

**DOMAIN
ERROR**

is not in the *domain* of the operator. With division there is the special case of zero appearing on the right as an argument, as in Figure 3.4B. Division by zero is not allowed—in fact, it has no meaning—so a zero on the right is not in the domain of the operator, unless there is also a zero on the left as in part C of the figure. (Making zero divided by zero have one for its value was an arbitrary, and somewhat questionable, choice by the designers of the language.)

reciprocal

Now refer back to Figure 3.2 for the definition of division as a monadic operator. It says that monadic division is the *reciprocal* operator—it yields for its value one *divided by* its argument. Figure 3.5 shows some examples.

At this point we have learned much more than how division works; we have really learned about almost all of the APL operators! Most of the operators can be used both monadically and dyadically. The definitions of the two forms usually bear some relationship to each other, although not always. The exercises are designed to give you some practice in using the dictionary and the terminal to find out how the other operators work.

Most of the operators which we will try in the exercises perform some sort of arithmetic function. We will mention briefly two other types of operators: *relational* and *logical*.

A)
      '*A*'÷3
DOMAIN ERROR
      '*A*'÷3
         ^

B)
      3÷0
DOMAIN ERROR
      3÷0
     ^

C)
      0÷0
1

FIGURE 3.4. Extreme cases for division.

     ÷4
0.25

     ÷.1
10

     ÷÷5
5

     ÷0
DOMAIN ERROR
     ÷0
    ^

FIGURE 3.5. The reciprocal operator.

relational operators

Relational operators are such things as *equals*, *less than*, *greater than or equal to*, or *not equal to*. They are always dyadic and produce the value 1 if the relationship that they express between their arguments is true, 0 if it is false. Figure 3.6A shows some examples.

logical operators

Logical operators work like logical connectives in language. Some examples are *and*, *or*, *not*: the first two are always dyadic; the third is always monadic. Just as with relational operators, APL uses the value 1 to represent "true" and the value 0 to represent "false." Thus, an expression involving the operator *and* will have value 1 (be true) only if both of its arguments have value 1. Since logical values must be either true or false, if a logical operator gets an argument which is not a 1 or a 0, an error message will occur. Figure 3.6B shows some examples.

A)

        3 = 3
1

        4 ≥ 6
0

        5 ≠ (6 + 2)
1

        (5 = 3) = (7 = 7)
0

B)

        1 ∧ 1
1

        1 ∧ 0
0

        ~1
0

        0 ∨ 1
1

        (5 < 3) ∨ (7 ≥ ⁻1)
1

        (~5 = 3) = (5 ≠ 3)
1

        5 ∨ (3 = 3)
DOMAIN ERROR
        5 ∨ (3 = 3)
          ∧

FIGURE 3.6. Relational and logical operators.

EXERCISES

(*Note*: all of these should be tried at the terminal. For most, you will want to consult the dictionary first, but try the starred exercises at the terminal first without the dictionary.)

*3–6. Evaluate the expressions in Figure 3.7A.

*3–7. Evaluate the expressions in Figure 3.7B.

3–8. Using the terminal, find the value of the expression in Figure 3.7C. Do *not* use multiplication. Are there different ways to do this? Which is simplest?

*3–9. Discover a monadic operator which, when applied to 3, produces 1.

*3–10. Discover a monadic operator which, when applied to 0, produces 1. Find two more.

*3–11. Find a monadic operator which does not always give the same result when applied to 150.

3–12. Discover a dyadic operator with the following properties: both arguments must be greater than 0 and the left argument must not be 1.

*3–13. Discover a dyadic operator which, when both arguments are 'A', produces 0.

*3–14. Find a monadic operator which does not work dyadically.

3–15. Find a dyadic operator which does not work monadically. Find many.

3–16. Which of the expressions in Figure 3.7D causes an error?

3–17. Find some operators which cannot take character arguments. Find some which can.

3–18. Write an expression involving three characters (and some operators) which produces a 1 if all three characters are the same and a 0 otherwise. Write a similar expression for the case when at least two are the same; exactly two are the same, all are different.

3–19. For each monadic operator shown in Figure 3.7E write an expression involving a number X which will produce a 1 if X is a valid argument to the operator.

3–20. Write an expression involving numbers X and Y which produces 1 if the expression shown in Figure 3.7F equals Y, 2 if it produces a DOMAIN ERROR and 0 otherwise.

A)

       ÷÷3
       ÷3÷3

B)

       3+2-÷.1
       6×3-÷5
       3+'A'='B'
       ('A'≠'B')-(8+~1)
       ×5
       +17
       ×2+'A'='A'
       (5<3)∨(3<5)∧(2<⁻1)
       17×3-(3+4)÷÷4-÷.25

C)

       9×8×7×6×5×4×3×2×1

D)

       ⁻⁻3
       -⁻3
       ÷0×2
       ~2
       ∧4
       ∨1
       'S'='T'
       ('S'='T')<(3=9)
       'S'≤'T'
       ~'T'≠'S'

E)

       ⊕
       ?
       ~

F)

       X|Y

FIGURE 3.7. Some exercises.

SCALAR OPERATIONS EXTENDED TO ARRAYS

So far we have only been discussing operations on scalars. Suppose that we wished to find the reciprocal of every element in a vector. We could, of course, find them one at a time, but in APL if we apply a monadic operator to any vector or array the operation is performed on the elements one at a time. So if we make the assignment in Figure 3.8A, and then type the expression in Figure 3.8B asking for the reciprocals of the elements of the vector VOLTAGE, the result is the vector shown in part C of the figure.

floor

Or suppose that we had the array GRID defined in Figure 3.8D and wished to take the floor of each element (the *floor* of a number X is the greatest integer less than or equal to X). Figure 3.8E shows how this is done: simply apply the monadic operator floor to the array GRID.

Notice that while we have only discussed two operators here, we have really learned how to work with any monadic operator which can be applied to a scalar. Such an operator can be applied monadically to any vector or array, and the result will be as if it had been applied element by element.

The dyadic operators can also be extended to arrays, but here we must take a small amount of care. There are two different cases to consider. The first is when one of the arguments to the operator has just one element, such as a scalar, or a vector or array with only one element.

If one of the arguments has only one element, and the other is an array, then the operation is performed between the single element and each array element in turn. Figure 3.9 shows some examples. In each case, the result of the operation is a vector or array of the same size as the original.

A)

  VOLTAGE ← 1 2 4 10 ‾5

B)

  ÷*VOLTAGE*

C)

1 0.5 0.25 0.1 ‾0.2

D)

  GRID ← (3,2)ρ 1 ‾.3 .5 7.7 ‾9 0
  GRID
 1   ‾0.3
 0.5   7.7
 ‾9   0

E)

  ⌊*GRID*
 1 ‾1
 0 7
 ‾9 0

FIGURE 3.8. Monadic operators applied to arrays.

  (5 2 ‾3 6 ‾5 9)+3
8 5 0 9 ‾2 12

  10-(3,3)ρ1 2 3 4 5 6 7 8 9
 9 8 7
 6 5 4
 3 2 1

  ((1,1,1,1,1)ρ12)÷1 2 3 4 6 12
12 6 4 3 2 1

FIGURE 3.9. Extensions of dyadic operators.

On the other hand, if both arguments are arrays then *their sizes must match exactly*. If the sizes do match, then the dyadic operation is performed between corresponding elements. For example, if we multiply a vector by itself, as in Figure 3.10A, the result is a vector whose elements are the squares of the elements of the original. Or, as in Figure 3.10B, we can use different arguments, if their sizes match.

However, if we forget the rule, as in Figure 3.10C, then an error message is printed. The caret shows the point at which APL finds the first indication of error. Let's reconstruct the process by which APL scans the first expression. Certainly the vector 7 5 6 9 is valid, and there is no reason that it cannot be the right argument of the multiplication operator. Likewise, the array on the left is, by itself, valid (had it not been, the caret would have pointed someplace inside the parentheses). But the array on the left cannot be the left argument of *any* dyadic operator if the vector is the right argument, so the error is detected only after all parts of the expression have been examined. In this case, APL finds the error when it realizes that there is an array on the left **RANK** and a vector on the right. The error is a RANK ERROR, meaning that **ERROR** the dimension of the item pointed to by the caret is incorrect (because it doesn't match the dimension of the other argument).

In the second example of part C, the dimensions of the arguments are the same, but even so the sizes do not match. The arguments are **LENGTH** vectors of different lengths, so the error is a LENGTH ERROR. **ERROR** In summary:

If one argument to a dyadic operator has one element, the size of the result is the size of the other argument.

If both arguments are vectors or arrays, the size of the result is the common size of the arguments.

A)
```
      (1 2 3 4 5 6)×1 2 3 4 5 6
1   4   9  16   25   36
```

B)
```
      (6 7 8)-4 0 ‾4
2   7  12
```

```
      'BOLOGNA'='SALAMI '
0   0   1   0   0   0   0
```

```
      ((2,3)ρ 1 0 0 0 1 1)∧(2,3)ρ 0 1 1 1 1 0
  0 0 0
  0 1 0
```

```
      ((2,2,1)ρ10 20 30 40)÷(2,2,1)ρ1 2 3 4
      10
      10

      10
      10
```

C)
```
      ((1,4)ρ1 2 3 8)×7 5 6 9
RANK ERROR
      ((1,4)ρ 1 2 3 8)×7 5 6 9
      ∧
```

```
      (2 5 9)×1 3 7 11
LENGTH ERROR
      (2 5 9)×1 3 7 11
      ∧
```

FIGURE 3.10. More extensions of dyadic operators.

reduction

There is another way to extend the scalar dyadic operators to vectors and arrays. Suppose that we wanted to add all the elements of a vector together. We use what looks like a monadic operator made up of two symbols, a plus followed by a slash. An example is shown in Figure 3.11A. This is the *sum reduction* of the vector, and is a shorthand way to add up the elements. In fact, the expression in Figure 3.11A has the same value as the one in Figure 3.11B. The difference, of course, is that we can take the sum reduction of a variable which has been assigned previously without having to write down all of its values. An example is given in Figure 3.11C.

The reason that two symbols are used for the sum reduction operator is that we can use any scalar dyadic function in place of addition. Some examples are shown in part D of the figure.

It is not necessary that the argument to a reduction be a vector: any array is permissible but, as will be seen in the exercises, the corresponding result may be surprising.

EXERCISES

3–21. What happens if we take the reciprocal of a vector which contains a 0?

3–22. In Figures 3.9 and 3.10, which of the parentheses are necessary? If some aren't needed, why were they used?

A)
```
      +/1  2  3  4
10
```

B)
```
      1+2+3+4
10
```

C)
```
      INTEGERS ← 1  2  3  4
      +/INTEGERS
10
```

D)

EXPRESSION	VALUE	EQUIVALENT TO
-/1 2 3 4	‾2	1-2-3-4
-/4 3 2 1	2	4-3-2-1
×/6 5 4 3 2 1	720	6×5×4×3×2×1
÷/12 3 4	16	12÷3÷4
=/5 5 3 0 1	0	5=5=3=0=1
⌈/3 ‾1 5 2	5	3⌈‾1⌈5⌈2
⌊/3 ‾1 5 2	‾1	3⌊‾1⌊5⌊2
∨/'DOG'='HOG'	1	∨/0 1 1
		0∨1∨1

FIGURE 3.11. Some reductions.

3-23. In each triple in Figure 3.12A, which two have the same value?

3-24. Using the logical operators and reduction, write expressions for each of the following statements about a vector TONES:

    a. All of the elements of TONES are equal to 'C'.

    b. None of the elements of TONES is greater than 8.

    c. At least one element of TONES is 'F'.

    d. Not more than five elements of TONES are negative.

3-25. How will you verify that the answers to Exercise 3-24 are correct?

3-26. Predict which expressions in Figure 3.12B will cause errors.

3-27. (*Note*: This is an "advanced" exercise in using the terminal to figure out the way that an operator works.) Try to discover the rules for the way that sum reduction is applied to arrays.

    a. What is the result of the sum reduction of an array FILE when all but one element in the size of FILE is a 1?

    b. In Exercise 3-27a, what is the size of the result? Compare the dimension of FILE with the dimension of its sum reduction.

    c. Predict and test a relationship between the dimension of any array and the dimension of its sum reduction.

    d. If you have gotten this far, you should be able to assign the correct value to each expression in Figure 3.12C without using the computer or knowing all about how sum reduction works for arrays.

    e. What have you learned so far about other reductions (times reduction, minus reduction, etc.) applied to arrays?

    f. Design a sequence of experiments like the ones above to determine the general rules for sum reduction of arrays.

3-28. Show that *and reduction* can be read "all of" and that *or reduction* can be read "any of." What interpretations can you give to reductions which use other logical operators? To reductions which use other operators?

MIXED OPERATORS

We come now to the so-called mixed operators. These are the irregular verbs of APL. They provide much of what is interesting, and like the irregular verbs in natural languages there is no one pattern which can describe them all. Some act on scalars to produce vectors, while others act on arrays to produce other arrays, often of a different size than the originals. Some of those which act on scalars extend to vectors, as in the previous section, while others do not.

A)

```
R                       S                       T
1  2  3=2               1  2  3<2               2>1  2  3
1  2  3=2               1  2  3=.5              0=3  2  1
1  2  3=2               3=2  3  4               1=‾1  0  1
×1  0  ‾5               (1,3)ρ1  0  ‾1          2  1  0+‾1
!6                      120                     ×/4  2  3  1  5
‾8                      -/3  5  2  8            ((3-5)-2)-8
(2,3)ρ'AX'='X'          (2,3)ρ0  1  0           (2,3)ρ0  1  0  1
÷/12  6  .5             ×3                      -/3  3  5
≠/3  4  5  1            ∧/1  0  0  1  1         ∨/'HI'='LO'
3ρ'HH'                  'HAT'                   'HAT'[×1  2  3]
```

B)

```
(3=1  2  3)∨(5≠1  2  3  4)
'ABCD'≤'E'
((2,3)ρ1  2  3  4)=(2,3)ρ4  +/1  2  3  4  5
6÷4-1  2  3  4
'ABCD'=1  2  3  4
(3ρρ1  2)=3ρ(1,3)ρ3
```

C)

EXPRESSION	CHOICES
+/(3,2)ρ1 2 3 4	10
	13
	6 7
	3 7 3
+/+/(1,1,1,1)ρ10	3
	10
	30
	40
ρ+/+/(2,2,2,2)ρ5	4
	2ρ2
	×(2,2)ρ5
	(2,2)ρ10

FIGURE 3.12. Exercises.

Due to the diversity among these operators, we will not examine each in detail. Rather, by looking at a few we can develop an idea of the sorts of details we must attend to in learning a new operator.

For our first example, see Figure 3.13. The operator here is called *iota* and, as we shall see, the monadic and dyadic forms do not have a great deal to do with each other.

iota

The monadic form is used to generate a vector from its scalar argument. Applying iota to a positive integer N yields the vector 1 2 3 ... N. Applying iota to 0 yields the empty vector. Applying iota to any other argument causes an error. Some examples are shown in Figure 3.14.

We should point out here that it is possible to set APL so as to change the *origin* for the iota operator. If we change the origin to 0 then iota N will be 0 1 2 ... N−1. Also, the first subscript of a vector will be the 0th instead of the first. For the purposes of examples, we will assume that the origin is 1 (*1 origin indexing*) unless otherwise specified.

origin

As a dyadic function, iota is quite different. As we can see from Figure 3.13 and Appendix Three, its left argument must be a vector while its right argument is not restricted. For this operator, the action can be demonstrated by showing its behavior with a scalar as right-hand argument; for any other right-hand argument the effect is then element by element.

ι (I)	ι (I)

INDEX

Mixed, dyadic, any/any
  AιB) has size (ρB). A must be a
  vector. Each element of the result
  is the location of the first occurrence in A of the corresponding
  element of B. "Nonoccurrence"
  is indicated by the value 1+(ρA):

  (9 17 15)ι(2,3)ρ9 17 11 15 6 28

  1 2 4
  3 4 4

Note: In 0 origin the result
would have been:

  0 1 3
  2 3 3

INDEX GENERATOR

Mixed, monadic, integer
  (ιB) is a vector of B successive
  integers, starting with the origin:

  ι3 [1 origin]

  1 2 3

  ι5 [0 origin]

  0 1 2 3 4

FIGURE 3.13. The definition of iota.

ι5
1   2   3   4   5

ι8
1   2   3   4   5   6   7   8

ι1
1

ι0
    NOTE-PRINTING THE EMPTY VECTOR CAUSES
        ONE LINE SKIP

ι2.3
DOMAIN ERROR
    ι2.3
    ∧

ι4 6 8
RANK ERROR
    ι4 6 8
    ∧

FIGURE 3.14. Examples of monadic iota.

Consider the first expression in Figure 3.15A. The argument on the left is a vector and the argument on the right is a scalar. Note that the scalar is the fourth element of the vector; this is the information that iota is designed to tell us. Thus, the *value* of the expression is 4. Similarly, the value of the second expression is 15. Note that there are many occurrences of the character 'U' in the left-hand argument, but that iota only gives the location of the leftmost. The third expression shows what happens if the right-hand argument does not appear on the left—the result is 1 plus the size of the vector.

If the right-hand argument is not a scalar, then the operator is applied element by element, always with the entire left-hand argument. Figure 3.15B shows more examples of dyadic iota.

Dyadic iota is quite different from any of the dyadic scalar operators, since it does not allow arbitrary left-hand arguments, even though any argument is acceptable on the right. You might even think of the operator plus its left-hand argument as a sort of "specialized operator" which can take any right-hand argument. A similar pattern exists for many of the mixed operators in that there are constraints placed on which left-hand arguments they permit. It is not, however, always the case that no constraints are placed on the right-hand arguments, as the next complementary pair of operators shows.

```
A)
      6  10  3  8  ⁻2  5ι8
4

      'THE MOON IS BLUE, HOW TRUE ARE YOU?'ι'U'
15

      1  2  3  4ι10
5


B)
      'DYADIC'ι'IOTA'
5   7   7   3

      1 2 3 4 5 6ι0 2 4 6 8
7   2   4   6   7

      '1  2  3'ι1
6

      LANGUAGES ← (4,3)ρ'APLPLIFAPASM'
      LANGUAGES
APL
PLI
FAP
ASM

      'COMPUTERS'ιLANGUAGES
   10    4   10
    4   10   10
   10   10    4
   10    9    3

      3ι3
RANK ERROR
      3ι3
       ∧

      (,3)ι3
1

      ((2,4)ρ1  2  3)ι2
RANK ERROR
      ((2,4)ρ1  2  3)ι2
                    ∧
```

FIGURE 3.15. Examples of dyadic iota.

Figure 3.16 is a summary of the forms available to us when using the operators *compress* and *expand*. Even though it doesn't tell us what the operators do, it does give us much useful information. First of all, it does tell us that the left-hand argument must be composed of zeros and ones. Furthermore, the figure shows six forms, three for compressing and three for expanding. Each form for compressing is matched by an analogous form for expanding, the only difference being the way that the slash marks tilt. We might expect, therefore, that there will be a great deal of similarity in the way that these two operators perform.

compress
We will begin with *compress*. The left-hand argument must be *logical* (made up of zeros and ones); a logical vector is sometimes called a *bit-string*. Furthermore, if this argument has more than one element, it must be a vector and not an array. As with many other operators, although it was not the case with iota, there are also restrictions on what right-hand arguments are permissible. In this case, the restriction derives from our choice of left-hand argument.

conform-able
Whenever an operator requires that its arguments possess certain similarities, we say that the arguments must be *conformable*. The meaning of conformable, however, varies from one operator to another. The simplest case to consider with compress is when the right-hand argument is a vector; then, conformable means that the two arguments must have the same size.

Consider the expression in Figure 3.17A. This is a compression expression: the vector on the left is logical, it has the same number of elements as the one on the right, and the two vectors are separated by the symbol for compression. Now, the first element on the left is a 1; this tells us to *select* the first element on the right. Similarly, since the second element on the left is a 0, we *ignore* the second element on the right. As the result shows, what we are doing is using the left-hand argument as a guide to tell us which of the elements on the right to take. Figure 3.17B shows some more examples of compression of vectors.

If the argument on the left has only a single element, whether it be a scalar or a one element array of many dimensions, the operation still makes sense: if the left-hand argument is 1, then the entire right-hand argument is taken, while if there is a 0 on the left, the result is the empty vector. Part C of the figure shows some examples.

X/Y	X (logical)* compressing along the last dimension of Y
$X/[Z/Y$	X (logical) compressing along the Zth dimension of Y
$X \neq Y$	X (logical) compressing along the first dimension of Y
$X \backslash Y$	X (logical) expanding along the last dimension of Y
$X \backslash [Z]Y$	X (logical) expanding along the Zth dimension of Y
$X \backslash Y$	X (logical) expanding along the first dimension of Y

*That X is *logical* means it is composed of zeros and ones.

FIGURE 3.16. Compression and expansion.

A)
```
      1 0 1 1 0/'APPLE'
APL
```

B)
```
      0 1 0 1 0/1 2 3 4 5
2   4

      PRESSURE ← 12 3 14 19 7 5 7 3 9 1 11
      (PRESSURE≤7)/PRESSURE
3   7   5   7   3   1
      (PRESSURE≤7)/ιρPRESSURE
2   5   6   7   8   10

      0 0 0 0 0 0/'FORTRAN'
    (EMPTY VECTOR)

      1 1 1 1 1/'KOALA'
KOALA
```

C)
```
      1/10 20 30
10   20   30

      0/'PANDA'
    (EMPTY VECTOR)

      ((1,1,1)ρ1)/'FILES'
FILES
```

FIGURE 3.17. Some compressions.

When the right-hand argument is an array, compression takes place along only one dimension. For example, consider the compression expression in Figure 3.18A. Compression acts on each row, so that as a result entire columns are either selected or ignored. This is a sort of element by element extension to the rule for vectors, except here the "elements" are entire rows of the array. If the array has more than two dimensions, the same rule holds: compression acts to select or ignore columns.

conforma-bility for compress

We can see, therefore, that for the right-hand argument to be conformable with the left, the following rule must hold: If there is more than one element on the left, then the number of elements on the left must be equal to the number of columns on the right.

When we compress an array, the size of the result is almost the same as the size of the right-hand argument. The only difference comes in the number of columns: the number of columns in the result is equal to the number of ones in the left-hand argument (unless, of course, the left-hand argument was a single 1, in which case the result is equal to the right-hand argument). Figure 3.18B shows some examples of compressing arrays.

compres-sion along coordinates

What we have been doing so far can also be called *column compression* or *compression along the last coordinate*. We can do compression along any coordinate of an array. For example, in a two-dimensional array, we could also do *row compression*: the left-hand argument would be applied to each column, so that entire *rows* would either be selected or ignored. To do compression along any coordinate other than the last, we must specify the coordinate inside brackets right after the compression sign. Figure 3.18C shows some examples.

expand

Expansion has an approximately opposite effect. We need only discuss the case where the right-hand argument is a vector, however, as the extension to arrays is very similar to the way that it is for compression.

```
A)
      GUIDE ← (3,6)ρι6
      GUIDE
  1   2   3   4   5   6
  1   2   3   4   5   6
  1   2   3   4   5   6
      1 0 0 1 1 0/GUIDE
  1   4   5
  1   4   5
  1   4   5

B)
      NAMES ← (2,7)ρ'J.SMITHA.JONES'
      INITIALS ← 1 0 1 0 0 0 0
      NAMES
J.SMITH
A.JONES
      INITIALS/NAMES
JS
AJ


      RACE ← (2,3,4)ρι24
      LAPS ← 1 0 0 1
      RACE
  1    2    3    4
  5    6    7    8
  9   10   11   12

 13   14   15   16
 17   18   19   20
 21   22   23   24
      LAPS/RACE
  1    4
  5    8
  9   12

 13   16
 17   20
 21   24


C)
      1 0 1/[1]GUIDE
  1   2   3   4   5   6
  1   2   3   4   5   6

      0 1 0/[2]RACE
  5    6    7    8

 17   18   19   20

      INITIALS/[2]NAMES
JS
AJ
```

FIGURE 3.18. Compressing arrays.

conforma-
bility for
expand

Again, the left-hand argument must be a logical vector and it must be conformable with the right-hand argument. However, conformable has a different meaning than it did for compression. For a vector as right-hand argument, there must be as many ones on the left as there are elements on the right. There will, in general, also be zeros on the left. These indicate places where the right-hand argument is to be expanded by the insertion of zeros (in numeric vectors) or blanks (in character vectors). Some examples are given in Figure 3.19.

```
      1 0 1 0 1\'APL'
A  P  L


      1 0 1 0 1\2 4 6
2   0   4   0   6


      NAMES ← (2,6)ρ'JSMITHAJONES'
      NAMES
JSMITH
AJONES
      1 0 1 1 1 1 1\NAMES
J SMITH
A JONES


      INTEGERS ← (2,5)ρι10
      INTEGERS
  1     2     3     4     5
  6     7     8     9    10
      1 1 0\[1]INTEGERS
  1     2     3     4     5
  6     7     8     9    10
  0     0     0     0     0
      1 0 1\[1]INTEGERS
  1     2     3     4     5
  0     0     0     0     0
  6     7     8     9    10
```

FIGURE 3.19. Expansions.

EXERCISES

3-29. Which expression in Figure 3.20A is different from the others?

3-30. Use each of the operators rho and iota, and compress to write an expression whose value is the empty vector.

3-31. Use compression to find the message hidden in Figure 3.20B.

3-32. Explain how compression can be used with other operators for each of the following:
  a. Removing all the vowels from a character vector.
  b. Finding the locations of the positive numbers in a numeric vector.
  c. Adding an 'S' to 'STICK' if the value of a variable named COUNT is greater than 1.

3-33. Given two variables LEFT and RIGHT, write an expression which produces the value 1 if the variables would be conformable for compression (with LEFT being the left-hand argument).

3-34. Formulate and verify a rule telling when two variables are conformable with respect to expansion.

3-35. Can the empty vector be a left-hand argument of a compression; of an expansion?

3-36. Evaluate the expressions in Figure 3.20C; check your results at the terminal.

3-37. Write an expression which, for any positive integer N, gives the vector N N—1 N—2 ... 1. What would be the result of your expression in 0 origin indexing?

3-38. Another special form of compression (or expansion) can be obtained by overstriking the operator sign with a subtraction sign, as shown for compression in Figure 3.20D. Use the terminal to discover along which coordinate this indicates compression (or expansion).

3-39. It is often convenient to be able to distinguish between character variables and numeric variables. To do this, we have to make a supposition. Suppose that when a variable has the empty vector for its value, APL has some way to distinguish whether it is an empty vector of numbers (see Figure 3.20E) or an empty vector of characters (Figure 3.20F). Let J be an empty vector. Following the definition of *expand* literally, what is the value of 0\J if J is an empty character vector; if J is an empty numeric vector? Now, write an APL expression involving a variable U which will produce 0 if U is made up of characters and 1 if it is made up of numbers. (*Hint*: we would first create an empty vector from U, then use expand to get either a blank or a 0, and finally check to

A)

```
    1  2  3  4⍳6
    'DOGGED'⍳'E'
    (1+⍳5)[5]
    +/'HA'⍳'MA'
```

B)

```
WAHBCADTE F G
 H IJFKOLOMLNS
TOHPQERSSET U
MVOWXRYTZA1L2S
 3 45B6E7 8 9
```

C)

```
    1  0  0  1  1  1/3+⍳6
    (5≤1  2  3  4  5  6  7)/'ONLYAPL'
    1  1  0  1/'THEY'
    1  1  0  1\'THY'

    XWORD ← (3,4)ρ'DUCKO O GOWN'
    1  0  1/[1]XWORD
    1  0  1  0/[2]XWORD
    (XWORD[2;]='O')/⍳ρXWORD[2;]

    ACCOUNT ← (3,2,2)ρ4×⍳19
    ρ1  0  1  0  0\[2]ACCOUNT
```

D)

```
    ≠
```

E)

```
    0ρ0
```

F)

```
    0ρ' '
```

FIGURE 3.20. Exercises.

see whether the value produced was a 0.) Verify the supposition by checking all this at the terminal.

The following exercises are intended to help you discover the way that some of the other mixed operators function. Other mixed operators will be discussed in the text when they are needed, but you are encouraged to try to become familiar with as many as you have time for.

3-40. Which expression(s) in Figure 3.21A have value 1?

3-31. Verify that the expression in Figure 3.21B differentiates between arbitrary numeric vectors L and vectors made up of only zeros and ones. Will the expression also work for arbitrary arrays? If so, explain why. If not, write one which will.

3-42. The *grade up* operator is shown in Figure 3.21C. Apply it to the first vector shown to produce each of the other two. (*Hint*: one of these requires subscripting.)

3-43. The *grade down* operator is shown in Figure 3.21D. Use it to produce the first vector shown from each of the others.

3-44. The monadic *reverse* operator is shown in Figure 3.21E. Insert it, and any appropriate parentheses, in the expression shown there to make the value of the expression equal to 12.

3-45. Verify that for any vector TIMES, each expression in Figure 3.21F will always have value 1. One of them will not work in the same way if TIMES is not a vector. Modify it so it does.

3-46. Which expression in Figure 3.21G is not equal to the other two?

3-47. Show that if S is a scalar and V is a vector then the expression in Figure 3.21H produces the vector V if S is an element of V, and the empty vector otherwise. Write an expression which gives all the indices where S appears in V, or the empty vector if S is not in V.

3-48. Using various of the symbols shown in the first line of Figure 3.21I, produce each of the other lines from the vector 1 2 3 4 5.

A)

```
      1↑ι5
      1↓ι5
      (3↑ι5)[1]
      5∊ι4
      4∊'1234'
```

B)

```
      (+/L∊0 1)=ρL
```

C)

```
      ▲
      3  7  1  9  4  ⁻6
       ⁻6  3  1  5  2  4
      ⁻6  1  3  4  7  9
```

D)

```
      ▼
      6  5  4  3·2  1
       1  2  3  4  5  6
       1  3  7  11  31  99
```

E)

```
      φ
      +/   ι3  +   ι3
```

F)

```
      ×/TIMES∊TIMES
      ~0∊TIMES∊TIMES
```

G)

```
      ⁻4φι10
      ⁻4φι10·
      ⁻6φι10
```

H)

```
      ((ρV)×S∊V)ρV
```

I)

```
      ∊▲▼φ↑↓\/ι
0
0  0
2
1  2
1  2  3  4
2  3  4  5
5  4  3  2
LENGTH ERROR
DOMAIN ERROR
SYNTAX ERROR
```

FIGURE 3.21. More exercises.

COMPOSITE OPERATORS

Suppose that two people each make certain purchases from a mailorder catalogue. Each row of the array AMOUNTS shown in figure 3.22A represents the purchases of one person—the 8 in the second row and third column indicates that eight of the third item were ordered by the second person. The costs *per item* can be represented in the vector COSTS; one unit of the first item costs $40 and so on.

It is simple to calculate the amount which each person must pay: take the amounts ordered, multiply each by the corresponding cost per item, and then add all the costs together. Figure 3.22B shows how easily this can be done in APL.

A large company, which may get hundreds of order forms each day, might have to perform exactly this sort of calculation on each one. It would surely be a tiring and somewhat error-prone process if someone had to repeat the calculations shown in the figure once for each row of the array. Clearly, what is needed is a way to extend these calculations from one row to the entire array in a row by row manner, just as other operators have been extended element by element from scalars to arrays.

While conceptually it is not difficult to see that an operation might be extended from rows (vectors) to arrays, we might have some problems in this particular case as we are not dealing with one operation but two—multiplication and sum reduction. The designers of APL solved this problem by creating a new type of operator—one which turns a pair of operators into a brand new one.

First, let's look at a specific case. Figure 3.23 shows the *inner product* of the array AMOUNTS with the vector COSTS. You can see that the result is a vector whose first element is the total cost associated with the first person (first row of AMOUNTS) and whose second element is the total cost associated with the second person (second row of

A)
```
      AMOUNTS ← (2,5)ρι10
      AMOUNTS
   1    2    3    4    5
   6    7    8    9   10

      COSTS← 40 30 20 10 1
      COSTS
40   30   20   10    1
```

B)
```
      +/AMOUNTS[1;]×COSTS
205
      +/AMOUNTS[2;]×COSTS
710
```

FIGURE 3.22. Calculations of total costs.

```
      AMOUNTS
   1    2    3    4    5
   6    7    8    9   10


      COSTS
40   30   20   10    1


      AMOUNTS+.×COSTS
205   710
```

FIGURE 3.23. An inner product.

AMOUNTS). If we call the inner product of AMOUNTS with COSTS by the name RESULTS, then RESULTS is a vector defined as shown in Figure 3.24A.

inner
product

You can see that in this case the period acts something like an operator which takes the arguments *plus* and *times*, producing the operator called inner product. In fact, there is some truth to this. APL lets you combine any two scalar operators in this way, to get a *generalized inner product*. Figure 3.24B shows how this might be defined. The two operator symbols used there are not real operators; they can be replaced with two dyadic scalar operators to get a valid definition.

The existence of generalized inner product is one of the very powerful features of the language. However, most of the applications are somewhat mathematical, and so outside of the scope of this book. For this reason, we have not discussed generalized inner product in detail; it can be used with other types of arguments—two arrays for example—and there are detailed definitions and conformability requirements for each case. We leave it to the interested reader to do further experimentation and exploration.

A)

```
      RESULTS ← AMOUNTS+.×COSTS

      ⍝-----RESULTS IS A VECTOR OF
      ⍝-----SIZE (ρAMOUNTS)[1]
      ⍝-----ITS I-TH ELEMENT IS

      RESULTS[I] ← +/AMOUNTS[I;]×COSTS
```

B)

```
      RESULTS ← AMOUNTS○.⊡COSTS

      ⍝-----○ AND ⊡ ARE TWO SCALAR OPERATORS
      ⍝----- THE I-TH ELEMENT OF RESULTS IS

      RESULTS[I] ← ○/AMOUNTS⊡COSTS
```

FIGURE 3.24. Definitions of inner products.

**outer
product**

It should be no surprise that where there is an inner product there is also an *outer product*. Again, we will not discuss this in detail, but will merely provide an example of how it can be used. Perhaps we have two vectors and want to know which elements in the first are equal to which elements in the second. Suppose that the first vector has five elements and that the second has eight. This requires 40 comparisons. Using an outer product, as shown in Figure 3.25A, we can do these comparisons and end up with a nice visual record of the results. For example, if we look at the fifth row, there is a 1 in column three. This means that the fifth element of OFFERS is equal to the third element of COSTS. The rest of Figure 3.25 gives the definitions for outer product.

The symbol for outer product looks very much like the symbol for inner product. The difference is that the little circle which appears before the period is not an operator. Any valid dyadic scalar operator can be placed after the period. Also, there is a great variety to outer product which we have not discussed; as with inner product, the exact definitions for different types of arguments, and the corresponding conformability rules, are left to the interested reader.

EXERCISES

3-49. Using the definitions in Figure 3.26A, evaluate and explain each expression in Figure 3.26B.

3-50. Using outer products, write expressions which yield each of the following:

a. A square (the same number of rows and columns) array with ones on the main diagonal (running from upper left to lower right) and zeros everywhere else.

b. A square array with ones above the main diagonal and zeros everywhere else.

3-51. We have purposely not discussed how to extend the comma, which is used to concatenate vectors, to arrays. Find out how to concatenate (or *laminate*) arrays. What are the conformability requirements? What happens when a number in brackets is placed right after the comma?

A)

```
     OFFERS ← 46 1 33 19 12
     COSTS ← 1 11 12 1 24 2 16 33
     OFFERS∘.=COSTS
 0 0 0 0 0 0 0 0
 1 0 0 1 0 0 0 0
 0 0 0 0 0 0 0 1
 0 0 0 0 0 0 0 0
 0 0 1 0 0 0 0 0
```

B)

```
     RESULT ← OFFERS∘.=COSTS

     ⍝-----RESULT IS AN ARRAY WITH (ρOFFERS) ROWS
     ⍝-----AND (ρCOSTS) COLUMNS. ITS [I;J] ELEMENT
     ⍝-----IS DEFINED BY
     RESULT[I;J] ← OFFERS[I]=COSTS[J]
```

C)

```
     RESULT ← OFFERS∘.⊡COSTS

     ⍝-----⊡ IS ANY SCALAR OPERATOR.
     RESULT[I;J] ← OFFERS⌊I⌋⊡COSTS⌊J⌋
```

FIGURE 3.25. Outer products.

A)

```
     PRODUCTS ← (3,4)ρ⍳12
     TAXES ←  1 10 100 2
```

B)

```
     PRODUCTS+.×TAXES
     PRODUCTS+.=TAXES
     PRODUCTS=.>TAXES
     PRODUCTS+.+TAXES
```

FIGURE 3.26. Inner product exercises.

Interlude Two

Workspaces

When you sign on to the machine there are usually many other users as well and you do not have the entire machine at your disposal. Instead, you are assigned a small piece of the machine called a *workspace*. We will not be concerned with the way that workspaces are actually handled by the machine but only with how they appear to us.

LOAD, CLEAR, COPY

Think of a workspace as a single sheet of paper on which you can write and erase at will. Initially, when you sign on, you are given a clean sheet of paper called a *clear workspace*. At any time, you can erase everything from your workspace and make it clear again by issuing the system command

)CLEAR

CLEAR WS

The system responds with the message CLEAR WS, as shown, to indicate that the erasing is completed.

The workspace that is available to you when you are working at the terminal is called your *active workspace*: this is the one in which you do your writing and erasing. There are, however, three "filing cabinets" containing workspaces which you can reference.

Why would you want to reference another workspace? Other workspaces can contain information about the computer; drills to help you learn APL; programs that you or other people have written to do a variety of tasks, games, puzzles; and even calendars containing nude pictures of your favorite cartoon strip dog.

Workspaces are collected together in *libraries*. Each library can have any number of workspaces. Every user has one library, and there are also many public libraries. Thus, the three sources of saved workspaces are your own library, other users' libraries and public libraries.

Every workspace (except possibly your active workspace) has a name and every library has a number. To be able to use a workspace you must know both its name and its library number. For example, to be able to use a workspace called APLNEWS from library number 1, type

)LOAD 1 APLNEWS

The load command has the following effect: it wipes out your active workspace and then puts an exact copy of APLNEWS as your new active workspace. The "file drawer" copy of APLNEWS in library 1 is left untouched, and what was in your active workspace before no longer exists (unless you previously made a copy of it someplace).

If there turns out not to be a workspace in library 1 called APLNEWS the system will return the message

WS NOT FOUND

and there will be no change to your active workspace.

When loading a workspace from your own library, it is not necessary to give a number. Simply type

)LOAD MYSPACE

and if you have a workspace named MYSPACE it will be loaded.

To find out what workspaces there are in your library enter the command

)LIB

For a list of all the workspaces in public library N, enter

)LIB N

It is also possible, as has been mentioned, to use a workspace belonging to another user. The number of the library in this case is the user's sign-on number (not including the lock, if there is one). However, you can not type

)LIB 092773820

and see all the workspaces belonging to 092773820, and 092773820 cannot see the list of yours.

There is another way to reference workspaces. You can copy all (or, as we will see later, part) of a workspace. When you execute the command

)COPY 1 APLNEWS

a copy is again made of that workspace, but it does *not* replace your active workspace; instead, it is added to whatever is already in your active workspace. Workspaces are limited in size, and if you begin copying too many things into them, you run the risk of filling up your active workspace to capacity. If you do, the system will let you know:

WS FULL

EXERCISES

(*Note*: To be able to use a workspace you must know what is in it. A public library workspace should contain directions for its own use, but these are no good unless you know how to find them. We will give you two "magic words" which will help you in your quest (they will be converted to "scientific formulae" later in the book, or you can investigate on your own). The magic words are)FNS and)VARS. If you type one of these after loading or copying a workspace, the system will respond by listing a lot of names. Most of them may seem meaningless. You will be looking for a name that sounds like it holds information about the workspace, like DESCRIBE or INFO or MANUAL. If you find one such, type it in and then follow the directions.)

I2-1. Find a printed list of the contents of all the public libraries which are in your computer.

I2-2. Is there a public workspace which contains news about the system, such as the hours that APL is available or what to do if you have problems? If so, load it and find out what it has to say. If not, perhaps you can persuade your computer center to put one in.

I2-3. Find an interesting game in one of the public libraries and play it.

I2-4. Find a public library with some kind of teaching drill, such as for a science course or a foreign language or some complicated set of programs on the system. Try to use it. Do you like that kind of teaching? How could it be improved?

I2-5. Find a public library which has a drill on the APL operators. Pick an operator which we haven't yet discussed and see if you can deduce what it does by using the drill program.

I2-6. Try to get a workspace full error by copying many workspaces into your active workspace. You can find out how much space is left in your workspace by typing *I-beam* 22 as in Figure I2.1. When you get a workspace full error does this mean there is no more room? Can you still create variables or do arithmetic in a full workspace? Are all full workspaces equally full?

I2-7. In what units is I-beam 22 on your system? How many of them are there in a clear workspace?

I2-8. What information does the system give when a workspace is loaded or copied?

SAVE

To save a copy of your active workspace in your library you must first give it a name. A workspace name must start with an alphabetic character and may not contain any blanks; there is also a limit on the total number of characters, which may differ from system to system. To

FIGURE 12.1. I-Beam 22.

name the active workspace CRUNCH type

)WSID CRUNCH

WAS MYSPACE

The message typed back indicates what the previous name of the workspace was. If it had no name, the message would have been

WAS CLEAR WS

To save the active workspace, type

)SAVE

The system will probably respond by giving the date and time. The effect of the SAVE command is opposite to that of the LOAD command. A copy is made of the active workspace and stuck off in a file drawer under the name CRUNCH. You may then go on making changes to the active workspace, without affecting the saved copy of it in any way.

Sometimes you will want to get rid of a workspace which has been saved. To do this, type

)DROP CRUNCH

to expurgate the saved copy of CRUNCH from the file drawer. This command has no effect on the active workspace, even if its name is also CRUNCH.

EXERCISES

12-9. Get a clear workspace, name it BILLS and assign to variable GAS the value 1. Save BILLS. Then perform the following steps:
   a. Assign to OIL and to GAS the value 2.
      Load BILLS.
      Find out the value of OIL and GAS.
   b. Assign to OIL and GAS the value 3.
      Copy BILLS.
      Find out the value of OIL and GAS.
   c. Assign to OIL and GAS the value 3.
      Execute the command)PCOPY BILLS.
      Find out the value of OIL and GAS.
   What conclusions can you draw about the relative effects of LOAD, COPY, and PCOPY?

12-10. Find out how to lock and unlock a workspace.

4

A First Program

"Introduce me, now there's a good fellow," he said,
   "If we happen to meet it together!"
And the Bellman, sagaciously nodding his head,
   Said,"That must depend on the weather."

APL is a language. APL expressions which we type in at the terminal are like sentences and a program in APL is a paragraph made up of sentences. The program is a list of APL expressions and anything which can be entered at the terminal can be part of a program. As part of a program, the APL expressions are not evaluated when you type them in. Instead, they are saved until you decide to use the program and then evaluated one at a time.

Reading and writing, in APL as much as in any natural language, are complementary processes and we will learn about them together.

READING A PROGRAM

del

line zero

We will begin by reading the program in Figure 4.1. Notice first of all the small point-down triangles at the beginning and end. These *dels* indicate the beginning and the end of the program; they also tell the system that the expressions being entered are part of the program and not to be immediately evaluated. All lines but the first are numbered, starting from 1; the unnumbered first line is referred to as *line zero*, or the *header line*.

Line zero always contains the name of the program, in this case TEMP. When we type the name *without* the del the expressions on the lines are evaluated one after the other, starting with line 1; at this point they will be treated just as if they had been simply entered in at the terminal. So, consider line 1. This line contains nothing but a simple character vector. Had we typed this in at the terminal it would have been typed back to us, and so when we *call* TEMP the first thing we should expect is to see the sentence THE TWELVE MONTHLY TEMPERATURES WERE printed by APL.

lamp

Line 2 contains a single name. This could be the name of a variable or of a program—we have no way of knowing. Until, that is, we look at lines 3–5. The symbol at the beginning of each line is called a *lamp*; it is the same symbol that we use to indicate a comment block in a structure chart and has the same function. APL ignores any line which begins with a lamp. Thus, these lines contain a message to the reader explaining what a particular part of the program is about. The program would run *exactly* the same without the comment, but might be much harder for us to understand.

Line 6 prints another character vector and then on line 7 there is an arithmetic operation: the elements of TEMPERATURE are added together and the sum is divided by 12. Since the result is not assigned to any variable, it will be printed too. Another character vector is printed on line 8 and then on line 9 a new symbol appears. Using the right-to-left rule we can understand part of that line: first the largest element of the vector TEMPERATURE is found and assigned to variable EXTREME, and then EXTREME is assigned to the box, called a

```
      ∇  TEMP
[1]      'THE TWELVE MONTHLY TEMPERATURES WERE'
[2]      TEMPERATURE
[3]      ⍝-----TEMPERATURE IS A VECTOR OF
[4]      ⍝------THE AVERAGE MONTHLY TEMPERATURES
[5]      ⍝------FOR A YEAR
[6]      'THE AVERAGE TEMPERATURE WAS'
[7]      (+/TEMPERATURE)÷12
[8]      'THE LARGEST TEMPERATURE WAS'
[9]      □←EXTREME←⌈/TEMPERATURE
[10]     'IT OCCURRED IN MONTHS'
[11]     (EXTREME=TEMPERATURE)/⍳12
[12]     'THE SMALLEST TEMPERATURE WAS'
[13]     □←EXTREME←⌊/TEMPERATURE
[14]     'IT OCCURRED IN MONTHS'
[15]     (EXTREME=TEMPERATURE)/⍳12
      ∇
```

FIGURE 4.1. A program to read.

quad. As we know, when a quantity is assigned to a variable it will not be automatically printed back. Sometimes, however, we want to do both: print a value *and* assign it to a variable. The quad is a special symbol used for output and input: in this context it means that the value of variable EXTREME should be printed.

The next line, line 10, shows another character vector, and then there is another arithmetic expression, involving compression. Its result, as you should check, will be the indices of those elements in the twelve element vector TEMPERATURE which are equal to the largest, EXTREME. Then lines 8–11 are almost repeated in lines 12–15, where the smallest temperature is found.

We should at this point, having read the program, be able to "abstract it." The program uses a vector TEMPERATURE, which must be defined outside the program. The program adds up the elements and divides the sum by 12, and then finds in turn the largest and smallest elements and their locations in the vector.

Of course, the final judge as to whether or not we are correct in our reading is the computer, to whom all programs must be submitted. Figure 4.2 shows a session at the computer with the program. The first time that the name TEMP was typed in, line 1 was executed but the machine was unable to execute line 2, as we had forgotten to give TEMPERATURE a value. When an error occurs in running a program it is much like when it occurs in a line that you type in: the error message is printed, followed by the offending line, and then APL gives an indication of where the error was found. The program is not "gone" now, as an expression would be. The system remembers that the program execution was *suspended* on line 2, and if we can correct the error we can go on from where we left off.

In this case, to correct the error we have only to give a value to the vector TEMPERATURE, which is the next thing done in the figure. To resume execution of the program, we type a right-pointing arrow, pointing at the number of the line on which the program was interrupted (read this as "continue with line 2").

From here on the behavior of the program is as we expected. We might try again, because the more test cases we try, the more confidence we can have (actually, it is not so much the number of test cases but the number of cases that they test which is important). We thus define a new vector TEMPERATURE, and call TEMP again. And again, everything works as expected.

A third test, in which all elements of TEMPERATURE are 100, does not fare so well. The program is interrupted at line 11 with a LENGTH ERROR. Before we look at line 11, however, look at the output which preceded it. The program says that the average value of the elements of TEMPERATURE is 91.66666667. But that is absurd: if there is one

```
        TEMP
THE TWELVE MONTHLY TEMPERATURES WERE
VALUE ERROR
TEMP[2] TEMPERATURE
        ∧
        TEMPERATURE←21 20 33 45 53 72 71 72 62 51 38 20
        →2
21  20  33  45  53  72  71  72  62  51  38  20
THE AVERAGE TEMPERATURE WAS
46.5
THE LARGEST TEMPERATURE WAS
72
IT OCCURRED IN MONTHS
6  8
THE SMALLEST TEMPERATURE WAS
20
IT OCCURRED IN MONTHS
2  12


        TEMPERATURE←31 30 43 55 63 82 81 82 73 61 48 30
        TEMP
THE TWELVE MONTHLY TEMPERATURES WERE
31  30  43  55  63  82  81  82  73  61  48  30
THE AVERAGE TEMPERATURE WAS
56.58333333
THE LARGEST TEMPERATURE WAS
82
IT OCCURRED IN MONTHS
6  8
THE SMALLEST TEMPERATURE WAS
30
IT OCCURRED IN MONTHS
2  12


        TEMPERATURE←100 100 100 100 100 100 100 100 100 100 100
        TEMP
THE TWELVE MONTHLY TEMPERATURES WERE
100  100  100  100  100  100  100  100  100  100  100
THE AVERAGE TEMPERATURE WAS
91.66666667
THE LARGEST TEMPERATURE WAS
100
IT OCCURRED IN MONTHS
LENGTH ERROR
TEMP[11] (EXTREME=TEMPERATURE)/ι12
        ∧
        ρTEMPERATURE
11
        1100÷12
91.66666667
```

FIGURE 4.2. Testing the program.

thing upon which we can depend it is that the average of a set of numbers, all of them equal to 100, is 100. The conclusion which we must draw is that we cannot depend on what is printed by a program to be true!

In this case the two errors, the one that APL caught and the one that we caught, are related. The LENGTH ERROR in line 11 indicates that the two arguments to the compression operator have different lengths: since the right hand argument has size 12, the first thing we should check is that TEMPERATURE may not have 12 elements. Indeed, as the next line of the figure shows, it has only 11. This might also explain the incorrect average: $(11 \times 100) \div 12$ is 91.66666667.

Since we only want our program to work for correct vectors TEMPERATURE, our first thought might be that it is all right if a bad vector causes the program to stop in this way. But actually, it is not. A program should never have an error in it. This goal may be impossible to realize, but we can at least never leave in an error that we know about. Our next step, therefore, is to correct our program.

EXERCISES

4-1. If, as we said, anything which can be entered as an APL expression directly can be put as a line of a program, it is not unreasonable to expect the opposite as well. Verify that every single line of the program TEMP can be entered directly to the terminal and that the same results will ensue as when they are executed as lines of the program.

4-2. Verify that the expressions in Figure 4.3 have the same effect.

4-3. List some different ways you might want to correct the error in the program. Sometimes a program you write will only be used by you and sometimes you will make it available to others. Evaluate each of your proposed corrections in each of these lights. Do not ignore the possibility that you may originally intend not to make a program available to others, and much later change your mind.

4-4. Reconsider Exercise 4-3 in case the program is part of a system for controlling airplanes at a large airport.

CORRECTING AND WRITING PROGRAMS

Of the many ways in which we could correct this program, one of the most reasonable is to modify it so that it will work for any size vector. To do this, we need only replace the twelves on lines 7, 11, and 15 by an expression giving the size of TEMPERATURE. The terminal session showing how these corrections are made is given in Figure 4.4.

```
       □←EXTREME←⌈/TEMPERATURE
EXTREME←□←⌈/TEMPERATURE
```

FIGURE 4.3. Two equivalent expressions.

```
       ∇ TEMP
[16]   [7](+/TEMPERATURE)÷ρTEMPERATURE
[8]    [7□]
[7]    (+/TEMPERATURE)÷ρTEMPERATURE
[7]    [11□18]
[11]   (EXTREME=TEMPERATURE)/ι12
                              //
[11]   (EXTREME=TEMPERATURE)/ιρTEMPERATURE
[12]   [15□21]
[15]   (EXTREME=TEMPERATURE)/ι12
                          3  //
[15]   (EXTREME=TEMPERATURE    )/ιρTEMPERATURE
[16]   [15□]
[15]   (EXTREME=TEMPERATURE)/ιρTEMPERATURE
[15]   [□]
     ∇ TEMP
[1]    'THE TWELVE MONTHLY TEMPERATURES WERE'
[2]    TEMPERATURE
[3]    ₳-----TEMPERATURE IS A VECTOR OF
[4]    ₳------THE AVERAGE MONTHLY TEMPERATURES
[5]    ₳------FOR A YEAR
[6]    'THE AVERAGE TEMPERATURE WAS'
[7]    (+/TEMPERATURE)÷ρTEMPERATURE
[8]    'THE LARGEST TEMPERATURE WAS'
[9]    □←EXTREME←⌈/TEMPERATURE
[10]   'IT OCCURRED IN MONTHS'
[11]   (EXTREME=TEMPERATURE)/ιρTEMPERATURE
[12]   'THE SMALLEST TEMPERATURE WAS'
[13]   □←EXTREME←⌊/TEMPERATURE
[14]   'IT OCCURRED IN MONTHS'
[15]   (EXTREME=TEMPERATURE)/ιρTEMPERATURE
     ∇
[16]   ∇
```

FIGURE 4.4. Correcting the program.

correcting

We will use different techniques to correct the lines. First we indicate to APL that we wish to make corrections to the program by typing the del and then the program name. The program responds by asking for the next line of the program; since we have not told it otherwise, it assumes we wish to add lines to the program. Instead we type line 7 in brackets and follow it by the corrected version of the line. To check that we made no typing errors, we can ask to see line 7 displayed by typing, inside the square brackets, a 7 followed by the quad symbol.

editing

Sometimes when fixing one mistake on a line we will make a different mistake, and it is therefore advisable to do as little typing as possible. APL provides us with a very efficient mechanism for making corrections. We type the line number we wish to change, followed by a quad, followed by another number, which is our estimate of where the first character we wish to correct is—this estimate need not be at all accurate. In the figure, our estimate was 18: the response of the system was to type the line, then skip a line and space in 18 spaces. We can now give APL directions of two types, after which it will retype the line. If we type a slash under a character, that character will be deleted; if we type a number under a character that character will be preceded by that number of spaces. (Note that we can do all the spacing and backspacing we want. One rule of APL that is not usually written down is that what is entered into the machine is the line *as you see it* and the order in which you type the characters does not matter.) When we are correcting at the very end of a line we don't need to indicate a number of spaces.

The response of the system is to retype the line with the deletions and spaces as indicated, and then position the typing element under the first space which was added (or at the end of the line if no spaces were added). We can make any additions we want in the spaces or at the end of the line and what we see when we hit return is the line that the machine will use in the program. We repeat the same correction technique for line 15. (Note that superfluous blanks are not retained.)

listing

Before we type a del to indicate that we are through changing the program, it is wise to read it once more. To do this, we would probably like a clean listing of the program, which we can get by typing a quad all by itself, in brackets. We should ask ourselves, what could we do now to make the program fail? We are asking for the size of the vector TEMPERATURE: suppose that TEMPERATURE is not a vector. Surely, the result will be strange. If TEMPERATURE is supposed to be a vector, we can ensure that it is one by using the monadic operator

ravel

ravel (a comma); the expression in Figure 4.5 makes a vector from TEMPERATURE. Of course, if TEMPERATURE was already a vector, this has no effect. We can add this to line 2, but before we make more changes, let's consider what else could go wrong. As we read the program, we see that it will always say that there are 12 temperatures, even though all the changes we have been making have been to correct

TEMPERATURE←,TEMPERATURE

FIGURE 4.5. Raveling a variable.

for the possibility that there will not always be 12. It would be reasonable to have the program be as truthful as possible. We would therefore

printing characters with numbers

like line 1 to print the actual number of elements in TEMPERATURE. To print characters and numbers on the same line, we must separate them by semicolons. It is *almost* like concatenating the numbers and characters, but that is something we cannot do.

We might, therefore, want to replace line 1 with Figure 4.6; then we have no need to make any changes to line 2. This version of the program is shown in Figure 4.7 and is the one we will continue working with.

We could, however, put a line ahead of line 1 to make TEMPERA-TURE a vector. We cannot make this line 0, since that is reserved for

inserting lines

the name of the program. We can, however, add lines between 0 and 1; these would be decimal numbered, such as 0.1, 0.00023, etc. The terminal session showing these corrections to the program is given in Figure 4.8 as a continuation to Figure 4.4. Note that to get a listing we first closed definition mode and then opened it again. After inserting decimal numbered lines, when you close definition mode the lines are automatically renumbered as 1, 2, 3, etc.

We have not yet said anything about how the program TEMP can

entering a program

be created. One of the beauties of APL is that creating (or *entering*) a program is extremely easy. First type a del followed by the name of the program and hit return. You are now in definition mode: the system prints

[1]

and expects you to enter the first line of the program. After that it prints

[2]

for the second line and so on. Once you are in definition mode, you can add and change (and delete—see Exercise 4-11) lines at will. When you are done, type a del to leave definition mode.

EXERCISES

4-5. Verify the rule that the order of typing things in a line does not matter. You might enter a line such as (three spaces), 7, (two backspaces), +, (two backspaces), 9, (return).

4-6. Find out the order in which elements of an array are taken when it is raveled and made into a vector.

```
      'THE ';ρTEMPERATURE←,TEMPERATURE;' MONTHLY TEMPERATURES WERE'
```

FIGURE 4.6. Mixed output.


```
      ∇ TEMP
[1]     'THE ';ρTEMPERATURE←,TEMPERATURE;' MONTHLY TEMPERATURES WERE'
[2]     TEMPERATURE
[3]     ⍝-----TEMPERATURE IS A VECTOR OF
[4]     ⍝------THE AVERAGE MONTHLY TEMPERATURES
[5]     ⍝------FOR A YEAR
[6]     'THE AVERAGE TEMPERATURE WAS'
[7]     (+/TEMPERATURE)÷ρTEMPERATURE
[8]     'THE LARGEST TEMPERATURE WAS'
[9]     □←EXTREME←⌈/TEMPERATURE
[10]    'IT OCCURRED IN MONTHS'
[11]    (EXTREME=TEMPERATURE)/⍳ρTEMPERATURE
[12]    'THE SMALLEST TEMPERATURE WAS'
[13]    □←EXTREME←⌊/TEMPERATURE
[14]    'IT OCCURRED IN MONTHS'
[15]    (EXTREME=TEMPERATURE)/⍳ρTEMPERATURE
      ∇
```

FIGURE 4.7. The program with revisions.


```
        ∇ TEMP
[16]    [0.5]TEMPERATURE←,TEMPERATURE
[0.6]   [1]'THE ';ρTEMPERATURE;' MONTHLY TEMPERATURES WERE'
[2]     ∇
        ∇ TEMP[□]∇
     ∇ TEMP
[1]     TEMPERATURE←,TEMPERATURE
[2]     'THE ';ρTEMPERATURE;' MONTHLY TEMPERATURES WERE'
[3]     TEMPERATURE
[4]     ⍝-----TEMPERATURE IS A VECTOR OF
[5]     ⍝------THE AVERAGE MONTHLY TEMPERATURES
[6]     ⍝------FOR A YEAR
[7]     'THE AVERAGE TEMPERATURE WAS'
[8]     (+/TEMPERATURE)÷ρTEMPERATURE
[9]     'THE LARGEST TEMPERATURE WAS'
[10]    □←EXTREME←⌈/TEMPERATURE
[11]    'IT OCCURRED IN MONTHS'
[12]    (EXTREME=TEMPERATURE)/⍳ρTEMPERATURE
[13]    'THE SMALLEST TEMPERATURE WAS'
[14]    □←EXTREME←⌊/TEMPERATURE
[15]    'IT OCCURRED IN MONTHS'
[16]    (EXTREME=TEMPERATURE)/⍳ρTEMPERATURE
      ∇
```

FIGURE 4.8. Alternate corrections.

4-7. Are the results of the two expressions in Figure 4.9 the same for any variable WAGES? If so, for which ones?

4-8. Make a copy of the program TEMP from Figure 4.7. To begin, type a del followed by the name of the program and then return. The system will ask for line 1, and when that is entered, line 2 and so on. When you are done, type a del to leave definition mode.

4-9. Write and run a program to count and print the number of 'E's in a character vector STRING.

4-10. Modify the program written in Exercise 4-9 so that it counts and prints the number of vowels in STRING.

4-11. To delete a line of a program, enter definition mode, type the number of the line in brackets, hit attention and then immediately hit return. Practice adding and deleting lines in some program. What happens if you space once before hitting RETURN?

4-12. In Figure 4.7, since TEMPERATURE may not have size 12, it may not represent a year. Correct the comment.

4-13. When correcting a line, what would happen if you unintentionally type a 'B' over a plus sign? Does the same thing happen for all unintentional overstrikes?

INPUT

While we may feel fairly confident that we have eliminated all the errors from the program, we still cannot say that it will always run without errors. The user of the program must remember to give a value to TEMPERATURE before running TEMP. The most efficient way to eliminate this source of error would be to have the program itself ensure that TEMPERATURE gets a value.

We cannot, unfortunately, have the program detect whether or not a value has been assigned to TEMPERATURE, for in doing so it would have to examine TEMPERATURE and would again run the risk of a value error. What we can do is make the assignment of a value to TEMPERATURE a necessary part of running the program. One way to do this is to have the program ask for the value of TEMPERATURE. The quad, which we have used for output to the terminal, can also be used to get input from the terminal. If we simply type a quad we can see the way it functions in getting input from Figure 4.10.

quad input

When APL sees a quad without an assignment arrow pointing into it, it proceeds to ask for input from the terminal. It prints a quad followed by a colon and uses the value or expression which is typed in as the value for the quad. In the example in Figure 4.10, after the vector 1 2 3 had been entered it was as if that vector had been typed originally, instead of the quad. Since there was no assignment of the quad to some variable, the value was printed.

,*WAGES*
(⍳0),*WAGES*

FIGURE 4.9. Are these equivalent?

⎕
⎕:
        1 2 3
1   2   3

FIGURE 4.10. Input with a quad.

For a slightly more complicated example, consider Figure 4.11.

There are two requests for input. The first is the rightmost. In responding to it we entered a valid APL expression which also assigned a value to V, so that when, proceeding from right to left, APL needed to find the value of V, it had already been assigned.

Returning to our program, we could have it request a value for TEMPERATURE with a statement like the one in Figure 4.12. Before adding this in, however, we look at the program again. In line 1 we have to ravel TEMPERATURE. Instead of this, we could simply ravel the input as soon as we get it (see Figure 4.13). Whenever we ask for input, we should have the program explain exactly what it is asking for. So, before the line which asks for input we would put a statement which would print a message explaining what sort of input is wanted. Note that we would probably go along with our original intention and have the program ask for a vector of 12 temperatures; however, our program is still protected no matter what the user actually enters.

It seems at this point that we will have to enter two new lines ahead of the ones we already have. While this simple step would certainly be acceptable, we will be a little fancier to illustrate a point about APL input and output. When APL has to print a line, it must first evaluate the entire line. Thus, in line 1 of Figure 4.7, APL does not first print the rightmost part of the line and then find the size of TEMPERATURE and so on. Just the opposite: it proceeds right to left evaluating every part of the line and building up an "image" of the line. Only when the image is complete is it printed. It follows from this that if there is a request for input on a line to be printed, the request for input will come before there is any printing.

```
            V  +  ▢  +  ▢÷5
▢:
            3  +  V←2
▢:
            1
4
```

FIGURE 4.11. Input within an expression.

TEMPERATURE←▢

FIGURE 4.12. A proposed modification.

TEMPERATURE←,▢

FIGURE 4.13. A better modification.

Consider therefore Figure 4.14, which shows a program and then a sample execution. When line 1 is executed the request is printed. When line 2 is executed, before anything can be printed, every expression on the line must be evaluated. Thus, the user at the terminal sees next a request for input, followed by the printing of the message on line 2 and then the rest of the program execution as before.

EXERCISES

4-14. Why can't the quad come on the same line as the message which asks for the 12 monthly temperatures?

4-15. When APL sees a quad, how does it know whether it is for input or for output?

4-16. What happens if you make an error in entering input? Try making VALUE ERRORS, DOMAIN ERRORS, and SYNTAX ERRORS.

```
      ∇ TEMP[☐]∇
    ∇ TEMP
[1]   'PLEASE ENTER A VECTOR OF 12 MONTHLY TEMPERATURES'
[2]   'THE ';ρTEMPERATURE←,☐;' MONTHLY TEMPERATURES WERE'
[3]   TEMPERATURE
[4]   ⍝-----TEMPERATURE IS A VECTOR OF
[5]   ⍝------THE AVERAGE MONTHLY TEMPERATURES
[6]   ⍝------FOR A YEAR
[7]   'THE AVERAGE TEMPERATURE WAS'
[8]   (+/TEMPERATURE)÷ρTEMPERATURE
[9]   'THE LARGEST TEMPERATURE WAS'
[10]  ☐←EXTREME←⌈/TEMPERATURE
[11]  'IT OCCURRED IN MONTHS'
[12]  (EXTREME=TEMPERATURE)/ιρTEMPERATURE
[13]  'THE SMALLEST TEMPERATURE WAS'
[14]  ☐←EXTREME←⌊/TEMPERATURE
[15]  'IT OCCURRED IN MONTHS'
[16]  (EXTREME=TEMPERATURE)/ιρTEMPERATURE
    ∇

      TEMP
PLEASE ENTER A VECTOR OF 12 MONTHLY TEMPERATURES
☐:
      1 2 3 4 5 6 7 8 9 10 11 12
THE 12 MONTHLY TEMPERATURES WERE
1   2   3   4   5   6   7   8   9   10   11   12
THE AVERAGE TEMPERATURE WAS
6.5
THE LARGEST TEMPERATURE WAS
12
IT OCCURRED IN MONTHS
12
THE SMALLEST TEMPERATURE WAS
1
IT OCCURRED IN MONTHS
1
```

FIGURE 4.14. A program which requests input.

PROGRAMS WITH ARGUMENTS

We can fix the program in Figure 4.7 in a different way to ensure that TEMPERATURE gets a value. In a sense, this program is like a monadic APL operator. It is of course very different from an operator in that it produces no value and just does a lot of printing, but there is a similarity in that TEMPERATURE resembles an argument to the program. In fact, APL gives us a mechanism for making this similarity precise. We can define the program in such a way that after typing the name we also type an argument. For example, see the output in Figure 4.15.

```
        TEMP 1 2 3 4 5 6 7 8 9 10 11 12
THE 12 MONTHLY TEMPERATURES WERE
1   2   3   4   5   6   7   8   9   10   11   12
THE AVERAGE TEMPERATURE WAS
6.5
THE LARGEST TEMPERATURE WAS
12
IT OCCURRED IN MONTHS
12
THE SMALLEST TEMPERATURE WAS
1
IT OCCURRED IN MONTHS
1
        TEMP 3+5×ι9
THE 9 MONTHLY TEMPERATURES WERE
8   13   18   23   28   33   38   43   48
THE AVERAGE TEMPERATURE WAS
28
THE LARGEST TEMPERATURE WAS
48
IT OCCURRED IN MONTHS
9
THE SMALLEST TEMPERATURE WAS
8
IT OCCURRED IN MONTHS
1
```

FIGURE 4.15. Running a function.

Whatever we type after the name TEMP is taken by the program to be the value of TEMPERATURE. In Figure 4.16 we show a program being changed to function in this manner and then a listing of the program.

When we make this change, TEMPERATURE acquires a very special property. There is really no variable named TEMPERATURE—it is a dummy name. One way to see this is to copy the program into a clear workspace and then invoke it, as in Figure 4.17. After the program finishes, try to find the values of EXTREME and TEMPERATURE. There will be a value for EXTREME; it is a variable created during the running of the program. But there will be no value for TEMPERATURE. TEMPERATURE is like the x in an equation. TEMPERATURE is just the name which you give to the argument to make it easy for you to write the program. In fact, you might try reading the program like this:

line 1: 'THE'; size of *the argument* (which gets made into a vector);
'MONTHLY TEMPERATURES WERE'
line 2: print *the argument*

.
.
.

line 7: print the sum of the elements in *the argument*, divided by the size of *the argument*

and so on.

```
      ∇TEMP[0□]
[0]   TEMP
[0]   TEMP TEMPERATURE
[1]   [□]∇
  ∇   TEMP TEMPERATURE
[1]   'THE ';ρTEMPERATURE←,TEMPERATURE;' MONTHLY TEMPERATURES WERE'
[2]   TEMPERATURE
[3]   ⍝-----TEMPERATURE IS A VECTOR OF
[4]   ⍝------THE AVERAGE MONTHLY TEMPERATURES
[5]   ⍝------FOR A YEAR
[6]   'THE AVERAGE TEMPERATURE WAS'
[7]   (+/TEMPERATURE)÷ρTEMPERATURE
[8]   'THE LARGEST TEMPERATURE WAS'
[9]   □←EXTREME←⌈/TEMPERATURE
[10]  'IT OCCURRED IN MONTHS'
[11]  (EXTREME=TEMPERATURE)/ιρTEMPERATURE
[12]  'THE SMALLEST TEMPERATURE WAS'
[13]  □←EXTREME←⌊/TEMPERATURE
[14]  'IT OCCURRED IN MONTHS'
[15]  (EXTREME=TEMPERATURE)/ιρTEMPERATURE
  ∇
```

FIGURE 4.16. A program which accepts an argument.

```
      TEMP ι12
THE 12 MONTHLY TEMPERATURES WERE
1   2   3   4   5   6   7   8   9   10   11   12
THE AVERAGE TEMPERATURE WAS
6.5
THE LARGEST TEMPERATURE WAS
12
IT OCCURRED IN MONTHS
12
THE SMALLEST TEMPERATURE WAS
1
IT OCCURRED IN MONTHS
1

      EXTREME
1
      TEMPERATURE
VALUE ERROR
      TEMPERATURE
      ∧
```

FIGURE 4.17. The argument is a dummy name.

In fact, this is the way that APL reads the program when it is executing it. Another way to see the special status of the variable is to assign a value to TEMPERATURE, as in Figure 4.18, and then to invoke the program with some different argument. After the program is finished, variable TEMPERATURE is still the original array; it has not even been raveled.

local variables

We say that the argument of the program is a *local* variable—it only exists while the program is being run, and if there is another variable with the same name, that variable is protected while the program is running so that after program execution its value will have been unchanged.

We can make other variables local to the program if we wish. In this case, the only other variable in the program is EXTREME. We write the name of the variable after a semicolon on line 0, as in Figure 4.19. If there were another variable we wanted to localize, we would write it after a semicolon after EXTREME and so on.

We should make every variable which is only used in one program local to that program. There are two reasons for this. First of all, when programs become more complicated, and when there are many of them, we would otherwise have to constantly be keeping track of variable names to make sure that we didn't accidentally modify a variable being used in program A when running program B. Secondly, it makes it much easier to read a program if we can see at the beginning which variables are used only within it. We then know that these variables are not going to have values assigned to them outside the program, and that the other variables we see *do* need to have values assigned before we run the program.

```
      TEMPERATURE←(3,3)ρι9

      TEMP 2 4 6 8 2 4 6 8 2 4 6 8
THE 12 MONTHLY TEMPERATURES WERE
2   4   6   8   2   4   6   8   2   4   6   8
THE AVERAGE TEMPERATURE WAS
5
THE LARGEST TEMPERATURE WAS
8
IT OCCURRED IN MONTHS
4   8   12
THE SMALLEST TEMPERATURE WAS
2
IT OCCURRED IN MONTHS
1   5   9

      TEMPERATURE
   1   2   3
   4   5   6
   7   8   9
```

FIGURE 4.18. The argument is a local variable.


```
∇ TEMP TEMPERATURE;EXTREME
```

FIGURE 4.19. Localizing a variable.

Just as operators can have one or two arguments, so can programs. For example, we might want to be able to have the program print out the name of the month associated with the first temperature in the vector—a datum which we would have to supply. A program which permits this and a sample run are shown in Figure 4.20.

EXERCISES

4-17. Make EXTREME local to the program of Figure 4.16 and verify that it has the stated properties.

4-18. In Figure 4.20, why isn't it necessary to separate MONTH in line 1 by semicolons?

4-19. What happens if the program in Figure 4.20 is run and MONTH has a numeric value?

4-20. Correct the program in Figure 4.20 so that no error will result if MONTH is not a vector or scalar.

DEALING WITH ERRORS

If it is true that anything which is legal as an APL expression is legal as a line of a program, then it follows that an invocation of a program is legal as a line of another program. The ability to invoke programs within other programs is one of the most important in computer programming. Among other things, it allows us to develop a collection of routines which we might want to use for a variety of purposes, without having to rewrite them for each new use. We will be introducing a number of such programs, which we will call utility programs, during the course of this book. It is never *necessary* to use these programs. The statements they contain could always be included directly in your program. However, we feel that a small collection of such routines is immensely valuable and contributes strongly to the ultimate goal of writing programs that do what they are supposed to do.

ERROR   One such program is the program ERROR, which is listed in Appendix Four. ERROR is a two argument program. the left argument is a character string and the right argument is numeric, with value 0 or 1. If the right-hand argument is a 0, the program will appear to do nothing, while if the right-hand argument is a 1, the program will print its left-hand argument, and then stop execution of *all* programs (that is, both itself and the program that invoked it, and, if there was one, the program that invoked *it*, and so on).

As a possible use of the program ERROR, consider Figure 4.20. If the argument MONTH is not a character string, there will be an error detected on line 1. While we could correct the program directly in this

```
        ∇TEMP[□]∇
    ∇  MONTH TEMP TEMPERATURE;EXTREME
[1]     'STARTING IN ',MONTH
[2]     'THE ';ρTEMPERATURE←,TEMPERATURE;' MONTHLY TEMPERATURES WERE'
[3]     TEMPERATURE
[4]     ᴀ-----TEMPERATURE IS A VECTOR OF
[5]     ᴀ------THE AVERAGE MONTHLY TEMPERATURES
[6]     ᴀ------FOR A YEAR
[7]     'THE AVERAGE TEMPERATURE WAS'
[8]     (+/TEMPERATURE)÷ρTEMPERATURE
[9]     'THE LARGEST TEMPERATURE WAS'
[10]    □←EXTREME←⌈/TEMPERATURE
[11]    'IT OCCURRED IN MONTHS'
[12]    (EXTREME=TEMPERATURE)/ιρTEMPERATURE
[13]    'THE SMALLEST TEMPERATURE WAS'
[14]    □←EXTREME←⌊/TEMPERATURE
[15]    'IT OCCURRED IN MONTHS'
[16]    (EXTREME=TEMPERATURE)/ιρTEMPERATURE
    ∇

        'MARCH' TEMP 33 45 48 63 69 71 74 84 72
STARTING IN MARCH
THE 9 MONTHLY TEMPERATURES WERE
33   45   48   63   69   71   74   84   72
THE AVERAGE TEMPERATURE WAS
62.11111111
THE LARGEST TEMPERATURE WAS
84
IT OCCURRED IN MONTHS
8
THE SMALLEST TEMPERATURE WAS
33
IT OCCURRED IN MONTHS
1
```

FIGURE 4.20. A program with two arguments.

case, by replacing the comma with a semicolon, we should ask if that is a realistic solution. If the left-hand argument is not a character string, it is certainly not the name of a month, so that the user has surely made some kind of error. It would probably be kinder to the user (who might be yourself) to indicate that an error has been made, rather than to permit something like

THE 5 MONTHLY TEMPERATURES STARTING IN 71 78 81 89 93 WERE MARCH

to happen.

We use ERROR by giving as its right-hand argument an expression which has value 1 if there is an error and value 0 if there is no error. The left-hand argument should be a message explaining what the error is and where it occurred.

We know from Chapter 3 that if a variable S has a numeric value then the expression in Figure 4.21 has value 1, and that its value is 0 if S is a character variable. Line 1 of Figure 4.22 then will stop the program and print an error message if MONTH is not character-valued. Line 2 will stop the program and print an appropriate message if MONTH is not a vector or scalar.

EXERCISES

4-21. Modify Figure 4.22 so that it will only run through to completion if TEMPERATURE is a numeric vector with 12 elements. Test your modifications.

4-22. Write a program called CHARACTER. CHARACTER should take one argument, returning a 1 if the argument is character-valued and 0 if the argument is numeric. Test your program for scalars, vectors and arrays.

4-23. We can cause a program to print the value of an expression by having that expression be a line of the program. Or we could assign the expression to a quad. Discuss the advantages to someone reading a program of adopting one of these as a standard form. Discuss the advantages of adopting no standard form.

4-24. When we enter character data to an input request we must place it in quote marks just as with any other use of character data. However, there is a special feature which allows us to enter the data without using the quotes: this is the *quote-quad* shown in Figure 4.23A. When quote-quad is used for input, the system does *not* print the quad to tell you it wants you to type something; it just moves to the next line and waits. Quad and quote-quad character input are illustrated in parts B and C of the figure.

quote-quad input

```
0∊0\0/S
```

FIGURE 4.21. Is S numeric or character?


```
      ∇ TEMP[□]∇
    ∇ MONTH TEMP TEMPERATURE;EXTREME
[1]    'TEMP:ARGUMENT NOT CHARACTER ' ERROR 0∊0\0/MONTH
[2]    'TEMP:CHARACTER ARGUMENT WAS ARRAY ' ERROR(1<ρρMONTH)
[3]    'STARTING IN ',MONTH
[4]    'THE ';ρTEMPERATURE←,TEMPERATURE;' MONTHLY TEMPERATURES WERE'
[5]    TEMPERATURE
[6]    ᴀ-----TEMPERATURE IS A VECTOR OF
[7]    ᴀ------THE AVERAGE MONTHLY TEMPERATURES
[8]    ᴀ------FOR A YEAR
[9]    'THE AVERAGE TEMPERATURE WAS'
[10]   (+/TEMPERATURE)÷ρTEMPERATURE
[11]   'THE LARGEST TEMPERATURE WAS'
[12]   □←EXTREME←⌈/TEMPERATURE
[13]   'IT OCCURRED IN MONTHS'
[14]   (EXTREME=TEMPERATURE)/ιρTEMPERATURE
[15]   'THE SMALLEST TEMPERATURE WAS'
[16]   □←EXTREME←⌊/TEMPERATURE
[17]   'IT OCCURRED IN MONTHS'
[18]   (EXTREME=TEMPERATURE)/ιρTEMPERATURE
    ∇
```

FIGURE 4.22. Protecting against two types of error.


```
A)
            ▯

B)
            INPUT←□
    □:
       'HELLO'
            INPUT
    HELLO

C)
            INPUT←▯
    HELLO
            INPUT
    HELLO
```

FIGURE 4.23. Quote-quad input.

Revise Figure 4.22 so that it uses quote-quad input to get the name of the month. What are the advantages and disadvantages of there not being any indication that the system is waiting for input?

4-25. Sometimes when input is being requested, you would prefer to stop the program and not give any input. With quad input you can stop the program by typing a right-pointing arrow. With quote-quad input you must type an O followed by a backspace followed by a U followed by a backspace followed by a T. What happens if you use the arrow with quote-quad input, or the O-U-T with quad input?

escape from input request

4-26. When we edit a line of a program, besides typing numbers 0-9 beneath letters to indicate that spaces should be inserted, we also have the option of typing characters; A, B, C, and so on. Find out how many spaces each of these characters indicates.

5

IF Statements —
Checking Out Books

" 'Tis the voice of the Jubjub!" he suddenly cried.
   (This man, that they used to call "Dunce.")
"As the Bellman would tell you," he added with pride,
   "I have uttered that sentiment once.

" 'Tis the note of the Jubjub! Keep count, I entreat;
   You will find I have told it you twice.
" 'Tis the voice of the Jubjub! The proof is complete,
   If only I've stated it thrice."

Many libraries, especially those in universities, are beginning to computerize their operations. Use of the computer has a number of benefits: the vast amounts of recordkeeping needed to keep track of hundreds of thousands of books is all kept up to date by the computer, which can then provide accurate information to the library staff or to library users about books which have been checked out. At the same time, the computer can also keep track of users: reminding them when books are about to become due, sending out fine notices or preparing letters thanking them for always returning their books on time. To examine all the facets of library organization would take us considerably out of our way; here we will just look at what might happen at one small but critical point in the system—the checkout desk.

STRUCTURING DECISIONS

A borrower comes up to the checkout desk, books in hand. The librarian enters the number of books onto a little computer terminal and feeds the borrower's identification card into a slot in the side of the machine. The machine responds by telling the librarian how many books this borrower may indeed take out, and for how many days.

Faculty members, whose identification numbers begin with an F, may take out any number of books at a time and have 200 days to return them. Students, whose numbers begin with R (for residential) or O (for off-campus), may take only six books at a time, and these for only 30 days.

It is not our concern how the information from the identification cards gets from the little slot to the program or how the program becomes activated at the proper time. Certainly, before the checkout desk program was put into the system it would be tested extensively in isolation from the system, and we will take it only that far.

Let's try to get an idea of what is involved in this program. First we look at the identification number. The library is concerned about theft, especially of rare books, so we must scrutinize the number carefully. It should begin with a letter—F, R, or O—and then should have six digits. If someone tries to use an invalid card, or if the librarian inserts the card into the slot upside down, it will not meet these criteria and we can reject it.

Once we know the number is valid, we should look at the number of books as entered by the librarian. This must certainly be a positive integer—anything else is surely a typing error and should be reported as such.

Only now, with data we know to be valid, are we ready to act. For a faculty card we need only print out some such message as "These books are due in 200 days." For a student card, though, the situation is a bit more complicated: we must again print out the number of days

the books may be borrowed, but must also indicate whether this patron is trying to borrow too many books. These considerations are all expressed in the structure chart in Figure 5.1.

It isn't hard to see how each box in the structure chart could be turned into an APL expression. But if we were simply to place these instructions one after another in a program we would surely not get the right results. The structure chart is two-dimensional: sometimes we do one thing and sometimes another and this is indicated by the way that things are placed on the page. We do not have the same freedom in placing lines in an APL program; they must be listed one below another. We therefore need some way to control the *order* in which the lines are performed. Depending on the data, we will sometimes want to execute this line, sometimes that one. This will require the ability to selectively skip over some statements as directed by the data.

Notice that if we are going to be able to selectively choose statements, we must have a way to refer to them. One way to refer to them is the line number, but this is not very reliable. If we add or remove lines from the program the numbers of the other lines will change, so that it will always be difficult to ensure that references to lines are correct. Instead, we can give a label to any line we wish to refer to. Such a labeled line is shown in Figure 5.2. The label appears at the beginning of the line and is separated from the actual APL expression by a colon. The label is treated just like any other name in APL; for example, a name which is used as a label cannot be used anyplace else in the program as a variable. In fact, labels are treated as local variables, although they need not (and should not) be listed on line 0.

Now, how can we actually control the way that lines are executed? The mechanism that APL uses is natural and corresponds to the way that we do many similar tasks ourselves. First of all, when one APL line is done, the one which is usually done next is the next-numbered line. We saw this in the previous chapter where we were not controlling the way that lines were performed at all. What APL provides us with is a mechanism for saying "after this line, instead of the next-numbered line do line X instead." In fact, we will be able to say such things as "after this line, *if* such and such is true, *then* do line X, but *otherwise* just do the next-numbered line."

Before we get into this, let's look at the other extreme and see how we could write "do the next-numbered line" explicitly. It seems silly to do this, since we don't really have to do anything to get the next-numbered line performed next, but APL provides us with a way to say it—and it will in fact turn out to be quite important to be able to do so. Figure 5.3A shows one way: it is read "branch to iota zero" and is just a very fancy way of saying "do nothing."

do
nothing

We could actually do something on a line and also say "do the next-numbered line" explicitly. Figure 5.3B gives an example. By the right-to-left rule, the first thing that happens is that HOURS is incremented

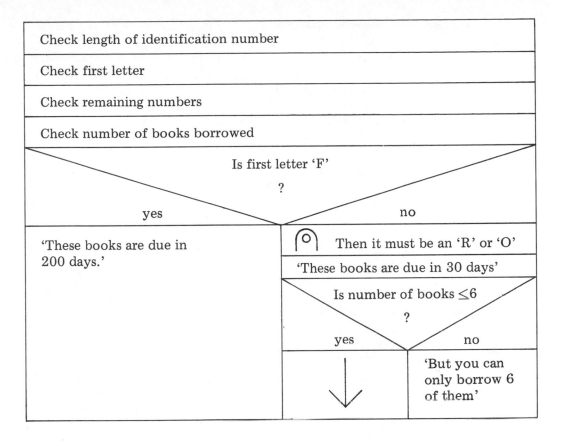

Check length of identification number	
Check first letter	
Check remaining numbers	
Check number of books borrowed	

Is first letter 'F'

?

yes	no
'These books are due in 200 days.'	⌐O⌐ Then it must be an 'R' or 'O'
	'These books are due in 30 days'
	Is number of books ≤6 ?
	yes no
	↓ 'But you can only borrow 6 of them'

FIGURE 5.1. At the checkout desk.

$$DEDUCTIONS:MEDICAL \leftarrow DOCTOR + HOSPITAL$$

FIGURE 5.2. A labeled line.

A)

    →ι 0

B)

    →ι (0×*HOURS*←*HOURS*+1)

FIGURE 5.3. Not branching.

by one. Then the line reads "branch to iota (zero times HOURS)" which, since zero times HOURS is zero, has the effect of "branch to iota zero."

Now let's look at a slightly more interesting example. Figure 5.4 shows a simple structure chart for determining if a vector X has seven elements. Figure 5.5 shows the corresponding program.

As we start to read the program we run up against a number of things on line 2 which we haven't seen before. There is the word NOTSEVEN, the word IF and a somewhat different use of the right-pointing arrow than we saw in Figure 5.3. If we quickly scan the rest of the program we see that NOTSEVEN is a line label. But what can IF be?

The line seems to read sensibly if we mix our English and APL: "branch to NOTSEVEN IF the size of X is not equal to seven." But this doesn't mean that APL will interpret it in the same way. We don't know what IF means to APL.

Although IF is not a grammatical form we have seen before, it is similar to one. It would make a certain amount of grammatical sense to replace the IF by a plus sign; then we would understand that we have a dyadic operator with two arguments. Thus, the line would make perfect (grammatical) sense if we knew that there was a dyadic operator called IF. However, there isn't one. Instead, we have created a program called IF which works just like a dyadic operator. It gets two arguments and has a value which depends in some way on the arguments.

IF

The expression on line 2 is evaluated just like any other APL expression: right-to-left. When APL sees an expression like $19-4+5$ it first evaluates $4+5$, getting 9, and then $19-9$, to get 10. In exactly the same way, APL first looks at the fragment shown in Figure 5.6. The result of this depends on the IF function. If the right-hand argument is false (value 0), the value of the fragment is the empty vector, so that we get a "do nothing" on line 2. But if the right-hand side is true (value 1), then the value returned is the left-hand argument (in this case, the label NOTSEVEN). At this time, the line means "branch to NOTSEVEN" and that is what happens: APL skips down to the line labeled NOTSEVEN and starts running the program from there. The function IF is listed in Appendix Four.

Figure 5.5 is now easy to read—or is it? Line 4 seems to say "branch to line 0." But this doesn't seem too sensible: line 0 is the header line, the name of the program. Are we supposed to start the program over again?

branch to line 0

Actually, because branching to line 0 doesn't make any sense, APL uses the command "branch to line 0" with a special meaning—stop the program. We need to be able to stop the program explicitly when, as in Figure 5.5, the last line that we want to perform is not the last-numbered line. With this understanding we can read all of Figure 5.5; as the output shows, it does exactly what we wanted.

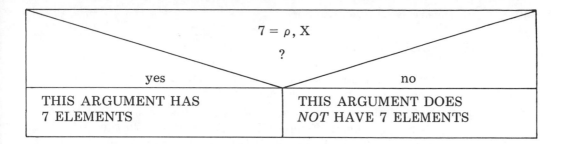

FIGURE 5.4. Examining the size of an argument.

```
     ∇  EXAMINE X
[1]     ᴀ-----CHECKS TO SEE IF X HAS 7 ELEMENTS
[2]     →NOTSEVEN IF 7≠ρ,X
[3]     'THIS ARGUMENT HAS 7 ELEMENTS'
[4]     →0
[5]   NOTSEVEN:'THIS ARGUMENT DOES NOT HAVE 7 ELEMENTS'
     ∇
```

```
      EXAMINE ι7
THIS ARGUMENT HAS 7 ELEMENTS

      EXAMINE (7,1,1,1)ρ4.5
THIS ARGUMENT HAS 7 ELEMENTS

      EXAMINE 'BOW WOW'
THIS ARGUMENT HAS 7 ELEMENTS

      EXAMINE 5
THIS ARGUMENT DOES NOT HAVE 7 ELEMENTS

      EXAMINE (3,3)ρ'ABC'
THIS ARGUMENT DOES NOT HAVE 7 ELEMENTS
```

FIGURE 5.5. How many elements?

```
      NOTSEVEN IF 7≠ρ,X
```

FIGURE 5.6. Invoking the function IF.

EXERCISES

5-1. Rewrite Figures 5.4 and 5.5 so that they also tell us whether X is a numeric vector or a character vector.

5-2. Note that we took some liberties in Figure 5.5. The structure chart question in Figure 5.7A was inverted into the question in Figure 5.7B which actually appeared in the program. Rewrite the program so that it corresponds exactly to the structure chart. Why do you think we did the inversion when we wrote the program?

5-3. Revise the program in Figure 4.24 by having it print explanatory messages to the user if the input is not a vector of size 12. For example, it should be able to give such information as

THIS INPUT HAS ONLY 9 ELEMENTS. IT SHOULD HAVE 12

or

THIS INPUT HAS 16 ELEMENTS, 4 TOO MANY.

WRITING THE PROGRAM

We are now ready to write a program CHECKOUT to implement Figure 5.1. The first question which we must ask is, What is the data that the program gets to work with? Certainly it gets the number of books, which is simply a number. But it also gets the identification "number," which has both letters and numbers—and as we know we cannot have both characters and numbers as part of the same data item in APL.

Actually, though, there is not much of a problem. We don't need to compute with the numbers on the identification card, so it will cause no trouble if we express them as numeric characters. Then the identification card can be represented by a character vector.

The structure chart in Figure 5.1 suggests that we perform the act of checking the data first. Figure 5.8 shows the part of the program which does this. We make a total of four checks, using the program ERROR. One line 1 we first ravel the identification number, ID, to make sure that it is a vector. Then we can ask for its size. If it is not exactly seven characters long then it must be a poor forgery and we reject it.

Next we check that the card has the proper information. The first character must be one of 'F', 'R', or 'O'. Third, the rest of the identification number (what we get by *drop*ping the first element, which is what the down-pointing arrow does) must be numeric characters. Finally, the number of books must be a positive integer; to verify this we ask if BOOKS remains the same when we take the absolute value and

A)

$7 = \rho , X$

B)

$7 \neq \rho , X$

FIGURE 5.7. Two related questions.

```
     ∇  BOOKS CHECKOUT ID
[1]    'INVALID ID CARD ' ERROR 7≠ρID←,ID
[2]    'INVALID ID CARD ' ERROR~ID[1]ε'FRO'
[3]    'INVALID ID CARD ' ERROR~∧/(1↓ID)ε'0123456789'
[4]    'NUMBER OF BOOKS ' ERROR(0=BOOKS)∨(BOOKS≠⌊|BOOKS)
     ∇
```

FIGURE 5.8. Testing for validity.

then drop off any fractional part using the operator floor. This tells us that BOOKS is nonnegative and an integer; we must also check for the specific case of BOOKS equal to 0.

Next we want to do the actual filtering of the identification number through the decisions. If it begins with an 'F' then the borrower gets the book for 200 days. This brings us up against an unfortunate feature of the language. We really want to do two things which are incompatible. The way that we think tells us in general to handle the first case first—that is, as we unfold Figure 5.1 into a program the part which deals with 'F'-type cards should appear first in the program. That's the first thing we've decided to do and the program will be much clearer if we do it first. But we also like to ask questions in a positive way. Ideally, we want to say "If the first character is an 'F' then give the borrower 200 days." Putting these two aims together would give a program something like this:

If the first character is 'F' do the next line

Give the borrower 200 days

Come here if, and *only if*, the first character wasn't 'F'

But it just doesn't work that way! We have to use the IF function to tell the program *not* to do the next line, since it always does the next line unless instructed otherwise.

We must compromise. Either we cannot do the first thing first or we must ask the negative of what we want. Here we will take the latter approach. We will use IF statements to say "If the condition does *not* hold, then continue processing someplace else." This approach will give us a program segment like the one shown in Figure 5.9.

If the first character is not 'F' then the borrower is a student; we will write the part of the program for students shortly. If the borrower is faculty we must print out the message saying how long the books may be borrowed. Then we are done and a "branch to zero" ends the program.

The entire program is shown in Figure 5.10. The only part that is new is the part that deals with student borrowers. First, the message giving the permitted borrowing time is printed. Then, if the borrower is taking only six or fewer books, that is all we need to do. However, if more than six books are being presented for checkout we must also print a message to warn the librarian. Figure 5.11 shows the program in action.

```
     →STUDENT IF ID[1]≠'F'
     'THESE BOOKS ARE DUE IN 200 DAYS'
     →0
     STUDENT: ...
```

FIGURE 5.9. Is it a faculty card?

```
       ∇  BOOKS CHECKOUT ID
[1]      'INVALID ID CARD ' ERROR 7≠ρID←,ID
[2]      'INVALID ID CARD ' ERROR~ID[1]ε'FRO'
[3]      'INVALID ID CARD ' ERROR~∧/(1↓ID)ε'0123456789'
[4]      'NUMBER OF BOOKS ' ERROR(0=BOOKS)∨(BOOKS≠⌊|BOOKS)
[5]      →STUDENT IF ID[1]≠'F'
[6]      'THESE BOOKS ARE DUE IN 200 DAYS'
[7]      →0
[8]    STUDENT:'THESE BOOKS ARE DUE IN 30 DAYS'
[9]      →0 IF BOOKS≤6
[10]    'BUT YOU MAY ONLY BORROW SIX OF THEM'
       ∇
```

FIGURE 5.10. The complete program.

```
       3 CHECKOUT 'F012345'
THESE BOOKS ARE DUE IN 200 DAYS

       7 CHECKOUT 'R987654'
THESE BOOKS ARE DUE IN 30 DAYS
BUT YOU MAY ONLY BORROW SIX OF THEM

       6 CHECKOUT  'O555121'
THESE BOOKS ARE DUE IN 30 DAYS

       5 CHECKOUT 'F1234567'
INVALID ID CARD  ERROR
```

FIGURE 5.11. Checking books out.

EXERCISES

5-4. We performed many checks on ID, but only one on BOOKS. Suppose that for some reason BOOKS is not a scalar: perhaps the librarian accidentally hit two keys on the terminal and BOOKS comes to the program as a vector. What happens? Is it worth checking for this? If so, do it; if not, explain why not.

5-5. Change CHECKOUT so that it always tells how many books are actually being borrowed.

5-6. Was it really necessary to ravel ID? What happens if ID comes in as a scalar and we don't ravel it before checking its size?

5-7. If there is an error in the identification card, the program says only INVALID ID CARD ERROR, even though it knows what the error is. Fix this.

5-8. The president of the university has decided to allow the citizens of the local community to borrow books for up to 15 days (but they may borrow as many as they wish). Rewrite the program to reflect this new policy. (*Hint*: Do a new structure chart first.)

FUNCTIONS

It may have occurred to you that the checks that we do on the validity of the identification card are rather simpleminded. Anyone who intended to forge an identification card would certainly get the number of characters right. This, as it turns out, has also occurred to the campus security consultants. Each identification number has an internal consistency check: the last number is derived from the others by a scheme which is supposed to be checked by the computer. The scheme works like this: sum the first five numbers; add 2 for a faculty card, 3 for an off-campus student and 5 for a residential student; square the result; and then take the last digit of that as the last digit of the identification number.

As an example, suppose that the identification number is F234127. Add up the first five digits to get 12, add 2 for faculty to get 14 and square that. The result is 196, so the last digit of the card should be 6—since it isn't, the card is invalid.

We want to include in our program a check as to whether or not the identification number passes this test. We will do it with a line like the one shown in Figure 5.12. This is another line which, at first glance, seems to follow a different grammar from what we have already learned. What is to the right of the name ERROR? ID is the name for the identification number, but what is TEST? We are supposed to have an expression to the right of ERROR, one which has value either 1 or 0.

`'SECURITY VIOLATION 'ERROR TEST ID`

FIGURE 5.12. Test is a function.

Since we know what ERROR does, we must conclude that TEST ID *is* an expression with value either 1 or 0. Since TEST is not an APL operator, it must be a function. TEST performs the checking of the identification number. It takes one argument, ID, and returns a value of 1 or 0 (1 when the ID is *in*valid). We talked about the concept of returning a value when we introduced IF, but now we need to go into a bit more detail. By "return a value" we mean that when the program runs it comes up with some value which replaces its name in the expression where it is used. This is not really mysterious. As we noted above, when APL evaluates a simple expression like 19−4+5 it first evaluates 4+5 and then replaces "4+5" by the result "9" in the expression, so that it is now evaluating the arithmetic expression "19−9."

A function program is handled the same way. When it appears in an expression, APL takes that part of the expression consisting of the program name and its arguments and replaces it with the value computed by the function. Naturally, we need a way to tell APL that certain programs are functions and must be treated in this way. Figure 5.13 shows a program to divide two numbers, checking for 0 as a divisor. The header line shows that the program returns a value. RESULT is the name that the program uses to specify that value. But the name RESULT has no meaning outside the program. Suppose we type 6 DIVIDEDBY 3. This calls the program, which sets up the value 2 in RESULT. When the program is done, APL knows (from the header line) to look at the value of RESULT and to use that as the value of the expression 6 DIVIDEDBY 3. There is nothing magic about the name RESULT—we could use any name at all.

Notice from Figure 5.13 that we can include references to DIVIDED-BY in expressions and it is just as if we had used the operator divide. Except, that is, for the very last call, where we get a VALUE ERROR. Looking closely at the program, we can see that it stops if the divisor is 0 but doesn't give any value to RESULT in that case. Thus, the expression 6 DIVIDEDBY 0 has no value.

We can correct for this. If we divide by 0 we will return something as a value. What we would want to do is return a value which is sure to be noticed, since division by 0 is usually a mistake. The value we use in Figure 5.14 should cause some strange things to happen in subsequent computations so that we would be likely to notice the error. But just to be sure, we also print a message warning that division by 0 has been attempted; this illustrates that we can do anything inside a function program that we can do in other programs.

```
      ∇  RESULT←DIVIDEND DIVIDEDBY DIVISOR
[1]      →0 IF DIVISOR=0
[2]      RESULT←DIVIDEND÷DIVISOR
      ∇
```

```
      6 DIVIDEDBY 3
2

      8 + 6 DIVIDEDBY 3
1 0

      6÷(6 DIVIDEDBY 3)
3

      6 DIVIDEDBY 0

      3 + 6 DIVIDEDBY 0
VALUE ERROR
      3 + 6 DIVIDEDBY 0
            ∧
```

FIGURE 5.13. Almost a function.

```
      ∇ RESULT←DIVIDEND DIVIDEDBY DIVISOR
[1]      →ZERODIVIDE IF DIVISOR=0
[2]      RESULT←DIVIDEND÷DIVISOR
[3]      →0
[4]    ZERODIVIDE:'DIVISION BY ZERO. RESULT SET TO ';RESULT←⁻999999999
      ∇
```

```
      6 DIVIDEDBY 3
2

      6 DIVIDEDBY 0
DIVISION BY ZERO. RESULT SET TO ⁻999999999
⁻999999999

      3 + 6 DIVIDEDBY 0
DIVISION BY ZERO. RESULT SET TO ⁻999999999
⁻999999996
```

FIGURE 5.14. A division function.

Now we can return to our program TEST. We will put Figure 5.12 after all the other checks on ID in Figure 5.10, so that we will not need to do the simple checks on ID inside TEST. The computation that we need to do is not difficult, except for the fact that it requires us to deal with the identification numbers as numbers, not as numeric characters. We can easily transform these six numeric characters to the corresponding six numbers by using the operator *index*. Examples are given in Figure 5.15: the location of each numeric character in the character string '0123456789' is itself a number.

index

The program TEST is shown in Figure 5.16. First we convert the numeric characters to numbers. Then we begin the consistency calculation. We add up the first five numbers and then add the number which represents the first character; this is selected by the compression expression. Finally, we square the result and take the last digit, which is just the remainder when we divide by 10 and can be found with the operator *modulus*. The result of the test, INVALID, is 1 if the calculated digit does not match the last digit of the card and is 0 otherwise.

modulus

Figure 5.17 shows the new CHECKOUT program.

EXERCISES

5-9. Figure 5.17 might seem to be a bit disconcerting, as some checks on the card are done right in CHECKOUT while others are "pushed down" into TEST. It would be much clearer if they were all kept together. Decide if we should do them all in TEST or if we should get rid of TEST and do them all in CHECKOUT. Explain your decision and then implement it.

5-10. Write a function which takes one argument, a character vector. The function returns that part of the vector beginning with the first element and ending with the second occurrence of that element. If the argument is 'STATE UNIVERSITY AT PODUNK' the program returns the value 'STATE UNIVERS'. If the first element is not repeated the program returns the empty vector.

COMPLICATING THE PROBLEM

In response to student statements that the library policy is not responsive to the actual needs of students, some changes have been made. Periodicals are now treated differently from books. No borrower may take out more than four periodicals at a time and they must be returned within 48 hours. Let's look at Figure 5.17 to see what changes this will engender.

```
        ¯1+'0123456789'ι'5'
5
        ¯1+'0123456789'ι'0'
0
        ¯1+'0123456789'ι'135245'
1 3 5 2 4 5
```

FIGURE 5.15. Numeric characters to numbers.

```
     ∇ INVALID←TEST ID;NUMERIC;DIGIT
[1]    NUMERIC←¯1+'0123456789'ι1↓ID
[2]    DIGIT←+/NUMERIC[ι5]
[3]    DIGIT←DIGIT+(ID[1]='FOR')/(2 3 5)
[4]    DIGIT←10|DIGIT*2
[5]    INVALID←DIGIT≠NUMERIC[6]
     ∇
```

FIGURE 5.16. Security testing.

```
     ∇ BOOKS CHECKOUT ID
[1]    'INVALID ID CARD ' ERROR 7≠ρID←,ID
[2]    'INVALID ID CARD ' ERROR~ID[1]ε'FRO'
[3]    'INVALID ID CARD ' ERROR~∧/(1↓ID)ε'0123456789'
[4]    'SECURITY VIOLATION ' ERROR TEST ID
[5]    'NUMBER OF BOOKS ' ERROR(0=BOOKS)∨(BOOKS≠⌊|BOOKS)
[6]    →STUDENT IF ID[1]≠'F'
[7]    'THESE BOOKS ARE DUE IN 200 DAYS'
[8]    →0
[9]  STUDENT:'THESE BOOKS ARE DUE IN 30 DAYS'
[10]   →0 IF BOOKS≤6
[11]   'BUT YOU MAY ONLY BORROW SIX OF THEM'
     ∇
```

FIGURE 5.17. A more secure system.

The program now needs to get separate numbers for books and periodicals. It still, of course, needs the identification number. Unfortunately, no APL program can have more than two arguments—there are only two sides (left and right) to the name. There is no serious problem, however, as there is no restriction of what the two arguments may be—only the program itself can decide, by explicitly rejecting arguments which are not proper for it. Thus, we could call the program in Figure 5.17 by passing a large two-dimensional array of numbers as the right-hand argument; only the error checks that we built in will reject the argument.

So to solve the problem of the books and periodicals we can decide that the left-hand argument will be a vector of size 2, the first element being the number of books and the second the number of periodicals. The first change that this suggests is to the name BOOKS—perhaps ITEMS would be better. (However, we don't *have* to change the name, and if we don't, we wouldn't have to make any changes at all to the header line.)

We will certainly need to perform more checks on ITEMS than we did on BOOKS: it must be a vector of size 2, each element must be a nonnegative integer and both elements cannot be 0.

We have some more decisions to make as well. Our new specifications treat all borrowers the same with respect to periodicals, so it seems reasonable to leave the handling of books as it is and to write code for the handling of periodicals afterwards. Naturally we do not want to let the faculty evade having their periodicals checked, so we can no longer stop the program when we finish checking faculty borrowers, as on line 8 of Figure 5.17; the same holds for students who don't try to borrow more than six books. Note also that a borrower may be taking only periodicals and we may not need to deal with the book part at all.

The modifications are simple to make. The new program is shown in Figure 5.18, and Figure 5.19 shows some runs.

EXERCISES

5-11. Play "twenty questions" with someone and write a structure chart as you proceed. When you ask a question, before it is answered, write down what you will ask if the response is "yes" and what you will ask if it is "no."

5-12. Write a structure chart and function which takes two three-character arguments, returning the alphabetically first of the arguments. Use the collating scheme: blank comes before A comes before B...comes before Z comes before 0 comes before 1... .

```
      ∇ ITEMS CHECKOUT ID
[1]     'INVALID ID CARD ' ERROR 7≠ρID←,ID
[2]     'INVALID ID CARD ' ERROR~ID[1]∈'FRO'
[3]     'INVALID ID CARD ' ERROR~∧/(1↓ID)∈'0123456789'
[4]     'SECURITY VIOLATION ' ERROR TEST ID
[5]     'ITEMS SIZE ' ERROR 2≠ρITEMS←,ITEMS
[6]     'ITEMS VALUES ' ERRORv/ITEMS≠⌊|ITEMS
[7]     'ITEMS VALUES ' ERROR 0=+/ITEMS
[8]     →PERIODICALS IF ITEMS[1]=0
[9]     →STUDENT IF ID[1]≠'F'
[10]    'THESE BOOKS ARE DUE IN 200 DAYS'
[11]    →PERIODICALS
[12] STUDENT:'THESE BOOKS ARE DUE IN 30 DAYS'
[13]    →PERIODICALS IF ITEMS[1]≤6
[14]    'BUT YOU MAY ONLY BORROW SIX OF THEM'
[15] PERIODICALS:→0 IF ITEMS[2]=0
[16]    'THESE PERIODICALS MAY BE BORROWED FOR 48 HOURS'
[17]    →0 IF ITEMS[2]≤4
[18]    'BUT YOU MAY ONLY BORROW FOUR PERIODICALS'
      ∇
```

FIGURE 5.18. Lending books and periodicals.


```
      2 3 CHECKOUT 'F132729'
THESE BOOKS ARE DUE IN 200 DAYS
THESE PERIODICALS MAY BE BORROWED FOR 48 HOURS

      6 9 CHECKOUT 'R821275'
THESE BOOKS ARE DUE IN 30 DAYS
THESE PERIODICALS MAY BE BORROWED FOR 48 HOURS
BUT YOU MAY ONLY BORROW FOUR PERIODICALS
```

FIGURE 5.19. Running the program.

5-13. Write a similar program for sorting, except let there be only one input, an array with three columns where each of the two rows represents a different word.

5-14. Can you write a program for Exercise 5-13 in the case where you don't know the number of rows in the array before you write the program? Can you write the structure chart?

5-15. A truly responsive library might change its borrowing time limits frequently, depending on the needs of the borrowers and the number of books in circulation. Modify CHECKOUT by including the various borrowing times as elements of a vector of size 3 (for the three borrower categories) which is assigned at the beginning of the program and then refer to this vector in the program instead of the absolute borrowing times. This way, changing a borrowing time involves changing only this one vector.

5-16. Follow up on Exercise 5-15 and modify the program to allow for the possibility that 'O'- and 'R'-type students have different borrowing times.

5-17. Modify Figure 5.18 so that the total number of books in the library is 100,000—so that no one could ever borrow more.

Interlude Three

Workspace Organization

We have already seen one form of the COPY command, for copying the entire contents of a saved workspace into the active workspace. Unlike LOAD, COPY does not copy the workspace itself, but only the programs and variables which it contains. Other forms of this command permit us to copy only parts of a workspace.

COPYING OBJECTS

The basic objects of a workspace are, of course, its programs and variables; one other object, the group, will be introduced below. To copy an object from a workspace it is necessary only to append the name of the object to the basic COPY command. Thus

)COPY ACCOUNTING PAYROLL

will copy (only) the object PAYROLL from the workspace ACCOUNTING. Of course, if the workspace is under a different sign-on number, that must be given too. In some systems, to copy two objects from a workspace it is necessary to give two separate COPY commands; in others, many names may be listed in the command. Note that if there is already an object PAYROLL in your active workspace the copied object will replace it.

Copying in this manner can be inconvenient when there are many objects to copy, so APL has a facility which lets you group a collection of objects under a common name and then, by copying the group name, get all the objects. For example, the command

)GROUP WEATHER TEMP TEMPERATURE CHECKOUT

creates a group called WEATHER consisting of the objects TEMP, TEMPERATURE and CHECKOUT. A group cannot be executed, but it can be copied. Note that a group must be created in the workspace that you are copying *from*, and so must be created before you need it. The ability to group objects is thus most useful for objects which you will be copying many times. Once you have a group though, copying it is no more difficult than copying any object. If WEATHER were a group in the workspace ACCOUNTING then the command

)COPY ACCOUNTING WEATHER

would copy the objects TEMP, TEMPERATURE and CHECKOUT.

We now have three major classes of objects: groups, variables, and programs. There is a system command which lets us list all of the objects of one of these types. To list all of the group names in your workspace, execute the command

)GRPS

This will tell you what the names of the groups are, but will not tell you the objects which comprise the groups. To find that out, use the command GRP, as

)GRP WEATHER

which results in a list of the objects contained in group WEATHER.

We have already seen the commands which cause APL to list all of the variable names or program names in your workspace: they are

)VARS

and

)FNS

As with GRPS, these commands will just give a list of the names of the variables or programs (all programs are sometimes called functions in APL even though all are not functions which return values—hence, the command FNS for FuNctionS). Using VARS will not get you the values of the variables and FNS will not run any programs.

EXERCISES

I3-1. What is the difference between the commands COPY and PCOPY?

I3-2. To add an object SNOW to group WEATHER use the command

)GROUP WEATHER WEATHER SNOW

What would be the result if you used the command

)GROUP WEATHER SNOW

instead?

I3-3. Define a group GUIDE, one object of which is another group. SAVE, CLEAR and then COPY GUIDE. Which objects are carried along in the copy?

I3–4. Define two groups, GUIDE and LEADER, and then include each group in the other. CLEAR and then copy one of the groups; which objects are carried along?

I3–5. To get rid of an object CODES from a workspace, enter the command

)ERASE CODES

If CODES is a program or a variable, it will indeed be erased. What objects will be erased if CODES is a group name? (Note that more than one object at a time can be listed in this command, as

)ERASE TEMP TEMPERATURE CHECKOUT

I3–6. If all the objects in a group are erased, what happens to the group?

I3–7. Which error messages can occur with a COPY command? How can you cause them to happen?

WORKSPACE FUNCTIONS

There are a number of other useful commands for workspace control. Three which we will mention briefly are WIDTH, DIGITS, and ORIGIN. Each command, like an operator, takes a single argument N. For WIDTH, the argument is the number of spaces across a line which APL will print. Of course, N cannot be larger than the number of physical spaces across your terminal, and there is usually a lower bound as well. For DIGITS, the number N is the maximum number of significant digits which will be printed for any number. Finally, for ORIGIN, N can be only 0 or 1 and is the new value of the origin for the operator *iota* and for subscripting. When you use one of these commands, APL will tell you what the previous value was, as in Figure I3.1.

Some of these same functions, and others as well, can also be accomplished by means of the I-beam operator. The I-beam looks and functions just like a primitive operator in that it has both monadic and dyadic forms, but each I-beam is really a request or command to the system. We have already seen that I-beam 22 returns the amount of space left in a workspace. Other monadic I-beams return the time of day, the date, the total number of users on the system and so on. There are also some dyadic I-beams for giving system commands. The 6 I-beam group contains the workspace commands which we mentioned above and a few other besides.

```
      )DIGITS 5
WAS 10
```

FIGURE I3.1. Changing digits.

The right-hand argument of the 6 I-beam is a vector of size 2. The first element is a control number, specifying which system command is being given, and the second is a new value being given to one of the system parameters (see the chart in Figure I3.2A). The line in Figure I3.2B sets the origin to the value of N. The 6 I-beam operator returns as a value the previous value of the system parameter. Thus, you can set these values as you wish inside a program and restore them to their previous values when the program finishes execution.

Two new system parameters are controlled by the 6 I-beam operator. One (with control number 1) is called the *link* or *seed* and is used by the random number generator to generate the next random number. Each time a number is generated by ? the seed is changed. The seed can be set with this 6 I-beam. This can be useful when you wish to rerun a program using random numbers.

When the control number is 4, the 6 I-beam lets you set the system's *fuzz*. Since the computer is only a finite machine it cannot accurately represent such numbers as 1/3, which have infinite decimal approximations. Furthermore, because of this, small errors are bound to creep in whenever arithmetic operations are done. For example, 14.026/7.013 is not likely to be exactly 2 after any computer gets done with it. But it would surely be undesirable if we had to worry about the machine's arithmetic problems, since the errors tend to be quite small. For all practical purposes, we would want the value of

$$2 = 14.026 \div 7.013$$

to be 1. APL takes care of this by keeping a very small number, called the fuzz, which it uses when comparing two numbers. If APL's internal representation of two numbers differs by less than the fuzz, then they are treated as though they were equal. Since the arguments to the 6 I-beam are integers, the number you give is not really the fuzz. Instead, it is an integer which is used to determine the fuzz.

Figure I3.3 shows a program which uses the 6 I-beam operator. The program's arguments are two numbers; the program sets the value of DIGITS to be the left-hand argument, prints the right-hand argument and then restores the value of DIGITS. Figure I3.4 shows some runs of the program.

EXERCISES

I3-8. Why does the expression in Figure I3.5 print the time of day in a recognizable form?

I3-9. How small can the value of DIGITS be? Of WIDTH?

A)

```
      COMMAND              ACTION
      6ɪ0,N                SETS ORIGIN TO N
      6ɪ1,N                SETS SEED TO N
      6ɪ2,N                SETS DIGITS TO N
      6ɪ3,N                SETS WIDTH TO N
      6ɪ4,N                SETS FUZZ TO N
```

B)

```
      SAVEΔORIGIN←6ɪ0,N
```

FIGURE I3.2. Some system commands.

```
     ∇ DIGITS PRINT NUMBER;SAVEΔDIGITS
[1]    SAVEΔDIGITS←6ɪ2,DIGITS
[2]    □←NUMBER
[3]    SAVEΔDIGITS←6ɪ2,SAVEΔDIGITS
     ∇
```

FIGURE I3.3. Changing DIGITS in a program.

```
      )DIGITS 10
WAS 10
      ÷19
0.05263157895
      5 PRINT ÷19
0.052632
      8 PRINT ÷19
0.052631579
      13 PRINT ÷19
0.05263157894737
      )DIGITS 10
WAS 10
```

FIGURE I3.4. The result of changing DIGITS.

```
      (24 60 60 60)Tɪ20
```

FIGURE I3.5. The time of day.

I3-10. How do small changes in the seed affect the values of the random numbers generated?

I3-11. What units are used for the fuzz?

I3-12. Can you create two numbers which print the same but are not considered equal by APL? Can you create two numbers which are considered the same but print differently?

6

DO Loops—
A Program
for Sorting

The Beaver had counted with scrupulous care,
    Attending to every word:
But it fairly lost heart, and outgrabe in despair,
    When the third repetition occurred.

If it became necessary, in the previous chapter, to add three or four new classes of library user, we would have to make major revisions in the programs. We would need a little piece of program to handle each particular user category. As the number of user categories grew larger, this would clearly become cumbersome. We could imagine a structure chart which had a large DO block, "DO for each user category in turn." We could then use the same instructions for each category; the differences between categories, such as maximum borrowing times, would be expressed by choosing the correct time from a vector according to the category number. We could do this easily in a structure chart but we have not yet found a way to translate the DO block into APL statements. The ability to repeat statements is what gives programming its power; we will illustrate it in this chapter, beginning with a program for finding the alphabetically first (smallest) row of a character array.

FROM DO BLOCKS TO DO LOOPS

We show in Figure 6.1 a structure chart for the problem of finding the smallest row of an array. Starting with JUMBLE as the array containing the various words, we let ROWS be the number of its rows and COLUMNS the number of columns. ALPHA is set to be the vector containing all the characters which we allow in JUMBLE, in alphabetical order, and POSSIBLE starts out as the vector 1, 2, ..., ROWS. Look first at the two statements inside the DO block, letting POSITION be 1 for the purposes of the example. The first statement produces a vector whose ith element is the order (according to ALPHA) of the symbol in the ith row and first column. Thus, if the first *column* is ' A BA C' then the first statement will produce 1 2 1 3 2 1 4 as the value of ORDER. The only rows which can possibly contain the alphabetically first word are those for which the corresponding values in ORDER are as small as possible. In this case, they would be the three rows beginning with blank, rows 1, 3 and 6. So, in the second statement, we replace POSSIBLE by the vector of numbers of those rows, 1, 3 and 6. And when we look at the next column, we know that we only have to look at the elements in rows which are still (elements of) POSSIBLE.

How long do we have to keep doing this procedure? Surely we can stop if POSSIBLE ever has only one element, for that will correspond to the alphabetically first row; we can also stop after examining all the columns. If, after looking at all the columns, POSSIBLE has more than one element, then all the rows whose indices are in POSSIBLE are equal and alphabetically before all the others.

The rest of the structure chart should now be clear. We set the variable POSITION to be 0 and then increment it by 1 just before performing the two statements in the scope of the DO block. The first time we do these statements, POSITION will have value 1, the next time value

⟨○⟩	JUMBLE is an array SMALLEST will be its alphabetically smallest row
	ROWS ← (ρJUMBLE)[1]
	COLUMNS ← (ρJUMBLE)[2]
	ALPHA ← ' ABC...YZ01...9'
	POSSIBLE ← ιROWS
⟨○⟩	Now loop through each column, eliminating rows which can't be smallest
	POSITION ← 0
	DO until (COLUMNS < POSITION ← POSITION+1) ∨ (1=ρ,POSSIBLE)
	ORDER ← ALPHAι JUMBLE[POSSIBLE;POSITION]
	POSSIBLE ← (ORDER = ⌊/ORDER)/POSSIBLE
	POSSIBLE ← 1↑POSSIBLE
	SMALLEST ← JUMBLE[POSSIBLE;]

FIGURE 6.1. The smallest row of an array.

2 and so on. When POSITION gets incremented to have value COL-UMNS+1, one more than the number of columns, the DO group is not entered. The DO group is also not entered when the size of POSSIBLE becomes 1. In either of these cases, the first statement below the DO group chooses the first element of POSSIBLE—if POSSIBLE has only one element, then that element will, of course, be chosen. The value of POSSIBLE is then the number of the row containing the alphabetically first word.

Before we write this program, let's first consider the simpler structure chart in Figure 6.2. This is a function of one scalar argument, called ARGUMENT, which returns the sum of the numbers from 1 to ARGUMENT. Of course, the same result could have been achieved in many simpler ways using APL's operators. The corresponding program is shown in Figure 6.3. The structure chart is very simple. We first set SUM to 0 so we can add to it, and then go through the loop with A having the values 1, 2, ..., successively and each time add A to SUM.

Now look at the program. In line 5, we initialize SUM. Lines 6, 7, 9 and 10 form the translation of the DO block and line 8 is its scope. Structurally they can be represented as in Figure 6.4.

loop

Line 7 is called the *loop control statement* and the entire group of statements is often called a *loop.*

WHEN

The utility program WHEN functions in much the same way as IF: for a 0 right argument, the result is the empty vector; for a right argument equal to 1, the result is the left argument. So each time line 7 is executed, A is incremented by 1. As long as its new value is less than or equal to ARGUMENT, the scope of the loop will be executed and control will then be returned to statement 7 by statement 9. However, once A becomes equal to ARGUMENT+1, control passes to statement 10, which in this case ends the program.

The statement labels used in the loop are chosen to mnemonically represent the action of the loop. The label on line 7 can be read "change A" since a delta is sometimes used in mathematics with a similar meaning, and the label on line 10 can be read "end change A." When, in other programs, the scope of the loop becomes complex, there will be other lines with labels besides those being used for the loop control and it will prove to be a significant help to have the labels for the loop control designated in this way so that we can easily see the structure of the program.

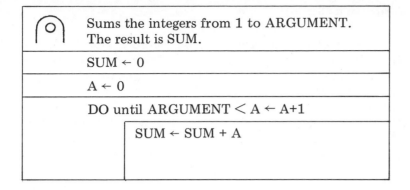

FIGURE 6.2. Repeated addition.

```
    ∇ SUM←SUMRED ARGUMENT;A
[1]    'SUMRED: ARGUMENT NOT SCALAR ' ERROR 1<ρ,ARGUMENT
[2]    'SUMRED: ARGUMENT NOT POSITIVE ' ERROR 0≥ARGUMENT
[3]    'SUMRED: ARGUMENT NOT INTEGER ' ERROR ARGUMENT≠⌊ARGUMENT
[4]    ⍝-----THIS PROGRAM FINDS SUM←1+2+...+ARGUMENT
[5]    SUM←0
[6]    A←0
[7] ΔA:→ENDΔA WHEN ARGUMENT<A←A+1
[8]    SUM←SUM+A
[9]    →ΔA
[10] ENDΔA:→0
    ∇
```

FIGURE 6.3. Translation of Figure 6.2.

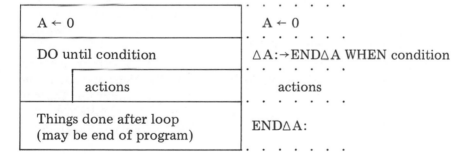

FIGURE 6.4. From structure chart to program.

We return now to the structure chart of Figure 6.1 and the program FIRST in Figure 6.5 which implements it. After checking that the argument is valid and setting up the collating sequence ALPHA we set ROWS and COLUMNS to be the number of rows and columns of the argument, respectively. We next start POSSIBLE off as the vector 1, 2, ..., ROWS, signifying that at this point all rows are equally likely as candidates for being the alphabetically first. Then we enter the loop. The loop variable POSITION is initialized at 0 and then incremented each time through. The loop ends when POSITION becomes larger than COLUMNS or when POSSIBLE has only one element. Inside the loop we find, as before, the indices in ALPHA of the elements in the column referred to by POSITION and the rows designated by POSSIBLE, and then replace POSSIBLE by the vector containing only the numbers of those rows which yield the smallest index. We then go back to increment POSITION and enter the loop again.

When one of the conditions in the loop control statement has been met, control passes to line 12, where the first element of POSSIBLE is chosen as the row number of the result and the function is given a value by assigning the alphabetically first row to SMALLEST.

EXERCISES

6-1. Write a program for finding the alphabetically last column of a character array.

6-2. In both Figure 6.5 and Exercise 6-1 we have made no check as to whether the array contains any characters not in ALPHA. Assume that the array contains exactly one such illegal character. Which, if either, of the programs will still produce the correct result—a row containing only legal characters?

6-3. Write a function of two character vector arguments which produces a 1 if the left argument appears in the right argument and a 0 otherwise. The response will be 1, for example, for the pair ('RAN', 'ARRANGE') but 0 for the pair ('CAT', 'CHAT').

6-4. Does line 1 of SUMRED really test if ARGUMENT is a scalar?

THE BUBBLE SORT

In most applications, we will seldom want only the alphabetically first row of the array. It is much more common to require the array to be sorted, so that the first row is alphabetically smaller than the second, which is smaller than the third, and so on. We could use the program FIRST to completely sort the rows in the obvious way. After finding the smallest row, place it at the top of the array. Then look at the remaining rows to find the next smallest and so on. Such a procedure

```
      ∇ SMALLEST←FIRST JUMBLE;ALPHA;POSITION;ORDER;ROWS;COLUMNS;POSSIBLE
[1]     'FIRST: ARGUMENT NOT ARRAY ' ERROR 2≠ρρJUMBLE
[2]     'FIRST: ARGUMENT NOT CHARACTER ' ERROR 0∈0\0/JUMBLE
[3]     ALPHA←' ABCDEFGHIJKLMNOPQRSTUVWXYZ0123456789'
[4]     ROWS←(ρJUMBLE)[1]
[5]     COLUMNS←(ρJUMBLE)[2]
[6]     POSSIBLE←ιROWS
[7]     POSITION←0
[8]   ΔPOSITION:→ENDΔPOSITION WHEN(COLUMNS<POSITION←POSITION+1)∨1=ρ,POSSIBLE
[9]     ORDER←ALPHAιJUMBLE[POSSIBLE;POSITION]
[10]    POSSIBLE←(ORDER=⌊/ORDER)/POSSIBLE
[11]    →ΔPOSITION
[12]  ENDΔPOSITION:POSSIBLE←1↑POSSIBLE
[13]   SMALLEST←JUMBLE[POSSIBLE;]
      ∇
```

FIGURE 6.5. Finding the smallest row.

would certainly work but it is far from the most efficient possible. To find the smallest element requires a large number of comparisons among rows; in making these comparisons we surely get some information about the relative rankings of some of the other rows which don't turn out to be first and yet we don't use any of this information to find the second smallest row.

There are a number of techniques available for taking advantage of the partial information which is developed during the sorting process. One such procedure is the *bubble sort*. With the bubble sort, we look at the first two rows and interchange them if they are not in the proper order. Then we look at rows two and three. If they are in the proper order, then we in fact know that all the first three rows are in proper order. Otherwise, we interchange the second and third rows. Now we must compare the first and second rows and perform another interchange if *they* are not in the proper order.

We continue the process, encompassing one more row each time. So, at some point, we are comparing a current row, say row i, with row $i-1$. If these two are correctly ordered, (row i is larger than or equal to row $i-1$), then in fact all of the first i rows are sorted: this is because the steps up to this point have been sorting the first $i-1$ rows. However, if row i is smaller than row $i-1$, we simply have to find where it belongs and put it there. We can do this by interchanging: we take row i and interchange it with row $i-1$, then row $i-2$ and so on, until we find the place where it belongs.

How do we know where this row belongs? Let's suppose that we have moved it until it is now row j, where j is less than i. If $j=1$, then our row was the alphabetically smallest. Otherwise, we only have to look at row $j-1$: we know from previous steps that rows 1 through $j-1$ are all in order, so if the row we have been moving is bigger than row $j-1$, it is in the proper place. The similarity of the way this row moves to that of a bubble moving in a column of water is what gives the method its name. It is much easier to see this work than to read about it: Figure 6.6 will get you started by showing how it works on a one column array of numbers and then you should try some more examples with both numeric and character arrays. Note that in the fourth step of Figure 6.6 the last element (2) bubbles up the column in three interchanges until it reaches the second position.

A structure chart for the bubble sort is given in Figure 6.7. Notice that there are two loops, one embedded in the other. The array being sorted is JUMBLE. The variable CURRENT represents i of the preceding discussion, so that at the ith step (CURRENT=i) we compare rows CURRENT and CURRENT−1. If they are properly ordered, we increment CURRENT by 1 and re-enter the outer loop. Otherwise, we first interchange rows CURRENT and CURRENT−1. The variable CURRENTΔVALUE is used in the interchange process and has the value which row CURRENT had before the interchange.

```
          3    1    1    1    1    1    1
         →1    3    3    3    3    3   →2
          4   →4    4    4    4   →2    3
          5    5   →5    5   →2    4    4
          2    2    2   →2    5    5    5
         ─────────────────────────────────
STEP NUMBER   1    2    3   4.1  4.2  4.3  END
```

FIGURE 6.6. A bubble sort.

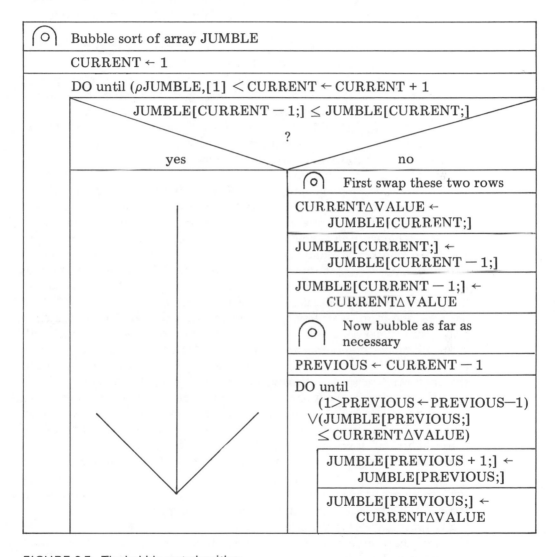

FIGURE 6.7. The bubble sort algorithm.

We then enter the inner loop to begin the bubbling process. Since we will want to first compare CURRENTΔVALUE with row CURRENT—2, we initialize the loop variable PREVIOUS to CURRENT—1. Notice that this loop counts down rather than up as the others we have seen. The loop is exited once row PREVIOUS and row PREVIOUS+1 (which has the same value as CURRENTΔVALUE) are properly ordered. Although APL is very fast anyway, we use CURRENTΔVALUE rather than JUMBLE[PREVIOUS+1;] in these comparisons because it takes a little less time to find the value of a variable than to find the value of one row of an array.

Notice that we have made no mention of how to compare two rows of the array. The less-than-or-equal operator will not work for character vectors (and even if it did, it would produce a vector of the same size as the arguments rather than a scalar). Looking at the program BUBBLE in Figure 6.8, you can see that we have assumed that there will be a function called LEQ which will produce a 0 if its right argument alphabetically follows its left argument and a 1 otherwise.

Assuming that such a function exists, let's look at the program BUBBLE.

The structure of the program follows that of the structure chart. Notice that it is quite easy to locate the two loops by means of the special line labels. There is one tricky difference between the structure chart and the program: the termination condition for the inner loop has been split into two lines, 9 and 10. Suppose we tried to combine them into one line. Consider first the expression in Figure 6.9A. By the right-to-left rule the comparison will be made before PREVIOUS is decremented. Since the preceding step, either through the loop or just before entering the loop, was designed to ensure that the relation on the right holds, we will never be able to enter the inner loop. If, on the other hand, we could make the comparison between JUMBLE[PREVIOUS—1;] and CURRENTΔVALUE, or, equivalently, write the line as in Figure 6.9B, consider what happens when we enter the line with the value of PREVIOUS equal to 1. We would want to have PREVIOUS decremented to 0, and then the loop would not be entered. But the entire expression must be evaluated before the decision not to enter the loop can be made. This will involve finding the value of JUMBLE[0;], which does not eixst in 1 origin indexing, and an INDEX ERROR will occur.

Thus, we break the condition into two parts, first checking PREVIOUS to see if it is still a valid index and then doing the comparison. We use the utility program WHEN on line 10 to remind us that this is really part of the loop control statement.

We still, of course, need a function LEQ. One candidate is presented in Figure 6.10. This is essentially the same as the program FIRST, changed to accept two vector arguments.

```
      ∇ SORTED←BUBBLE JUMBLE;CURRENT;PREVIOUS;CURRENTΔVALUE
[1]     'BUBBLE: ARGUMENT NOT ARRAY ' ERROR 2≠ρρJUMBLE
[2]     CURRENT←1
[3]   ΔCURRENT:→ENDΔCURRENT WHEN(ρJUMBLE)[1]<CURRENT←CURRENT+1
[4]     →ΔCURRENT IF JUMBLE[CURRENT-1;] LEQ JUMBLE[CURRENT;]
[5]     CURRENTΔVALUE←JUMBLE[CURRENT;]
[6]     JUMBLE[CURRENT;]←JUMBLE[CURRENT-1;]
[7]     JUMBLE[CURRENT-1;]←CURRENTΔVALUE
[8]     PREVIOUS←CURRENT-1
[9]   ΔPREVIOUS:→ENDΔPREVIOUS WHEN 1>PREVIOUS←PREVIOUS-1
[10]    →ENDΔPREVIOUS WHEN JUMBLE[PREVIOUS;] LEQ CURRENTΔVALUE
[11]    JUMBLE[PREVIOUS+1;]←JUMBLE[PREVIOUS;]
[12]    JUMBLE[PREVIOUS;]←CURRENTΔVALUE
[13]    →ΔPREVIOUS
[14] ENDΔPREVIOUS:→ΔCURRENT
[15] ENDΔCURRENT:SORTED←JUMBLE
      ∇
```

FIGURE 6.8. A bubble sort.

A)
```
    ΔPREVIOUS:→ENDΔPREVIOUS WHEN (1>PREVIOUS←PREVIOUS-1)∨(JUMBLE[PREVIOUS;]LEQ CURRENTΔVALUE)
```

B)
```
    ΔPREVIOUS:→ENDΔPREVIOUS WHEN (JUMBLE[PREVIOUS;]LEQ CURRENTΔVALUE)∨(1>PREVIOUS←PREVIOUS-1)
```

FIGURE 6.9. Two incorrect versions of a condition.

```
      ∇ TRUE←LEFT LEQ RIGHT;ALPHA;POSITION;POSSIBLE;ORDER
[1]     'LEQ: LEFT ARGUMENT NOT CHARACTER ' ERROR 0∈0\0/LEFT
[2]     'LEQ: RIGHT ARGUMENT NOT CHARACTER ' ERROR 0∈0\0/RIGHT
[3]     'LEQ: LEFT ARGUMENT NOT VECTOR ' ERROR 1≠ρρLEFT
[4]     'LEQ: RIGHT ARGUMENT NOT VECTOR ' ERROR 1≠ρρRIGHT
[5]     'LEQ: ARGUMENTS NOT CONFORMABLE ' ERROR(ρLEFT)≠ρRIGHT
[6]     ALPHA←' ABCDEFGHIJKLMNOPQRSTUVWXYZ0123456789'
[7]     POSSIBLE←ι2
[8]     POSITION←0
[9]   ΔPOSITION:→ENDΔPOSITION WHEN((ρLEFT)<POSITION←POSITION+1)∨(1=ρ,POSSIBLE)
[10]    POSSIBLE←(ORDER=⌊/ORDER←ALPHAι2ρLEFT[POSITION],RIGHT[POSITION])/POSSIBLE
[11]    →ΔPOSITION
[12] ENDΔPOSITION:TRUE←1=1↑POSSIBLE
      ∇
```

FIGURE 6.10. Comparing two character vectors.

EXERCISES

6-5. Notice that the check that the items being sorted are character-valued is made in LEQ rather than in BUBBLE. Thus, it is necessary only to change LEQ in order to have a bubble sort for numeric arrays. Make such a change.

6-6. A much more useful version of LEQ would examine the inputs to see if they were both numeric or both character and perform a correct comparison in either case. Write and use such a program. Don't forget to check for the case of one argument being numeric and the other one being character.

6-7. Can the problem which caused us to break the termination condition for the inner loop into two statements be rectified by using 0-origin indexing?

6-8. How do we know what the less-than-or-equal operator *would* produce for character vector arguments even though it doesn't accept such arguments?

A DIFFERENT APPROACH

The version of BUBBLE which we now have still has at least one rather unfortunate feature—it may move the rows of the array around a number of times. Moving rows of an array can become expensive for arrays with many rows and columns and it would be preferable to do as little moving as possible. The function BUBBLE in Figure 6.11 has the same structure as Figure 6.8, but works somewhat differently. In line 2 we set a vector INDICES to be the vector of row numbers. Then, instead of interchanging rows of JUMBLE, the program interchanges corresponding elements of INDICES. Thus, when line 16 is reached, the vector INDICES indicates the order in which the rows of JUMBLE should be taken so that the result will be sorted properly. (Note the similarity between this and the way that the grade-up operator works on numeric vectors.) In line 16 the array is sorted by indexing with the vector INDICES; then the sorted array is assigned to SORTED to give the result of the function.

It would be interesting to see which version of the bubble sort is, in fact, faster. To do this, we need to be able to find out how much computation time (CPU time) is taken by a program, which we can do with the system operator I-beam 21; this has for its value the number of sixtieths of a second of CPU time used since the beginning of the sign-on session. The program TIMER in Figure 6.12 can be used to investigate the amount of CPU time used between two events.

Calling TIMER 0 saves the value of I-beam 21 at that instant. Later, when TIMER 1 is invoked, the saved value of I-beam 21 is subtracted

CPU time

```
      ∇ SORTED←BUBBLE JUMBLE;CURRENT;PREVIOUS;CURRENTΔVALUE;INDICES
[1]     'BUBBLE: ARGUMENT NOT ARRAY ' ERROR 2≠ρρJUMBLE
[2]     INDICES←ι(ρJUMBLE)[1]
[3]     CURRENT←1
[4]   ΔCURRENT:→ENDΔCURRENT WHEN(ρINDICES)<CURRENT←CURRENT+1
[5]     →ΔCURRENT IF JUMBLE[INDICES[CURRENT-1];] LEQ JUMBLE[INDICES[CURRENT];]
[6]     CURRENTΔVALUE←INDICES[CURRENT]
[7]     INDICES[CURRENT]←INDICES[CURRENT-1]
[8]     INDICES[CURRENT-1]←CURRENTΔVALUE
[9]     PREVIOUS←CURRENT-1
[10]  ΔPREVIOUS:→ENDΔPREVIOUS WHEN 1>PREVIOUS←PREVIOUS-1
[11]    →ENDΔPREVIOUS WHEN JUMBLE[INDICES[PREVIOUS];] LEQ JUMBLE[CURRENTΔVALUE;]
[12]    INDICES[PREVIOUS+1]←INDICES[PREVIOUS]
[13]    INDICES[PREVIOUS]←CURRENTΔVALUE
[14]    →ΔPREVIOUS
[15] ENDΔPREVIOUS:→ΔCURRENT
[16] ENDΔCURRENT:SORTED←JUMBLE[INDICES;]
      ∇
```

FIGURE 6.11. Another bubble sort.

```
      ∇ TIMER X
[1]     →REPORT IF X=1
[2]     SAVETIME←ι21
[3]     →0
[4]   REPORT:'THE CPU TIME IN SECONDS IS ';((ι21)-SAVETIME)÷60
      ∇
```

FIGURE 6.12. A timing routine.

from the current value, giving the amount of time elapsed. Notice that the variable SAVETIME cannot be made local to the function, since it would then cease to exist after the program is exited at line 3. A variable which is not local is called *global*. We will adopt the convention here that all global variable names which appear in programs are underlined, so that in reading the program we can differentiate immediately between those variables whose values are assigned by the program and those whose values are assigned before the program is called.

global variable

We can embed TIMER and the bubble sort programs in a routine like COMPAREΔBUBBLES in Figure 6.13 to compare the amount of CPU time taken by each of the bubble sorts; so that both sorting programs can exist in the same workspace we have temporarily renamed the one in Figure 6.11 (the later one) as BUBBLE2.

On the small examples in Figure 6.14 the times are very close; it is probably more interesting to note the way that small changes in the data can affect the times rather than to look at the times themselves.

On the larger sorting tasks, differences do appear between the two routines, but the second one is not always faster. We can see the reason by examining BUBBLE2 more closely. Each time we find a row of the array JUMBLE, we have to do double indexing through the vector INDICES, as on line 5. This is bound to be more costly than single indexing and can overtake the gain we make by not actually moving rows. When the number of columns is small, it is not very expensive to move rows around and the first program does a little better. When there are many columns, then the second program does perform slightly faster. Clearly, if you knew which kind of array you had to sort, you could pick the program accordingly. This is true in general: a program's design should be tailored to the data on which it will operate.

EXERCISES

6-9. Does one of the two bubble sort programs use significantly less workspace room than the other? Why or why not? (*Note*: When a program is running, it may take up more space than when it is inactive.)

6-10. Write a program which sorts the elements of a numeric vector and compare its performance with the grade-up operator.

6-11. While we cannot use the comparison (except for = and ≠) and grade-up operators with character vectors, we can use them with numeric vectors. Write a sorting program which sorts the rows of a numeric array.

```
     ∇ COMPARE∆BUBBLES JUMBLE;NO∆PRINT
[1]    TIMER 0
[2]    NO∆PRINT←BUBBLE JUMBLE
[3]    TIMER 1
[4]    TIMER 0
[5]    NO∆PRINT←BUBBLE2 JUMBLE
[6]    TIMER 1
     ∇
```

FIGURE 6.13. Comparing the bubble sort.

```
     COMPARE∆BUBBLES (5,5)ρ'EVERYGOOD BOY  DOES FINE '
THE CPU TIME IN SECONDS IS 1.216666667
THE CPU TIME IN SECONDS IS 1.316666667


     COMPARE∆BUBBLES (5,5)ρ'EVERY GOOD BOY DOES  FINE'
THE CPU TIME IN SECONDS IS 1.63333333
THE CPU TIME IN SECONDS IS 1.56666667


     Z←17ρ'Z'
     COMPARE∆BUBBLES (30,100)ρZ,Z,'Y',Z,Z,'X',Z,Z,'W',Z,'V',Z,Z,'U',Z
THE CPU TIME IN SECONDS IS 169.5166667
THE CPU TIME IN SECONDS IS 159.1333333


     COMPARE∆BUBBLES (50,20)ρZ,'Y',Z,'X',Z,'W',Z
THE CPU TIME IN SECONDS IS 235.5833333
THE CPU TIME IN SECONDS IS 240.7166667
```

FIGURE 6.14. Comparisons of the two algorithms.

6-12. Write a sorting program for character arrays which first transforms the array to a numeric one, by replacing each character with its index in the vector ALPHA. Compare the performance of this program with a similar one which does not transform the array.

6-13. Rewrite TIMER so that it rounds off the time to two digits after the decimal place. Does this give less significant information?

6-14. In LEQ the common size of the arguments is evaluated on line 9 every time through the loop. How much more efficient does the bubble sort become if we assign this size to a variable before entering the loop and then reference that variable in line 9?

6-15. Donald Knuth, in his book *Sorting and Searching* (Reading, Mass.: Addison-Wesley, 1973), compares the bubble sort with a number of different algorithms for sorting and concludes, "In short, the bubble sort seems to have nothing to recommend it, except a catchy name and the fact that it leads to some interesting theoretical problems." Theoreticians might wish to investigate some of those "interesting" problems. However, if you need to sort some data, we recommend taking a look at the book and finding out which algorithms are considered better.

Interlude Four

Debugging Aids

As you will probably have discovered by now, no matter how carefully one writes a program and enters it into the machine, there is a good chance that it will not behave as expected. Sometimes the errors are typographical, sometimes logical, and sometimes due to a misunderstanding of some feature of APL, but errors there always are. Rooting out and eliminating errors is called *debugging*. Programming and debugging are often complimentary arts: a person may be especially talented at one and only barely acceptable at the other. The following statement expresses some of the differences in these tasks:

Different programming phases give different programmers a chance to shine. For example, when we are making the overall design of a program, what we most need is the ability to create new programming ideas and to screen them on the basis of broad principles. Examples of such screening ideas are symmetry of structure and generality of function—one leads to simple coding of difficult problems and the other leads to the solution of difficult problems with simple coding. Still, these critical abilities are useless if there is a paucity of ideas to which to apply them. Nothing cannot be criticized. Thus, a programmer lacking in either ability—creativity or selectivity—will be handicapped in attempting to design programs.

When coding, however, different abilities come to the fore. Instead of the broad, sweeping mind, the mind which is clever at small things now excels. Then, when testing, the programmer must switch to yet another group of gifts—particularly the eye for wholeness, or *gestalt*. Consider the following tale.

"I was eating breakfast and reading an article by Stephen Spender called 'The Making of a Poem.' On page 120, I reached the end of one section and set the book down to put some more sugar on my cereal. When I picked the book up again to start reading a section called 'Memory,' I immediately had a feeling that there was something wrong in the first sentence which started:

'If the art of concentrating in a particular way. . . .'

I felt, more or less simultaneously, that the trouble was in the word 'particular' and that it involved a misprint. The misprint, however, was rather confusing for I sensed that it was letter inversion but I also sensed—a little bit more weakly, though, I have a definite impression of that—that there was a letter missing. I examined the word 'particular'—which, by the way, I often mistype as 'particluar'—first for the inversion and, failing to find that, for the omitted letter. I spent a rather long time looking for the error—I could measure that because I ate five or six spoonfuls of cereal in the process, the amount I ordinarily eat between sips of water. But I could not find anything wrong, and when I reached for the water glass, I was rather confused.

"The water glass was empty, so I set down the book and went to the sink to fill it. Upon returning, I drank some water, picked up the book, and started to read. I finished the paragraph without further difficulty, but when I commenced reading the next, I immediately saw that the line:

'All poets have this highly devolped sensitive apparatus. . . .'

contained the misprint of the word 'devolped', which stood in the same position in that sentence as 'particular' had stood in the first sentence of the preceding paragraph. I had the right impression, but I had 'focussed' wrongly."

Although this error was in printing, its discovery and location followed very closely the process by which many programming errors are found. First, there is only the *gestalt*, a general feeling that something is out of place without any particular localization. Then follows the ability to shake loose from an unyielding situation—the ability to change one's point of view, even by employing external devices such as going for a glass of water. Then, however, one must go from the general to the particular—'focussing,' as it was called here. Although one does not find errors efficiently by a detailed search of each line, or word, or character, the ability to get down to details is essential in the end. Thus, for debugging, an almost complementary set of mental powers is needed. No wonder good debuggers are so rare![1]

Unfortunately, very few of us can avoid having to debug our own programs at least once in a while. Debugging can make one feel like Dr. Watson in a Sherlock Holmes story—there are clues falling all around and yet they just won't point to the murderer. Anyone who has been programming for as long as two weeks has a stock of anecdotes about debugging tasks and it can be very interesting (for a while) to listen to some of these. While debugging is usually a bit difficult, it can sometimes be close to impossible. Almost always, when a program is impossible to debug it is because the program is impossible to understand. The best defense is to write programs that are clear and readable. All the techniques which we introduce in this book are designed to help you write programs that will be both easy to read and easy to debug.

[1]Reprinted with permission of the VanNostrand Reinhold Company, from *The Psychology of Computer Programming* by Gerald M. Weinberg, copyright 1971 by Litton Educational Publishing, Inc.

TRACING AND STOPPING

In debugging, there is no substitute for working out a program by hand, keeping track of every variable and every computation and every branch. Start with the lowest level programs, those which don't call any others, and don't move to higher level programs until the lower level ones are correct. This method, followed with care, is usually sufficient. Sometimes, however, we need to go to the machine for help.

Suppose that one of our test cases has produced an incorrect answer or an error message. We trace through the program using the test data and can't locate the error. It then occurs to us that we could get more insight into the problem if we knew the value being assigned to the variable on line 13, or whether the branch in the IF condition on line 6 is being taken. One way to find these things out is to insert statements in the program that print the values of some variable, or simply messages identifying their location. If the message AT LINE 7 is printed when we expected to branch around it, this certainly gives us more information.

However, APL is provided with tools that let us do exactly this sort of tracing without our having to make temporary changes to the program. One of these is the *trace* command. With one exception, every line of a program, when executed, results in some value being generated. The value may be something that is being printed, a value which is being assigned to a variable, or a line number which is being branched to. The exception is an invocation of another program which is not a function. We can instruct the system so that whenever certain lines are executed the value associated with those lines is to be printed. In Figure I4.1A we list the program SUMRED of Chapter 6. The command in Figure I4.1B is the trace command. It can be read, "trace lines 7 and 8 of SUMRED." The result of the trace is shown by the call SUMRED 3 in part C.

The first line being traced which is encountered is line 7. This time, the result of the utility program WHEN is the empty vector, so nothing is printed after the identification SUMRED[7]. Next, line 8 is executed. Since the value of A, 1, is being added to SUM, which is still 0, the value evolved on the line is 1, as indicated by the trace. The next two times through the loop are similar. No branch is taken from line 7 and, in succession, the numbers 2 and 3 are added to SUM, giving partial sums 3 and 6. Finally, when A receives the value 4 on line 7 the condition is true, so the branch is taken to line 10.

When you are no longer interested in tracing, you can assign either 0 or the empty vector to the trace "command variable" as shown in Figure I4.1D.

A)

```
      ∇ SUM←SUMRED ARGUMENT;A
[1]    'SUMRED: ARGUMENT NOT SCALAR ' ERROR 1<ρ,ARGUMENT
[2]    'SUMRED: ARGUMENT NOT POSITIVE ' ERROR 0≥ARGUMENT
[3]    'SUMRED: ARGUMENT NOT INTEGER ' ERROR ARGUMENT≠⌊ARGUMENT
[4]    ⍝-----THIS PROGRAM FINDS SUM←1+2+...+ARGUMENT
[5]    SUM←0
[6]    A←0
[7]  ΔA:→ENDΔA WHEN ARGUMENT<A←A+1
[8]    SUM←SUM+A
[9]    →ΔA
[10] ENDΔA:→0
      ∇
```

B)

```
      TΔSUMRED←7 8
```

C)

```
      SUMRED 3
SUMRED[7]
SUMRED[8] 1
SUMRED[7]
SUMRED[8] 3
SUMRED[7]
SUMRED[8] 6
SUMRED[7] 10
6
```

D)

```
      TΔSUMRED←0
      TΔSUMRED←⍳0
```

FIGURE I4.1. An example of tracing.

Occasionally you will want a bit more information than can be gotten by tracing. You might have a complicated APL expression in your program and want to see exactly what it is doing, using exactly the same values it is getting in the program. While you could simply enter the expression, that might not be sufficient if, for example, you suspect that one of the variables in it is a vector of size 1 when it should be a scalar. A trace will not show any distinction between these two cases. What we can do is ask APL to suspend execution of the program. This is done with the *stop* command. In Figure I4.2 we list the function LEQ from Chapter 6 and then instruct the system to suspend the program just *before* executing line 10; this is like the trace command but begins with 'S' instead of 'T'.

When line 10 is reached, a message is printed telling us where the program is, in case more than one line was given for the stop command. The program has *not* been exited. As you can see from the figure, all the local variables still have their values and when we are done examining them we can instruct the program to continue execution with line 10.

state
indicator

Notice that after the third time the program is suspended, we issue the system command)SI. SI stands for *state indicator*, and this is a request for a listing of the names of all suspended programs. The first line says that LEQ has been suspended in line 10, and the second that it was called from line 10 of BUBBLE.

```
      ∇ TRUE←LEFT LEQ RIGHT;ALPHA;POSITION;POSSIBLE;ORDER
[1]     'LEQ: LEFT ARGUMENT NOT CHARACTER 'ERROR 0∊0\0/LEFT
[2]     'LEQ: RIGHT ARGUMENT NOT CHARACTER 'ERROR 0∊0\0/RIGHT
[3]     'LEQ: LEFT ARGUMENT NOT VECTOR 'ERROR 1≠ρρLEFT
[4]     'LEQ: RIGHT ARGUMENT NOT VECTOR 'ERROR 1≠ρρRIGHT
[5]     'LEQ: ARGUMENTS NOT CONFORMABLE 'ERROR(ρLEFT)≠ρRIGHT
[6]     ALPHA←' ABCDEFGHIJKLMNOPQRSTUVWXYZ0123456789'
[7]     POSSIBLE←⍳2
[8]     POSITION←0
[9]    ΔPOSITION:→ENDΔPOSITION WHEN((ρLEFT)<POSITION←POSITION+1)∨(1=ρ,POSSIBLE)
[10]    POSSIBLE←(ORDER=⌊/ORDER←ALPHA⍳2ρLEFT[POSITION],RIGHT[POSITION])/POSSIBLE
[11]    →ΔPOSITION
[12]  ENDΔPOSITION:TRUE←1=1↑POSSIBLE
      ∇


      SΔLEQ←⍳0
      BUBBLE (5,5)ρ'EVERY GOOD  BOY DOES FINE'

LEQ[10]
      POSITION
1
      LEFT
EVERY
      RIGHT
 GOOD
      →10


LEQ[10]
      LEFT
EVERY
      RIGHT
  BOY
      POSITION
1
      POSSIBLE
1   2
      →10


LEQ[10]
      LEFT
 GOOD
      RIGHT
  BOY
      POSITION
1
      )SI
LEQ[10] *
BUBBLE[10]
     ̣SΔLEQ←⍳0
      →10
  BOY
 DOES
 FINE
 GOOD
EVERY
```

FIGURE I4.2. Using the stop command.

Figure I4.3 shows another request, at a later time, for the state indicator: there are three groups exactly the same. What probably happened is that LEQ was suspended, possibly because APL detected an error, and the user corrected the error and called BUBBLE again. This left copies of the programs LEQ and BUBBLE still pending. Then, no doubt, there was another error and another suspension. The lower sets of programs are just sitting there, taking up valuable space in the workspace, and should have been released. To release a suspended program and all the unstarred programs directly below it, type a right-pointing arrow. In this case, to clear the state indicator we would have to type three right-pointing arrows in succession (on three different lines).

EXERCISES

I4-1. Use the system operator I-beam 22 to find out how much space is taken up by a stack of suspended programs.

I4-2. Find an I-beam operator which is similar to the system command)SI.

I4-3. How many suspended programs are there in your workspace?

I4-4. In Figure I4.2, why is it that POSITION always has the value 1? If we had allowed the program to stop on line 10 once more, what would the value of POSITION have been?

```
LEQ[10]
      )SI
LEQ[10] *
BUBBLE[10]
LEQ[10] *
BUBBLE[10]
LEQ[10] *
BUBBLE[10]
```

FIGURE I4.3. Many suspended programs.

7

Learning to Play the Game of NIM:

An Example of Program Construction

"Taking Three as the subject to reason about—
  A convenient number to state—
We add Seven, and Ten, and then multiply out
  By One Thousand diminished by Eight.

"The result we proceed to divide, as you see,
  By Nine Hundred and Ninety and Two:
Then subtract Seventeen, and the answer must be
  Exactly and perfectly true."

The game of NIM is one which received a good deal of publicity after the movie "Last Year in Marienbad" appeared. Supposedly, it was the "in" thing at the parties of the very chic. We will use this game as an example to tie together some of the concepts we have been learning. In doing so, we will also write a program which figures out the winning strategy, although it is not too hard to figure out the strategy without the computer's aid.

AN INTERACTIVE NIM PLAYING PROGRAM

NIM is played by two people using some number, say 17, of sticks. The players alternate, removing one, two or three sticks from the pile. The player who removes the last stick loses. Our ultimate goal is to write a program for NIM which will learn to play a good game: in fact, NIM turns out to be so simple that the program will eventually play perfectly. Before we become involved in the details of a learning program, we should first try simply to write a program which plays the game and then add the more sophisticated features afterwards.

As a first attempt, we might write a program which will play NIM with the user at the terminal. The program should make only legal moves and should not allow its opponent to make any illegal moves. An important question is, who will make the first move? We could let the user decide, or the machine for that matter, but since we don't know whether it is important who goes first, we should let that decision depend on the toss of a coin.

We can imagine that the program is really playing two roles: it is both a player and the referee, and the two roles should be distinct. If we were writing a program to play a card game, such as blackjack ("21"), we wouldn't want the part of the program which was betting against us to be able to ask the part of the program which was dealing what the next card was.

Figure 7.1 gives a rough outline of the way we might expect the game to proceed. First we would decide which player went first and set up the 17 sticks. Then the referee would tell the player to go ahead. Entering the loop, the first player would propose a move. If the move was not legal, the player would try again. If it was legal, then the move would be made and the next player would be designated. Looking at the structure chart, we see first that it is really impartial: there is no distinction between the computer player and the human player. Of course, there must be some distinction between them when their moves are requested by the referee, but the structure of the program suggests that there be a separate program to request moves and that this separate program be the one which makes the distinctions.

We'll call the program which gets the moves INPUT. INPUT must have some way to know if it is to ask the human opponent or the

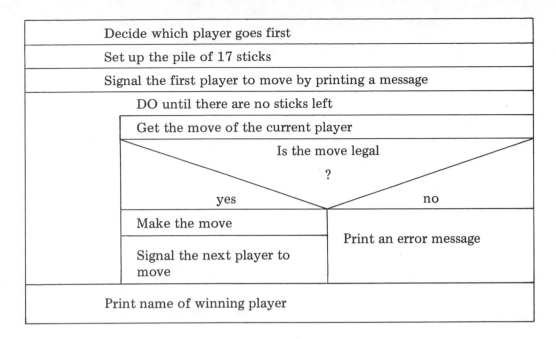

FIGURE 7.1. Design for a NIM program.

machine opponent for a move, so we will pass to INPUT one argument, an 'M' if the computer is to move next and a 'P' if the person is to move. Naturally, INPUT will be a function, which returns as its value the next move. For the human player we need only use a quad to request input. For the computer, while we eventually may have a very complex algorithm for its next move, at the moment it is playing randomly and so **roll** we can let it make a random move with the *roll* operator. A version of this program is shown in Figure 7.2.

There are only two features of the main program which might not be completely straightforward. The first is the detection of an illegal move. We know that a move is illegal if it is not one, two or three. But it is also illegal if it is larger than the number of sticks remaining. Since there are two different ways in which a move might be illegal, it seems reasonable to print different error messages, depending on which type of move is made. This calls for a decision which is not part of our original structure chart and so we will write a separate program to take care of it. Program ILLEGAL will have two arguments, the number of sticks remaining and the proposed move. If the move is illegal, the program will print an appropriate error message; otherwise it will do nothing.

We will incorporate ILLEGAL into the IF-THEN block in Figure 7.1. We can do this by making it be a function and having it return a 1 if the move was illegal and 0 if it was legal. Incorporating ILLEGAL with the IF function, we can cause a branch to the loop control statement if the move was illegal and continue on with the move if it was legal. Program ILLEGAL is shown in Figure 7.3.

```
     ∇ MOVE←INPUT PLAYER
[1]    ⍝-----IF PLAYER = 'P' HUMAN OPPONENT MOVES
[2]    ⍝-----IF PLAYER = 'M' MACHINE MOVES
[3]    'INPUT: ARGUMENT SIZE ' ERROR 1≠ρ,PLAYER
[4]    'INPUT: ARGUMENT MEANINGLESS ' ERROR~PLAYER∈'MP'
[5]    →MACHINE IF PLAYER='M'
[6]    →0×MOVE←□
[7]    MACHINE:MOVE←?3
     ∇
```

FIGURE 7.2. Input for a NIM program.

```
     ∇ RESULT←STICKS ILLEGAL MOVE
[1]    ⍝-----STICKS IS NUMBER OF STICKS REMAINING
[2]    ⍝-----MOVE IS PROPOSED MOVE
[3]    ⍝-----RETURNS 0 FOR LEGAL MOVE
[4]    ⍝-----RETURNS 1 AND PRINTS APPROPRIATE MESSAGE FOR ILLEGAL MOVE
[5]    'LEGAL:LEFT ARGUMENT NOT NUMERIC ' ERROR~0∈0\0/STICKS
[6]    'LEGAL:RIGHT ARGUMENT NOT NUMERIC ' ERROR~0∈0\0/MOVE
[7]    'LEGAL:LEFT ARGUMENT WRONG SIZE ' ERROR 1≠ρ,STICKS
[8]    'LEGAL:RIGHT ARGUMENT WRONG SIZE ' ERROR 1≠ρ,MOVE
[9]    RESULT←0
[10]   →IN∆RANGE IF MOVE∈ 1 2 3
[11]   'ILLEGAL MOVE: ONLY 1 2 OR 3 IS PERMISSIBLE'
[12]   →0×RESULT←1
[13]  IN∆RANGE:→0 IF MOVE≤STICKS
[14]   'ILLEGAL MOVE:CANNOT TAKE MORE THAN ';STICKS
[15]   RESULT←1
     ∇
```

FIGURE 7.3. Checking for illegal moves.

One of the simplest ways to keep track of which player goes next is by means of a *switch*. A switch is a variable which alternates between some set of values: the change in value occurs when some operation is performed on it. Here, we will let the switch alternate between values 1 and 2. In this way, using the switch to index the vector 'MP' gives the proper argument. A first version of the NIM program is shown in Figure 7.4. Notice how we use the variable PLAYERS, indexed by the switch, NEXT, to print the proper message indicating who moves and who wins. A sample game is shown in Figure 7.5.

```
      ∇ NIM;NEXT;STICKS;PLAYERS;PROPOSAL
[1]    NEXT←?2
[2]    ⍝-----NEXT DETERMINES WHICH PLAYER MOVES NEXT
[3]    PLAYERS←(2,3)ρ' I YOU'
[4]    STICKS←17
[5]   ΔSTICKS:→ENDΔSTICKS WHEN 0=STICKS
[6]    PLAYERS[NEXT;],' MOVE'
[7]    PROPOSAL←INPUT 'MP'[NEXT]
[8]    →ΔSTICKS IF STICKS ILLEGAL PROPOSAL
[9]    STICKS←STICKS-PROPOSAL
[10]   NEXT←3-NEXT
[11]   ⍝-----TRANSFORMS 1 TO 2 AND 2 TO 1
[12]   →ΔSTICKS
[13]   ⍝-----AT END, NEXT POINTS TO WINNER
[14] ENDΔSTICKS:PLAYERS[NEXT;],' WIN!'
      ∇
```

FIGURE 7.4. The NIM program.

```
      NIM
 I   MOVE
YOU MOVE
□:
       3
 I   MOVE
YOU MOVE
□:
       4
ILLEGAL MOVE: ONLY 1 2 OR 3 IS PERMISSIBLE
YOU MOVE
□:
       1
 I   MOVE
YOU MOVE
□:
       3
 I   MOVE
ILLEGAL MOVE: CANNOT TAKE MORE THAN 1
 I   MOVE
ILLEGAL MOVE: CANNOT TAKE MORE THAN 1
 I   MOVE
YOU WIN!
```

FIGURE 7.5. A game of NIM.

One unfortunate feature becomes immediately apparent: after the machine moves, its opponent has no way of knowing how many sticks remain. This is easily corrected by inserting an appropriate message. We might also consider the possibility that the machine's opponent does not know the rules of the game. It is easy enough to write a small program which explains how the game works and to have NIM ask the user to find out if it is necessary to call it. The RULES program and the revised NIM program are shown in Figure 7.6, followed

```
      ∇ RULES
[1]     'THE GAME OF NIM IS PLAYED WITH 17 STICKS'
[2]     'YOU AND I TAKE TURNS REMOVING 1,2 OR 3 STICKS'
[3]     'WHICHEVER OF US REMOVES THE LAST STICK LOSES'
[4]     'MAKE YOUR MOVE WHEN I ASK FOR IT BY TYPING'
[5]     '□:'
      ∇


      ∇ NIM;NEXT;STICKS;PLAYERS;PROPOSAL;YES;NO
[1]     'DO YOU WISH TO SEE THE RULES? ANSWER YES OR NO'
[2]     →START IF□=NO←~YES←1
[3]     RULES
[4]   START:NEXT←?2
[5]     ⍝-----NEXT DETERMINES WHICH PLAYER MOVES NEXT
[6]     PLAYERS←(2,3)ρ' I YOU'
[7]     STICKS←17
[8]   ΔSTICKS:→ENDΔSTICKS WHEN 0=STICKS
[9]     STICKS;'  STICKS LEFT'
[10]    PLAYERS[NEXT;],' MOVE'
[11]    PROPOSAL←INPUT 'MP'[NEXT]
[12]    →ΔSTICKS IF STICKS ILLEGAL PROPOSAL
[13]    STICKS←STICKS-PROPOSAL
[14]    NEXT←3-NEXT
[15]    ⍝-----TRANSFORMS 1 TO 2 AND 2 TO 1
[16]    →ΔSTICKS
[17]    ⍝-----AT END, NEXT POINTS TO WINNER
[18]  ENDΔSTICKS:PLAYERS[NEXT;],' WIN!'
      ∇
```

FIGURE 7.6. Revised NIM with rules.

by a sample of the play in Figure 7.7.

EXERCISES

7-1. Correct line 9 of the latest NIM program so that it will not plural-
ize and write STICKS when only one is left.

7-2. As the program is now written, the machine can make an illegal
move by taking more sticks than are left and a message will be
printed. Correct the program INPUT by adding as an argument
the number of sticks and then ensuring that the machine never
makes an illegal move of this form.
Note: Having done this, it would be logical to move the entire
program ILLEGAL and check for legality of the person's move
inside INPUT. We will, for the sake of continuity only, keep the
structure which we have developed so far for the program.

7-3. Propose an alternate method of asking whether the player wants
to see the rules. You should analyze ways in which the current
scheme is unsatisfactory before proposing an alternate.

7-4. Is it possible to reconstruct the machine's moves in Figure 7.5?

A LEARNING MACHINE

The technique we will use to give the program some learning ability is
reward-and-punishment. We cannot directly reward or punish a move,
since we don't know until the game is over whether the move led to a
win or to a loss; we can, however, reward or punish the entire sequence
of moves the machine made during one game. Before we try to design
a technique for doing this, we might look ahead to ask how we will
keep the program's memory of which moves have, on the average, been
better and how we will use this memory to play the game.

One reasonable way to proceed is to define a 17-by-3 array to be
the memory. The entries of the array will correspond in some way to
the relative worth of the various moves. When it comes time to move,
if there are t sticks in the pile, the program will examine the tth row of
the array and choose one of the three possible moves in accordance
with the values in that row. We would probably not want to use any
well-determined algorithm, such as "make the move corresponding to
the largest entry," because this does not give the learning program
enough chance to experiment with different possibilities. Instead, we
will use a simple form of what is called a Monte Carlo technique.

In each row of the array, the entries will be nonnegative and will
sum to 1. We will choose a random number between 0 and 1; if the first
element in the row is at least as large as this random number, the machine will remove one stick; if the sum of the first and second elements

```
        NIM
DO YOU WISH TO SEE THE RULES? ANSWER YES OR NO
☐:
        NO
17 STICKS LEFT
 I  MOVE
16 STICKS LEFT
YOU MOVE
☐:
        3
 I  MOVE
11 STICKS LEFT
YOU MOVE
☐:
        1
10 STICKS LEFT
 I  MOVE
7 STICKS LEFT
YOU MOVE
☐:
        3
4 STICKS LEFT
 I  MOVE
3 STICKS LEFT
YOU MOVE
☐:
        3
 I  WIN!


        NIM
DO YOU WISH TO SEE THE RULES? ANSWER YES OR NO
☐:
        YES
THE GAME OF NIM IS PLAYED WITH 17 STICKS
YOU AND I TAKE TURNS REMOVING 1,2 OR 3 STICKS
WHICHEVER OF US REMOVES THE LAST STICK LOSES
MAKE YOUR MOVE WHEN I ASK FOR IT BY TYPING
☐:
17 STICKS LEFT
 I  MOVE
14 STICKS LEFT
YOU MOVE
☐:
        3
11 STICKS LEFT
 I  MOVE
9 STICKS LEFT
YOU MOVE
☐:
        3
6 STICKS LEFT
 I  MOVE
3 STICKS LEFT
YOU MOVE
☐:
        2
1 STICKS LEFT
 I  MOVE
YOU WIN!
```

FIGURE 7.7. Two more NIM games.

is at least as large, then the machine removes two sticks; otherwise, it takes three sticks.

The revised program INPUT is shown in Figure 7.8. The memory array is called HISTORY: notice that it is a global variable. This is because it must exist independently of the program INPUT. It is now necessary to know the number of sticks remaining, so we have added a second argument to INPUT. (Of course, this change will have to be reflected in the calling program, NIM.) Lines 10–14 are an implementation of the Monte Carlo procedure.

Our aim is to get a vector whose first element is the first element of the appropriate row of HISTORY, whose second element is the sum of the first two elements in the row and whose third element is the sum of all the elements in the row. One way to do this is to produce a three-by-three array in which the first column contains the first element of the row of HISTORY and two zeros, the second column contains the first two elements of the row and one zero and the third column contains all the elements of the row: doing a sum reduction would then yield the appropriate vector.

The array formed on line 10 is not quite the one we want. Above the main diagonal (the left-to-right diagonal formed by the elements whose row and column indices are equal), the array does have the proper form but there is an unwanted nonzero element below. We correct for this and then take the sum reduction of the result. Line 13 chooses a number randomly between 0 and 1 and then in line 14 the move made is taken to be the first position in which the vector of successive sums is at least as large as the random number.

In line 14 we actually take the minimum of the calculated move and 3. We do this because no computer can do its calculations perfectly. Any computer is limited to some finite number of decimal places, but there are some numbers which cannot be so expressed: 1/3 is not equal to the number with 16 (or 60) threes after the decimal point. While APL arithmetic is so good that we rarely see problems arising from this limitation, they can occur. If the sum of the elements of some row of HISTORY were slightly smaller than 1, for a sufficiently large random number the result of the index operation on line 14 might be 4, so we correct for this possibility by ensuring that the move chosen is never larger than 3.

We now need a scheme for remembering the moves made in a game and modifying HISTORY as a result of the outcome. An easy way to modify it is to add some number to positions corresponding to winning moves and to subtract some quantity from positions corresponding to losing moves. This suggests that we remember the moves by creating, at the beginning of each game, another 17-by-3 array. This array, GAME, will be initially 0, but when the machine takes MOVE sticks from a pile containing CURRENT, we reset GAME[CURRENT;MOVE] to 1. Then, at the end of the game, we have only to add or subtract GAME from

```
     ∇ MOVE←CURRENT INPUT PLAYER;DISTRIBUTION;RANDOM
[1]     ⍝-----CURRENT IS NUMBER OF STICKS REMAINING
[2]     ⍝-----IF PLAYER = 'P' HUMAN OPPONENT MOVES
[3]     ⍝-----IF PLAYER = 'M' MACHINE MOVES
[4]     'INPUT: RIGHT ARGUMENT SIZE ' ERROR 1≠ρ,PLAYER
[5]     'INPUT: LEFT ARGUMENT SIZE ' ERROR 1≠ρ,CURRENT
[6]     'INPUT: RIGHT ARGUMENT MEANINGLESS ' ERROR~PLAYERε'MP'
[7]     'INPUT: LEFT ARGUMENT NOT NUMERIC ' ERROR~0ε0\0/CURRENT
[8]     →MACHINE IF PLAYER='M'
[9]     →0×MOVE←□
[10] MACHINE:DISTRIBUTION←(3,3)ρHISTORY[CURRENT;],0
[11]    DISTRIBUTION[3;1]←0
[12]    DISTRIBUTION←+/[1] DISTRIBUTION
[13]    RANDOM←(¯1+?101)÷100
[14]    MOVE←3⌊(DISTRIBUTION≥RANDOM)⍳1
     ∇
```

FIGURE 7.8. Revised input program.

HISTORY. Setting the elements of GAME can be done in INPUT and we can write a new routine, UPDATE, to modify HISTORY at the end of a game. We should be careful here, as it is not sufficient to simply add or subtract GAME from HISTORY. First of all, we assume in IN-PUT that the sum of each row of HISTORY is 1, so that we will have to normalize HISTORY to make this true again each time we modify it with GAME. A second problem is that when we subtract, we run the risk of making some element of HISTORY negative. We can correct for this in a simply way: instead of adding or subtracting some fixed value from the elements of HISTORY, we can subtract some fraction of their values.

Figure 7.9 shows the program UPDATE. The sum reduction of HISTORY at the right of line 8 produces a vector with 17 elements, the row sums of HISTORY. To normalize HISTORY, we have only to divide the elements by the corresponding row sum. Unfortunately, we cannot divide the array by the vector, as their sizes do not match. We can, however, divide the array by another array of the same size in which all the elements of a row are equal to the corresponding row sum of HISTORY. To create such an array, we have to create a 3-by-17 array for which all the elements of each column are equal to the correspond-

transpose

ing row sum of HISTORY and then take its *transpose* (interchange rows and columns). Notice also that the fraction of HISTORY which we add or subtract is set as a variable MODIFIER near the beginning of the program. Since we don't know what values are good (if, indeed, it makes any difference), this makes it easy to make changes and try different values.

The modified INPUT and NIM programs are shown in Figures 7.10 and 7.11 respectively. This package of programs will learn to play NIM, but if you try it out you will see that it is abysmally slow. What we need, to get the program to learn faster, is to remove the human element, as much of the slowness is involved in the printing and the requests for the human player's move. We could substitute a random move for the human input, but, logically, the program will not learn to play much better than its opponent and so having it play a random player will also result in slow learning. If we knew the best possible way to play, we could certainly replace the human player by a program which played as

```
      ∇ UPDATE WINNER;MODIFIER
[1]     ⍝-----WINNER IS 1 IF MACHINE WON, 0 FOR HUMAN
[2]     ⍝-----MODIFIER IS FRACTION USED TO CHANGE HISTORY
[3]     MODIFIER←0.25
[4]     →MACHINE IF WINNER=1
[5]     HISTORY←HISTORY-MODIFIER×HISTORY×GAME
[6]     →NORMALIZE
[7]   MACHINE:HISTORY←HISTORY+MODIFIER×HISTORY×GAME
[8]   NORMALIZE:HISTORY←HISTORY÷⍉(3,17)⍴+/HISTORY
      ∇
```

FIGURE 7.9. Updating memory.

```
      ∇ MOVE←CURRENT INPUT PLAYER;DISTRIBUTION;RANDOM
[1]     ⍝-----CURRENT IS NUMBER OF STICKS REMAINING
[2]     ⍝-----IF PLAYER = 'P' HUMAN OPPONENT MOVES
[3]     ⍝-----IF PLAYER = 'M' MACHINE MOVES
[4]     'INPUT: RIGHT ARGUMENT SIZE ' ERROR 1≠⍴,PLAYER
[5]     'INPUT: LEFT ARGUMENT SIZE ' ERROR 1≠⍴,CURRENT
[6]     'INPUT: RIGHT ARGUMENT MEANINGLESS ' ERROR~PLAYER∊'MP'
[7]     'INPUT: LEFT ARGUMENT NOT NUMERIC ' ERROR~0∊0\0/CURRENT
[8]     →MACHINE IF PLAYER='M'
[9]     →0×MOVE←⎕
[10]  MACHINE:DISTRIBUTION←(3,3)⍴HISTORY[CURRENT;],0
[11]    DISTRIBUTION[3;1]←0
[12]    DISTRIBUTION←+/[1] DISTRIBUTION
[13]    RANDOM←(¯1+?101)÷100
[14]    MOVE←3⌊(DISTRIBUTION≥RANDOM)⍳1
[15]    GAME[CURRENT;MOVE]←1
      ∇
```

FIGURE 7.10. More revisions to INPUT.

```
      ∇ NIM;NEXT;STICKS;PLAYERS;PROPOSAL;YES;NO;GAME
[1]     ⍝-----GAME IS THE RECORD OF MOVES MADE BY MACHINE IN INPUT
[2]     GAME←(17,3)⍴0
[3]     'DO YOU WISH TO SEE THE RULES? ANSWER YES OR NO'
[4]     →START IF⎕=NO←~YES←1
[5]     RULES
[6]   START:NEXT←?2
[7]     ⍝-----NEXT DETERMINES WHICH PLAYER MOVES NEXT
[8]     PLAYERS←(2,3)⍴' I YOU'
[9]     STICKS←17
[10]  ∆STICKS:→END∆STICKS WHEN 0=STICKS
[11]    STICKS;'  STICKS LEFT'
[12]    PLAYERS[NEXT;],' MOVE'
[13]    PROPOSAL←STICKS INPUT 'MP'[NEXT]
[14]    →∆STICKS IF STICKS ILLEGAL PROPOSAL
[15]    STICKS←STICKS-PROPOSAL
[16]    NEXT←3-NEXT
[17]    ⍝-----TRANSFORMS 1 TO 2 AND 2 TO 1
[18]    →∆STICKS
[19]    ⍝-----AT END, NEXT POINTS TO WINNER
[20]  END∆STICKS:PLAYERS[NEXT;],' WIN!'
[21]    UPDATE NEXT
      ∇
```

FIGURE 7.11. More revisions to NIM.

well as possible. Barring that, we can still do better than random by replacing the human player by one which uses all the information about the game which we have—the array HISTORY. The program NEWΔIN-PUT in Figure 7.12 does exactly this. Since the modification we have proposed would have resulted in our having the same code for choosing a move from HISTORY appear twice in NEWΔINPUT, we instead wrote a program MAKEΔMOVE to pick a move from HISTORY, and call it in two different places from NEWΔINPUT. MAKEΔMOVE appears in Figure 7.13.

This goes some way toward speeding up the learning, but it would be much better if we could have some large number of games played one right after another, without any printing at all, except perhaps for a message every five games to indicate that the program is still running and that the machine has not "hung up."

The program MANYΔNIM in Figure 7.14 implements these changes It accepts one argument, the number of games to be played. It runs through the loop which begins on line 6 to play that many games. On lines 20 and 21, if the number of games played so far is a multiple of 5, a message is printed. After each game, the array HISTORY is updated and, at the end of the session, the array is printed. To make the array more legible, we have added on numbers for the rows by concatenating HISTORY with the one column array whose elements are 1, 2, ..., 17.

```
     ∇ MOVE←CURRENT NEW∆INPUT PLAYER
[1]    ⍝-----CURRENT IS NUMBER OF STICKS REMAINING
[2]    ⍝-----IF PLAYER = 'P' HUMAN OPPONENT MOVES
[3]    ⍝-----IF PLAYER = 'M' MACHINE MOVES
[4]    'NEW∆INPUT: RIGHT ARGUMENT SIZE ' ERROR 1≠ρ,PLAYER
[5]    'NEW∆INPUT: LEFT ARGUMENT SIZE ' ERROR 1≠ρ,CURRENT
[6]    'NEW∆INPUT: RIGHT ARGUMENT MEANINGLESS ' ERROR~PLAYERε'MP'
[7]    'INPUT: LEFT ARGUMENT NOT NUMERIC ' ERROR~0ε0\0/CURRENT
[8]    →MACHINE IF PLAYER='M'
[9]    →0×MOVE←MAKE∆MOVE CURRENT
[10] MACHINE:MOVE←MAKE∆MOVE CURRENT
[11]   GAME[CURRENT;MOVE]←1
     ∇
```

FIGURE 7.12. Using memory for both players.

```
     ∇ MOVE←MAKE∆MOVE CURRENT;DISTRIBUTION;RANDOM
[1]    ⍝-----CURRENT IS THE NUMBER OF STICKS
[2]    DISTRIBUTION←(3,3)ρHISTORY[CURRENT;],0
[3]    DISTRIBUTION[3;1]←0
[4]    RANDOM←(¯1+?101)÷100
[5]    DISTRIBUTION←+/[1] DISTRIBUTION
[6]    MOVE←3⌊(DISTRIBUTION≥RANDOM)⍳1
     ∇
```

FIGURE 7.13. Generating a move.

```
     ∇ MANY∆NIM PLAYS;MOVE;STICKS;GAME;ROUND;NEXT
[1]    ⍝-----PLAYS IS THE NUMBER OF GAMES TO BE PLAYED
[2]    ⍝-----GAME IS THE RECORD OF MACHINE MOVES MADE IN NEW∆INPUT
[3]    'MANY∆NIM: ARGUMENT NOT NUMERIC ' ERROR~0ε0\0/PLAYS
[4]    'MANY∆NIM: ARGUMENT NOT SCALAR ' ERROR 1<ρ,PLAYS
[5]    'MANY∆NIM: ARGUMENT NOT POSITIVE INTEGER ' ERROR(PLAYS≠⌊PLAYS)∨PLAYS<0
[6]    ROUND←0
[7]  ∆ROUND:→END∆ROUND WHEN PLAYS<ROUND←ROUND+1
[8]    GAME←(17,3)ρ0
[9]    NEXT←?2
[10]   ⍝-----NEXT DETERMINES WHICH PLAYER MOVES NEXT
[11]   STICKS←17
[12] ∆STICKS:→END∆STICKS WHEN 0=STICKS
[13]   MOVE←STICKS NEW∆INPUT 'MP'[NEXT]
[14]   STICKS←STICKS-MOVE
[15]   NEXT←3-NEXT
[16]   ⍝-----TRANSFORMS 1 TO 2 AND 2 TO 1
[17]   →∆STICKS
[18]   ⍝-----AT END NEXT POINTS TO WINNER
[19] END∆STICKS:UPDATE NEXT
[20]   →∆ROUND IF 0≠5|ROUND
[21]   ROUND;' GAMES HAVE NOW BEEN PLAYED'
[22]   →∆ROUND
[23] END∆ROUND:'THE LEARNING ARRAY IS NOW'
[24]   ((17,1)ρ⍳17),HISTORY
     ∇
```

FIGURE 7.14. A NIM tournament.

In Figure 7.15, we show a simple program to start the array HIS-TORY off with equal probabilities for all legal moves. (Note that since only legal moves can now be made, the class to program ILLE-GAL has been eliminated from MANY△NIM.) Figures 7.16, 7.17 and

```
      ∇ INITIALIZE
[1]     HISTORY←(17,3)ρ(1 0 0 0.5 0.5 0),(45ρ÷3)
      ∇
```

FIGURE 7.15. Initializing the memory array.

```
 5 GAMES HAVE NOW BEEN PLAYED
10 GAMES HAVE NOW BEEN PLAYED
15 GAMES HAVE NOW BEEN PLAYED
20 GAMES HAVE NOW BEEN PLAYED
THE LEARNING ARRAY IS NOW
       1              1              0              0
       2              0.7596439169   0.2403560831   0
       3              0.2744163888   0.6098141972   0.115769414
       4              0.2057142857   0.4285714286   0.3657142857
       5              0.3333333333   0.3333333333   0.3333333333
       6              0.2432432432   0.3243243243   0.4324324324
       7              0.4444444444   0.3555555556   0.2
       8              0.3333333333   0.4166666667   0.25
       9              0.4324324324   0.2432432432   0.3243243243
      10              0.3293310463   0.4391080617   0.2315608919
      11              0.4604316547   0.1942446043   0.345323741
      12              0.3921568627   0.2941176471   0.3137254902
      13              0.3636363636   0.2727272727   0.3636363636
      14              0.5714285714   0.1542857143   0.2742857143
      15              0.2195121951   0.3902439024   0.3902439024
      16              0.2195121951   0.3902439024   0.3902439024
      17              0.1293929712   0.3594249201   0.5111821086
```

FIGURE 7.16. After 20 games.


```
THE LEARNING ARRAY IS NOW
       1              1              0              0
       2              0.9905896161   0.009410383883 0
       3              0.0832067461   0.8816904079   0.03510284601
       4              0.02770587435  0.01662352461  0.955670601
       5              0.3277848912   0.3841229193   0.2880921895
       6              0.5396290051   0.1365935919   0.323777403
       7              0.4888156275   0.4296231101   0.08156126232
       8              0.1217957891   0.1522447364   0.7259594745
       9              0.225205946    0.3624296511   0.412364403
      10              0.2807017544   0.2807017544   0.4385964912
      11              0.3940110323   0.4925137904   0.1134751773
      12              0.1257023106   0.2157823172   0.6585153723
      13              0.5395683453   0.1657553957   0.294676259
      14              0.1884597487   0.476500698    0.3350395533
      15              0.3803863299   0.2852897474   0.3343239227
      16              0.4739336493   0.355450237    0.1706161137
      17              0.2406617006   0.2115190728   0.5478192266
```

FIGURE 7.17. After 100 games.

7.18 show the results of running MANYΔNIM.

After the first session of 20 games the results are still rather uniform, although it has at least learned to remove only one stick from a pile of two. After 100 games there are clearer proclivities, especially for smaller numbers of sticks. If there are four left, it is sure that three should be removed; if six, then it usually removes one and so on.

scientific notation

The numbers after 300 trials have been printed differently from what we have seen before. This is the so-called "scientific" or "exponential" notation. A number is represented as a *mantissa* between 1 and 10 (or 0) before the E and a *characteristic* after the E which represents a power of 10. Thus, 2.5E3 means 2.5×10^3 or 2500. APL will convert to this notation when the numbers it has to present have too many digits to be written exactly: sometimes this may mean that you are not seeing all of the digits which APL is keeping.

After 300 games, it has a clear strategy. It tries to leave the opponent with one, five, nine or thirteen sticks. Indeed, this is a winning strategy. If you can leave your opponent with thirteen sticks, then no matter what the opponent's move, you can always move to leave nine. Then, you can move to leave five, and, finally, whether the opponent takes one, two or three, you can move to leave one—and win. Notice that this strategy only works for the second player; the first player cannot win against this strategy. This is also reflected in the array; the values in rows 5, 9, 13 and 17 are not as clearly defined as the others, since it tends not to matter what move is made from these positions.

Obviously, it is not always this easy to find the perfect strategy for a game. Nevertheless, heuristic techniques such as the one we used here are used in many learning situations and form an integral part of the field called Artificial Intelligence.

EXERCISES

7-5. In UPDATE, why do we need to create a 3-by-17 array and then use the transpose operator? Why not start with a 17-by-3 array directly?

7-6. Find out how the value of MODIFIER affects the rate at which the program learns.

7-7. We could have created the array DISTRIBUTION element by element in only a few lines of program. What do we gain by being fancy? What would we lose by doing it the simple way if we permitted each player to take 20 sticks from a pile which starts at 297?

7-8. The assignment of DISTRIBUTION can be done in a slightly different way as well. To get rid of the nonzero elements below the diagonal, we could simply multiply DISTRIBUTION by an array

THE LEARNING ARRAY IS NOW

$1.000000000E0$	$1.000000000E0$	$0.000000000E0$	$0.000000000E0$
$2.000000000E0$	$9.999037470E^{-1}$	$9.625295193E^{-5}$	$0.000000000E0$
$3.000000000E0$	$2.976772423E^{-6}$	$9.999940465E^{-1}$	$2.976772423E^{-6}$
$4.000000000E0$	$3.612688552E^{-6}$	$5.292024246E^{-6}$	$9.999910953E^{-1}$
$5.000000000E0$	$2.026202213E^{-1}$	$3.602137268E^{-1}$	$4.371660519E^{-1}$
$6.000000000E0$	$9.998641880E^{-1}$	$7.974284824E^{-5}$	$5.606919017E^{-5}$
$7.000000000E0$	$2.820161878E^{-3}$	$9.953208447E^{-1}$	$1.858993425E^{-3}$
$8.000000000E0$	$8.759527861E^{-5}$	$1.946561747E^{-4}$	$9.997177485E^{-1}$
$9.000000000E0$	$2.208287895E^{-1}$	$2.208287895E^{-1}$	$5.583424209E^{-1}$
$1.000000000E1$	$9.986782589E^{-1}$	$9.550152592E^{-4}$	$3.667258595E^{-4}$
$1.100000000E1$	$7.035770524E^{-3}$	$9.874993849E^{-1}$	$5.464844528E^{-3}$
$1.200000000E1$	$3.357930161E^{-2}$	$6.182356063E^{-2}$	$9.045971378E^{-1}$
$1.300000000E1$	$5.460079990E^{-1}$	$2.236448764E^{-1}$	$2.303471246E^{-1}$
$1.400000000E1$	$9.979010538E^{-1}$	$8.995483519E^{-4}$	$1.199397803E^{-3}$
$1.500000000E1$	$8.159561211E^{-2}$	$8.646182178E^{-1}$	$5.378617009E^{-2}$
$1.600000000E1$	$2.075675676E^{-1}$	$1.167567568E^{-1}$	$6.756756757E^{-1}$
$1.700000000E1$	$4.925909815E^{-1}$	$2.204539735E^{-1}$	$2.869550450E^{-1}$

FIGURE 7.18. After 300 games.

of the same shape which had all ones on and above the main diagonal and all zeros below. This array can be created with an outer product operator. Try to do it.

7-9. When the program plays itself, we are only using the information from half of the moves (one player) to update <u>HISTORY</u>. Change the program so that it uses all the information to learn.

7-10. Modify the programs so that the number of sticks in the starting pile is determined by a global variable <u>HEAP</u> which is requested by the program INITIALIZE.

7-11. Modify the programs so that the largest number of sticks which can be taken at one time is a global variable requested by the program INITIALIZE.

7-12. Now that we know the strategy, we can write a program which plays perfectly. Do so and then use it as the opponent for the learning program. Does this speed up or retard learning?

7-13. Analyze the programs we have written for instances of poor design. For example, when MANYΔNIM prints its little message every five games, it could also print the score (say, the number of times the first player won versus the number of times the second player won). This would be easy to do and would give us more information about how fast the program is learning. Correct each design problem you find.

7-14. Try to develop some other learning strategies for this game.

7-15. Write a program that plays SUPERNIM: there are A piles, each with B sticks. On a move a player cannot take more than D from any one pile. Write a program for SUPERNIM and have it learn to play for some interesting settings of the values.

7-16. If Exercise 7-15 was too easy, try generalizing SUPERNIM even further. Alternately, try to write learning programs for other games.

8

Formatting Output
An Example of Program Design

The Beaver brought paper, portfolio, pens,
And ink in unfailing supplies:
While strange creepy creatures came out of their dens,
And watched them with wondering eyes.

It is not always sufficient to get the right answers. Often, the way the solution is presented can be as important as the solution itself. This can be especially true when the solution is in the form of a report of some kind, such as a financial report, a bill, or a summary of scientific data. Sometimes for necessary reasons of format or style, and sometimes only for convenience, we expect even numeric data to be presented in a uniform style. Unfortunately, APL does not always provide the kind of output we would like, as Figure 8.1 illustrates.

The first array shows the results of some calculations as printed by APL. This could be unsatisfactory for a variety of reasons. If the calculations were dollars and cents figures, we might want only two digits after the decimal point, and, perhaps, less space between the columns, as in part B. On the other hand, these might be results of a calculation which are known to be accurate to five decimal places; then output as in the third part of the figure would be desired. APL does not provide any ready facility for such formatting of output.[1]

SYSTEM DESIGN

One of the difficulties in trying to format numeric output is in the need for filling out the right side of the number with zeros (and sometimes adding a decimal point) and for providing the desired number of spaces between columns; APL gives us very little control of how numbers will be printed, while we have a great deal of control over the way that characters are printed. This suggests that we could deal with the formatting problem much more easily if we could translate numeric data to character data.

In designing a program package to do such formatting, we should first decide on the design criteria:

What sort of data do we want the programs to process?

What sort of instructions do we want to be able to give?

What pathological cases may develop and how do we want to deal with them?

For the first criterion, it seems not unreasonable to ask that any numeric data structure be acceptable to the system, whether it be a scalar, a vector or an array. As for the sort of instructions we might want to give, we should first ask the related question, What should the final output look like? Clearly it should look as much like the numeric data as

---

[1] It is true, however, that programs similar to the ones to be developed here are supplied with many APL systems. Also, because of the importance of this type of formatting, the facility we will design here is beginning to appear as a primitive operator in some systems.

A)

0.19	‾3.12	1.73	2.07
0.6	‾0.2	2.011	2.76
13.9601	1.37	2.01	3.47
0.779	12.792	7.093	8.487
2.46	‾0.82	8.2451	11.316
57.23641	5.617	8.241	14.227

B)

0.19	‾3.12	1.73	2.07
0.60	‾0.20	2.01	2.76
13.96	1.37	2.01	3.47
0.77	12.79	7.09	8.48
2.46	‾0.82	8.24	11.31
57.23	5.61	8.24	14.22

C)

0.19000	‾3.12000	1.73000	2.07000
0.60000	‾0.20000	2.01100	2.76000
13.96010	1.37000	2.01000	3.47000
0.77900	12.79200	7.09300	8.48700
2.46000	‾0.82000	8.24510	11.31600
57.23641	5.61700	8.24100	14.22700

FIGURE 8.1. Different formats for printing.

possible—if the input is an array with 3 planes, 5 rows and 6 columns, the output should look the same. This leaves us with only a few possible decisions about the output: the amount of space to be devoted to any single number, the amount of space between columns, the number of digits after the decimal point and the actual position of the decimal point. In fact, however, these four decisions reduce to two.

Suppose that we fix the total number of spaces allotted to a number and that we also fix the position of the decimal point. Consider the example of printing the vector

$$(25.0245, \ 321.23)$$

where each number is to be allotted 10 spaces and the decimal point comes in the seventh place. The output would be as shown in Figure 8.2; the second line of the figure, and the arrows, are there only to show how the numbers line up according to the specifications. Spacing is forced between elements by allotting sufficient space to each number. Likewise, the position of the decimal point exactly defines the number of digits after it, since only so much room is allotted for the entire number.

Before we fix upon these two quantities as the ones to specify, we should note one inconvenience. If we wished to print only integers and hence not show the decimal point, we might have to specify, for example, 10 spaces for each number with the decimal point being the eleventh. While we could surely write a program which functioned with these data, there is something illogical about such a specification and, very probably, confusing to a potential user. Instead, therefore, we will specify the amount of space allotted for a number, and the number of spaces before the decimal point.

The one remaining design decision is the problem of pathological cases. Suppose that one of the numbers we want to print will not fit within the desired space; clearly, this would occur only because the integer part before the decimal point (including the minus sign if there is one) will not fit in its assigned space. We have two choices: either we could decide to preserve the alignment of decimal points and chop off the beginning of the number or we could move the decimal point over as much as possible to accommodate the entire number. While the first approach might be reasonable in certain applications, the second seems preferable as a universal rule.

To carry the problem a bit further, however, suppose that the integer part of the number is too large to fit even in the space provided for the entire number. This is a bit more difficult to resolve, as printing even the integer part of the number would involve invading the space reserved for other numbers. Whether or not this is even practical, let alone desirable, will depend on the way that the output data is handled by the program. So, while we will have to flag this problem for later

```
   25.024    321.230
12345678901234567890
     ↑          ↑
```

FIGURE 8.2. Lining numbers up for printing.

consideration, we can at least decide that whatever its resolution as much information as possible should be presented to the user.

EXERCISES

8-1. If your system has a function or operator for formatting as described above, find out how it works. Does it meet all the criteria we have described above? If not, does it have other properties which we have not mentioned? How does it handle pathological cases?

8-2. If your system has a function for formatting, read it to find out how it works.

8-3. Find other sets of two parameters which completely determine the output form; are there any pairs of parameters which are not complete in this sense?

PROGRAM DESIGN

The decisions we have made so far imply that the program which the user will see, which we may as well call FORMAT, will have two arguments. One will of course be the data to be formatted, while the other will be a vector of size 2 called PLAN, giving the amount of space allotted to each number and the amount allotted to the integer part of the number. However, a user who is formatting integer data will then have to enter a vector in which both elements are the same. This is hardly a major problem, but nevertheless is an inconvenience which we can remove within the program. We could permit a single number to be entered as the format specification, with the understanding that this would imply that only integers, or integer parts, were to be printed.

Figure 8.3 shows a reasonable first approximation to the structure chart for FORMAT. The arguments are the specification vector PLAN and the numeric DATA, and the result is the character-valued variable OUTPUT. The approach taken in this structure chart is quite straightforward. The size of OUTPUT will be the same as that of DATA, except in the last dimension, where a column of DATA will be expanded to be a vector of length PLAN[1]; thus, if DATA has n columns, OUTPUT will have nPLAN[1] columns, and if DATA is a scalar, OUTPUT will be a vector of length PLAN[1]. Ignoring for this "first draft" the mechanics of shaping OUTPUT, we begin by raveling DATA, so that it becomes a vector. Then, one at a time, we translate the elements of DATA into character strings and concatenate them onto OUTPUT, which was initialized as the empty vector. When this is done, we simply shape OUTPUT with the variable OUTPUTΔSIZE.

⊙	PLAN is the vector of specifications
	DATA is the numeric input
	OUTPUT will be the resulting character output

Set up OUTPUT△SIZE as the eventual size of the output

OUTPUT ← ⍳0

⊙ Now loop through the elements of DATA

DATA ← 0,,DATA

DO until 0 = ρDATA ← 1↓DATA

> Concatenate character version of
> DATA[1] onto OUTPUT

OUTPUT ← OUTPUT△SIZE ρ OUTPUT

FIGURE 8.3. A design for a program.

Of course, Figure 8.3 is not nearly complete enough to program, although it does convey the general approach. In fact, before proceeding we can settle our last design decision. This approach makes it definitely impractical to let a number which is too large run on into the space allotted the next number, for that would then be forced to run into the next and so on. Neither, however, would we want to print a portion of the integer part, for that would be very misleading. A more reasonable approach is not to include a number which is too large in the output at all. Instead, we could replace it by a string of asterisks, to indicate that the number which was supposed to go in that location did not fit. In order not to completely lose the number, though, we could print it out, as a number, some place during the program's execution, so that the user would not lose any information.

As usual, we must make some assumptions about the program's arguments, although they may not be explicit yet in the structure chart. We will be assuming, for example, that PLAN is either a vector of size 2 or a scalar, that its first element is a positive integer and that the second element, if there is one, is a nonnegative integer. If there is a second element, it should not be larger than the first. Rather than constantly requiring two cases, depending on whether PLAN is a vector or a scalar, we could, early in the program, expand a scalar PLAN to be a vector with two equal elements.

Another point worth checking, for the convenience of the user, is whether or not the eventual output will be too wide for the terminal. Recall that one of the 6 I-beam system operators enables us to find the number of characters which APL will print on one line, while the width of the output will be easily calculable from OUTPUTΔSIZE.

Finally, we need some way to translate a single numeric scalar into a character string of the proper format. We may assume that it is to be done by a program called REWRITE, which will have as its arguments the scalar and PLAN.

A second, slightly more detailed structure chart appears in Figure 8.4. One process box, which indicates four conditions to be checked, clearly represents many APL statements, while two others, the one reshaping PLAN and the one defining OUTPUTΔSIZE, may or may not require more than one statement; other than that, this is a fairly accurate representation of our plan for the program FORMAT. Since the program cannot be tested until we have written REWRITE, we will postpone coding of FORMAT until REWRITE has been considered.

EXERCISES

8-4. Write and test code which will expand a scalar PLAN to a vector of size 2.

PLAN is the vector of specifications DATA is the numeric input OUTPUT will be the resulting character output
Check that PLAN is a scalar or a vector of size 2
If PLAN is scalar, expand to a vector

Check: PLAN is all integers
           PLAN[1] > 0
           PLAN[2] ≥ 0
           PLAN[1] ≥ PLAN[2]

Set up OUTPUT$\triangle$SIZE as the eventual size of the output
OUTPUT ← ι0
Now loop through the elements of DATA
DATA ← 0,,DATA
DO until 0 = ρDATA ← 1↓DATA
OUTPUT ← OUTPUT, PLAN REWRITE DATA[1]
OUTPUT ← OUTPUT$\triangle$SIZE ρ OUTPUT

FIGURE 8.4. Filling in some details.

8-5. Write and test the code to find the value for OUTPUT△SIZE.

8-6. Another approach to the problem of numbers which are too large is to print them, where they are supposed to go, in exponential notation. As you read the chapter, consider how this could be done (and in which cases it would not help); at what points in the development of the program would this scheme have an effect?

NUMBERS TO CHARACTERS

In designing REWRITE we should note that the essential problem is in translating an integer to a character string; the problems of taking care of decimal points, minus signs, leading blanks and trailing zeros are relatively minor, as the structure chart in Figure 8.5 shows. However, even these latter problems, and the matter of deciding if the eventual character string fits in the allotted space, are not trivial. In this planning stage, it is easiest to again separate the problem of translating a number to a character string from the other incidentals.

How would we go about doing this translation? Consider a number such as 15. How can we produce the character string '15' from it? If we could separate its digits, producing the vector 1 5, we could then use the vector to subscript '123456789' and the result would be the character string we seek. In fact, we can do exactly that separation using the operator *encode*. The expression in Figure 8.6A will produce the vector 1 5. Figure 8.6B shows some other examples of encoding.

encode

To use encode in this manner we need to put exactly as many tens in front of the operator as the number has digits. We can find the number of digits in 15, for example, by taking its base 10 logarithm, which is 1.17609, and then using the *ceiling* operator to get 2. This will not work, of course, for zero or negative numbers, where there is no logarithm defined, or even for numbers which are not integers—how many digits there are in 3.14159 cannot be determined in just this way. This reinforces our decision to first concentrate on positive integers: translating 0 can be handled as a special case, while negative numbers and fractions will first have to be processed by REWRITE, as is suggested by Figure 8.5.

ceiling

The logarithm will not, however, work exactly even for all positive integers. The logarithm of 1 is 0, although 1 has one digit; for 10 it is 1, for 100 it is 2 and so on. Of a number of ways to correct for this, one of the simplest takes advantage of the fact that we are only dealing with integers; if we take the logarithm of the number *plus* .1, the ceiling will be increased by 1 only for powers of 10.

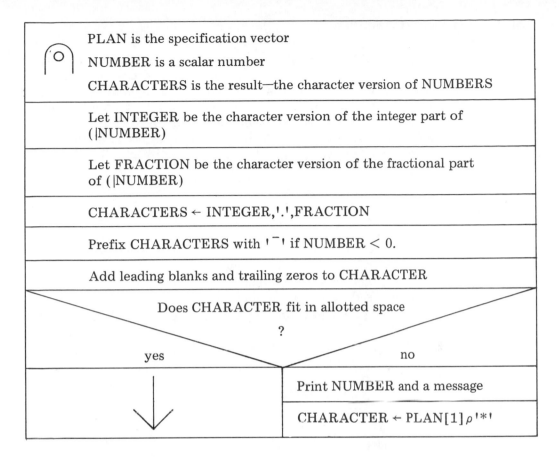

FIGURE 8.5. A first design for REWRITE.

A)

        10 10 ⊤ 15

B)

        10 10 ⊤ 3
    0   3
        10 10 10 ⊤ 863
    8   6   3
        2 2 2 ⊤ 7
    1   1   1
        2 2 2 ⊤ 6
    1   1   0

FIGURE 8.6. Examples of encode.

The program TRANSLATE is shown in Figure 8.7: this transforms a positive integer to characters. The reason we assume that the argument is scalar will be clear from the exercises. Rather than check this on each entry to the program, we will make sure that only arguments of the proper form are passed to TRANSLATE by REWRITE. Notice that, since the output of TRANSLATE is sometimes a vector, we ensure that it will *always* be a vector, avoiding corresponding checks in the calling program.

EXERCISES

8-7. What are the dangers inherent in permitting WHOLE to be a vector, even of size 1? (*Hint*: examine the size of the result of the encode function when its right-hand argument is a vector of size 1, as opposed to the case when it is a scalar.)

8-8. What advantages do we gain by not checking the input to TRANSLATE?

8-9. What dangers are there in not checking the arguments to any function? Does the answer to Exercise 8-8 outweigh these disadvantages? Can you formulate a rule of thumb for when it is permissible not to check the arguments to a program?

TRANSLATING FRACTIONS

Having written the program TRANSLATE leads us to reevaluate the structure chart in Figure 8.5. For example, we cannot simply find the translation of the fractional part of NUMBER, since TRANSLATE will only work for integers. We can get an integer from the fractional part if we multiply it by an appropriate power of 10 and then use the *floor* operator. Which power of 10 should we use? Clearly, the proper power of 10 is the one which will produce exactly enough digits to fit in the space after the decimal point—if the fractional part terminates in fewer places than this, the remaining space will be filled out with low order zeros. The proper power of 10 is therefore PLAN[1] − (PLAN[2]+1). This quantity, which we might call DECIMAL, gives us other information as well. If DECIMAL = ¯1, then PLAN[1]=PLAN[2] and neither the fractional part nor a decimal place is to be printed. If DECIMAL=0, there is to be a decimal point after each number but no digits following the decimal point.

```
      ∇ CHARACTERS←TRANSLATE WHOLE
[1]    ⍝-----WHOLE IS A NONNEGATIVE SCALAR INTEGER
[2]    →ZEROΔCASE IF WHOLE=0
[3]    CHARACTERS←,'0123456789'[1+((⌈10⍟WHOLE+0.1)ρ10)⊤WHOLE]
[4]    →0
[5]  ZEROΔCASE:CHARACTERS←,'0'
      ∇
```

FIGURE 8.7. Formatting an integer.

The structure chart in Figure 8.8 expresses the logic of the program. First, DECIMAL is defined, and then INTEGER is the character string version of the integer part of NUMBER, prefixed by a minus sign if necessary. Then, if DECIMAL is nonnegative, FRACTION is initialized to be '.', since if DECIMAL is not ¯1 there will at least be a decimal point in the character string version of NUMBER; if DECIMAL is negative, then FRACTION is the empty vector.

**exponen-
tiation**

Now, if DECIMAL is not positive, that is all we need to do with FRACTION. Otherwise, we first scale the fractional part, multiplying it by 10*DECIMAL, and then translate it to a character string. While the result should have size DECIMAL, it may not. If the fractional part was 0, for example, the character string will only have size 1. Also, if the fractional part itself has any leading zeros, they will be lost in the scaling process, as can be easily verified at the terminal. Thus, we need to insert zeros between the decimal point and the character string. Notice how our original problem of having to add trailing zeros has been replaced by one in which we add leading zeros!

PLAN[1] is the total amount of space available

PLAN[2] is the number of positions before the decimal

NUMBER is a scalar number

CHARACTERS is the result—the character version of NUMBER

DECIMAL ← PLAN[1] − (PLAN[2]+1)

INTEGER ← TRANSLATE ⌊ |NUMBER

INTEGER ← ((NUMBER<0)ρ'¯'),INTEGER

FRACTION ← (DECIMAL≥0)ρ'·'

DECIMAL ≤ 0
?

yes | no

(yes: ↓)

FRAGMENT ← TRANSLATE
⌊(10*DECIMAL) × (|NUMBER)−
⌊|NUMBER

FRACTION ← FRACTION,
((DECIMAL−ρFRAGMENT)ρ'0'),
FRAGMENT

PLAN[2] ≤ ρINTEGER
?

yes | no

FRACTION ← (PLAN[2]−
ρINTEGER)↓FRACTION

INTEGER ← ((PLAN[2]−
ρINTEGER)ρ' '),INTEGER

CHARACTER ← INTEGER,FRACTION

PLAN[1] = ρCHARACTER
?

yes | no

(yes: ↓)

CHARACTER ← PLAN[1]ρ'*'

Print NUMBER and message.

FIGURE 8.8. REWRITE redesigned.

223

We now have to consider whether or not INTEGER is too large to fit into the allotted space. If it is, we truncate the appropriate number of character spaces from the *end* of FRACTION (note that in this case PLAN[2] is less than the size of INTEGER). Otherwise, we precede it by the appropriate number of leading blanks. The resulting concatenation of INTEGER and FRACTION is the result, unless it is still too large to fit in the allowed space. If so, we print the numeric value of NUMBER and return a string of asterisks. The program for REWRITE is shown in Figure 8.9.

EXERCISES

8-10. If a number must be replaced by asterisks and printed separately, it would be more useful to the user to know exactly which element is being printed (if the input to FORMAT is a vector or array) in case more than one needs to be replaced. Since the variables of FORMAT are available to this program, use them to determine the exact location of NUMBER (second plane, third row, fourth column, etc.) when it is being printed.

8-11. Use the structure chart of Figure 8.8 to design a comprehensive set of tests for the program in Figure 8.9.

8-12. Prove that in line 10 of Figure 8.9 DECIMAL is never less than the size of FRAGMENT.

COMBINING THE PIECES

We now have all the pieces we need to complete the program FORMAT, which is shown in Figure 8.10. Line 2 expands PLAN, if necessary, to have size 2. Line 7 calculates DATA△SIZE, which is the size of DATA, or 1 if DATA was a scalar. Then, OUTPUT△SIZE is the size of the eventual output. On lines 9 and 10 we check to see if the width of the output will be too large for the line; each time we reference the 6 I-beam, once to discover its value and once to reset, we must ensure that its value is not printed. The remainder of the program is just as we had planned.

```
      ∇ CHARACTER←PLAN REWRITE NUMBER;INTEGER;FRACTION;DECIMAL;FRAGMENT
[1]    ⍝-----PLAN IS A VECTOR OF SIZE 2 GIVING
[2]    ⍝------(TOTAL LENGTH, POSITIONS BEFORE DECIMAL)
[3]    ⍝-----NUMBER MUST BE A SCALAR
[4]    DECIMAL←PLAN[1]-(PLAN[2]+1)
[5]    INTEGER←TRANSLATE⌊|NUMBER
[6]    INTEGER←((NUMBER<0)ρ'‾'),INTEGER
[7]    FRACTION←(DECIMAL≥0)ρ'.'
[8]    →ADD∆BLANKS IF DECIMAL≤0
[9]    FRAGMENT←TRANSLATE⌊(10*DECIMAL)×(|NUMBER)-⌊|NUMBER
[10]   FRACTION←FRACTION,((DECIMAL-ρFRAGMENT)ρ'0'),FRAGMENT
[11]  ADD∆BLANKS:→TRUNCATE IF PLAN[2]<ρINTEGER
[12]   INTEGER←((PLAN[2]-ρINTEGER)ρ' '),INTEGER
[13]   →PUT∆TOGETHER
[14]  TRUNCATE:FRACTION←(PLAN[2]-ρINTEGER)↓FRACTION
[15]  PUT∆TOGETHER:CHARACTER←INTEGER,FRACTION
[16]   →0 IF PLAN[1]=ρCHARACTER
[17]   ⍝----OTHERWISE, EVEN (⌊NUMBER) CANNOT FIT IN
[18]   ⍝------PLAN[1] SPACES.  INSERT STARS AND PRINT
[19]   ⍝------VALUE OF NUMBER HERE
[20]   CHARACTER←PLAN[1]ρ'*'
[21]   '----> ';NUMBER;'  DID NOT FIT '
      ∇
```

FIGURE 8.9. Formatting a scalar.

```
      ∇ OUTPUT←PLAN FORMAT DATA;DATA∆SIZE;OUTPUT∆SIZE;LINE
[1]    'FORMAT: IMPROPER SPECIFICATION' ERROR(1<ρρPLAN)∨2<ρ,PLAN
[2]    PLAN←PLAN,(0=ρρPLAN)ρPLAN
[3]    'FORMAT:SPECIFICATION NOT INTEGER' ERROR∨/PLAN≠⌊PLAN
[4]    'FORMAT:WIDTH NOT POSITIVE' ERROR PLAN[1]≤0
[5]    'FORMAT:INTEGER PART NEGATIVE' ERROR PLAN[2]<0
[6]    'FORMAT:INTEGER PART TOO LARGE' ERROR PLAN[1]<PLAN[2]
[7]    DATA∆SIZE←(ρDATA),(0=ρρDATA)ρ1
[8]    OUTPUT∆SIZE←(‾1↓DATA∆SIZE),PLAN[1]×‾1↑DATA∆SIZE
[9]    LINE←6⍳ 3 120
[10]   LINE←LINE,(0ρ6⍳3,LINE)
[11]   ⍝-----TO DISCOVER AND THEN RESTORE LINE WIDTH
[12]   'FORMAT:OUTPUT DOES NOT FIT ACROSS LINE' ERROR LINE<‾1↑OUTPUT∆SIZE
[13]   OUTPUT←⍳0
[14]   DATA←0,,DATA
[15]  ∆DATA:→END∆DATA WHEN 0=ρDATA←1↓DATA
[16]   OUTPUT←OUTPUT,PLAN REWRITE DATA[1]
[17]   →∆DATA
[18]  END∆DATA:OUTPUT←OUTPUT∆SIZEρOUTPUT
      ∇
```

FIGURE 8.10. Formatting any numeric data.

Figure 8.11 shows some calls to FORMAT. It seems to be behaving properly in the first four cases. However the last case, which asked for the printing of some base 2 logarithms, caused a DOMAIN ERROR in TRANSLATE. We found out the value of WHOLE and it was ⁻1. TRANSLATE never changes the value of WHOLE so it must have gotten the ⁻1 from REWRITE, even though we wrote REWRITE to only pass nonnegative numbers to TRANSLATE! We ask for the *state indicator* to find out that TRANSLATE was called from line 9 of RE-WRITE (which was called from line 16 of FORMAT).

```
A)
      10 3 FORMAT (4,5)ρι20
   1.000000   2.000000   3.000000   4.000000   5.000000
   6.000000   7.000000   8.000000   9.000000  10.000000
  11.000000  12.000000  13.000000  14.000000  15.000000
  16.000000  17.000000  18.000000  19.000000  20.000000


B)
      6 6 FORMAT 100 10 1 0 .1 .01
    100      10       1      0       0       0


C)
      7 4 FORMAT .0001 .001 .01 .1 0 10 100
   0.00      0.00    0.01    0.10     0.00   10.00  100.00


D)
      12 0 FORMAT ÷3
0.3333333333


E)
      10 3 FORMAT 2⊕ι10
DOMAIN ERROR
TRANSLATE[3] CHARACTERS←,'0123456789'[1+(([10⊕WHOLE+0.1)ρ10)⊤WHOLE]
                                                ∧
      WHOLE
¯1
      )SI
TRANSLATE[3] *
REWRITE[9]
FORMAT[16]
```

FIGURE 8.11. Using the format package.

Figure 8.12 shows a run with a stop command placed on line 9 of REWRITE. Each time, we look at NUMBER and at the quantity which is supposed to be its nonnegative fractional part; the latter is to be multiplied by an appropriate power of 10, rounded down and passed to TRANSLATE.

The fourth time through, the value of NUMBER is (apparently) 2 and yet the quantity indicated by arrows, supposedly its fractional part, has a very small negative value. This is due to the fuzz—the fact that numbers are not always represented exactly. In this case, the value 2 is the result of a call (invisible to us) to the routines which APL uses to find logarithms. The value produced was slightly less than 2, but was so close that it is printed as 2 by APL; and this is correct—the logarithm of 4 should be 2. What is strange is that while NUMBER is equal to its floor and ceiling, and the absolute value of NUMBER is equal to the absolute value of the floor of NUMBER, the difference between these last two values is considered to be less than 0; the two numbers are equal but their difference is not 0!

When problems like this arise there is not always an easy way to get around them, and there certainly are no general rules: the action taken must depend on an analysis of the particular case. Certainly, this problem will only arise if the fractional part of NUMBER is supposed to be 0. In any other case, even if the numbers which APL produces are slightly off from their true values, at least it will be true that a nonnegative number is passed to TRANSLATE.

```
      SΔREWRITE←9
      10 3 FORMAT 2●ι10

REWRITE[9]
      NUMBER
0
      (|NUMBER)-L|NUMBER
0
      →9

REWRITE[9]
      NUMBER
1
      (|NUMBER)-L|NUMBER
0
      →9

REWRITE[9]
      NUMBER
1.584962501
      (|NUMBER)-L|NUMBER
0.5849625007
      →9

REWRITE[9]
      NUMBER
2
      (|NUMBER)-L|NUMBER
¯2.220446049E¯16                    ←←←←←←←←←←←←←←
      NUMBER=2
1
      NUMBER=LNUMBER
1
      NUMBER=⌈NUMBER
1
      (|NUMBER)=L|NUMBER
1
      0=(|NUMBER)-L|NUMBER)
0
      0>(|NUMBER)-L|NUMBER)
1
```

FIGURE 8.12. Locating the cause of the error.

Here, the problem is not too difficult to resolve. If the number we are about to pass to TRANSLATE is ever less than 0, we pass 0 instead. The version of REWRITE in Figure 8.13 (see line 10) implements this and the output in Figure 8.14 shows that the program does work now.

EXERCISES

8-13. Verify that the revised REWRITE takes care of the problem.

8-14. Why are there two commas on line 14 of FORMAT?

8-15. On line 16 of FORMAT, we could get the first element of DATA with the *take* operator instead of subscripting. Would that have worked?

8-16. Rewrite FORMAT so that the line width is first set to its maximum value before checking if there is room for the output on a line, and then is reset to its original value after program execution.

8-17. If your system has a library function similar to FORMAT, compare the running times of the two. Then, in each program, make a change so that the number 0 is represented as a string of zeros of length PLAN[1].

8-18. Write a program called EFORMAT which produces all its output in scientific notation. All nonzero numbers printed should be fractions with a nonzero digit immediately following the decimal place. The first element of PLAN could be the total amount of space allocated for a number and the second could be the number of digits printed after the decimal point. Remember to leave a space before the number for a sign, and three spaces after the E for a sign and two digits.

8-19. Design and write a version of FORMAT which allows the user to specify that different columns of the data will be printed according to different formatting schemes. In the output from the NIM program of the last chapter we might have wanted the first column (the row numbers) of Figures 8.16–8.18 printed in (2,2) format while the other columns would have been in, say, (8,1) format.

8-20. The method of building our program which we used here is called *bottom-up* because we first wrote the program at the very bottom, TRANSLATEd and then worked our way up. A different scheme is *top-down*. If we were doing this project top-down, we would first design and write FORMAT and test it out, before writing the lower level routines. How can we test FORMAT if the routines it calls have not yet been written? We write very small programs called *stubs*. For example, a stub for REWRITE would have the same name, REWRITE, and the same arguments,

top-down

stub

```
      ∇ CHARACTER←PLAN REWRITE NUMBER;INTEGER;FRACTION;DECIMAL;FRAGMENT
[1]     ᴀ-----PLAN IS A VECTOR OF SIZE 2 GIVING
[2]     ᴀ------(TOTAL LENGTH, POSITIONS BEFORE DECIMAL)
[3]     ᴀ-----NUMBER MUST BE A SCALAR
[4]     DECIMAL←PLAN[1]-(PLAN[2]+1)
[5]     INTEGER←TRANSLATE⌊|NUMBER
[6]     INTEGER←((NUMBER<0)ρ'‾'),INTEGER
[7]     FRACTION←(DECIMAL≥0)ρ'.'
[8]     →ADDΔBLANKS IF DECIMAL≤0
[9]     FRAGMENT←(|NUMBER)-⌊|NUMBER
[10]    FRAGMENT←TRANSLATE⌊(10*DECIMAL)×FRAGMENT×(FRAGMENT≥0)
[11]    FRACTION←FRACTION,((DECIMAL-ρFRAGMENT)ρ'0'),FRAGMENT
[12] ADDΔBLANKS:→TRUNCATE IF PLAN[2]<ρINTEGER
[13]    INTEGER←((PLAN[2]-ρINTEGER)ρ' '),INTEGER
[14]    →PUTΔTOGETHER
[15] TRUNCATE:FRACTION←(PLAN[2]-ρINTEGER)↓FRACTION
[16] PUTΔTOGETHER:CHARACTER←INTEGER,FRACTION
[17]    →0 IF PLAN[1]=ρCHARACTER
[18]    ᴀ----OTHERWISE, EVEN (⌊NUMBER) CANNOT FIT IN
[19]    ᴀ------PLAN[1] SPACES.  INSERT STARS AND PRINT
[20]    ᴀ------VALUE OF NUMBER HERE
[21]    CHARACTER←PLAN[1]ρ'*'
[22]    '----> ';NUMBER;'  DID NOT FIT '
      ∇
```

FIGURE 8.13. REWRITE revisited.

```
       10 3 FORMAT ⍉(4,12)ρ(⍳12),(2⍟⍳12),(⍟⍳12),(10⍟⍳12)
 1.000000   0.000000   0.000000   0.000000
 2.000000   1.000000   0.693147   0.301029
 3.000000   1.584962   1.098612   0.477121
 4.000000   2.000000   1.386294   0.602059
 5.000000   2.321928   1.609437   0.698970
 6.000000   2.584962   1.791759   0.778151
 7.000000   2.807354   1.945910   0.845098
 8.000000   3.000000   2.079441   0.903089
 9.000000   3.169925   2.197224   0.954242
10.000000   3.321928   2.302585   1.000000
11.000000   3.459431   2.397895   1.041392
12.000000   3.584962   2.484906   1.079181
```

FIGURE 8.14. A table of logarithms.

but would do very little, if anything. The point is to have some little "do-nothing" program so that we can test the *logic* of FORMAT without worrying about the details of TRANSLATE or REWRITE. This sounds complicated, and it is for the small programs in this book. For larger programs, it can work very well—if your design for FORMAT, say, is incorrect, would you rather find out before or after you put in all the work of writing all the lower level routines? For practice, write a stub for TRANSLATE which will allow you to check out the logic of FORMAT and of REWRITE without worrying about the details of TRANSLATE.

Interlude Five

Documenting a Workspace
for Other People

Adapted from "How to document an APL workspace"
by Dennis P. Geller *APL Quote Quad*, vol. 5, issue 4.

Most programs are written by programmers for other people to use. It is important that the programs be accompanied by good documentation which will enable the intended audience to make maximum and effective use of the programs. Careful documentation should be a part of the entire programming process; unfortunately this is not always the way that things are done.

A very revealing experiment has been conducted a number of times in introductory programming classes, with consistent results. The students were told to pick a program from a public library workspace, one which seemed interesting, and to use it. Invariably the workspace that the student picked was faulty: either the documentation was nonexistent, or it was there but incomplete or wrong, or, after struggling through all this, the programs simply did not work.

It may seem strange, and rather difficult to believe, but there are countless examples of programs which are in the public libraries which could not possibly have been run by their authors. (Perhaps they were run, and then modified and not run again before being saved into the library—no other conclusion is possible in the case of programs which, for example, cannot list their own instructions without errors.) Ideally, a program should never fail through an APL error, no matter what the user does, but *certainly* it should never fail if the user follows instructions exactly. (Obviously, there should be no programs in the public libraries which fail *all the time*, but there are.)

This is not the place to discuss the ways to make a program failproof—the point is that if you write documentation with the aim of being perfectly accurate, it will force you to test out what you say, and will probably improve the quality of your programming. The first and most important principle is, therefore: be accurate.

Now that we know how to do it (accurately), we can begin to explore what it is we need to do. The guidelines we will look at should be satisfactory, but it is not so much the forms that you use that are important as the principles behind them: clear communication, accuracy, and convenience.

DONT'S

First, let's look at two common mistakes that should not be repeated.

1. Do not use variables for descriptions. A number of workspaces have a variable named DESCRIBE. This is invariably an extremely long character string with imbedded carriage returns: the author types a quote mark, all of the desired text (often pages of it) and then a second quote mark to close the character string. This is probably the easier way to set up descriptive text, but there really are things wrong with it. For example, now that you have it, how do you modify it? Such long strings are almost impossible to change once set up, due to the difficulty of

locating specific positions within them: once set up such descriptions are never changed, despite the modifications that may go on in the program.

2. Do not make descriptions part of the working program. Do not make the descriptive material an actual part of the program. Rather, write a function that gives the necessary instructions and let it be called from the working program if the user so requires: the working program can ask "Do you want to see the instructions?" and then print them out only if the answer is yes. There is nothing more frustrating than waiting for a program to stop printing the same 30 lines of instructions that you have seen ten times before. Doing it this way also lets the user erase the descriptive information in case space is limited.

DESCRIBE AND INFO

Now that we have looked at two important don'ts, we can begin to examine some of the things that we should do. Most people expect to find instructions in a function (or variable) named DESCRIBE. There should therefore be such a function (not a variable), but it shouldn't do very much. Use the DESCRIBE program to give a brief abstract of the workings of the programs. This should be followed by a table listing the other documentation functions (which we will discuss below) and what they tell. A user now has enough information to get into the workspace and use it, or to decide it is uninteresting and do something else. A sample DESCRIBE is shown in Figure I5.1.

Before we go on to create more documentation functions, a general comment is in order. As the programmer, you know all about this particular workspace. You probably don't even need to look at the documentation—but other users do. You are not going to sit around cutting up the descriptions and pasting them in a notebook, but other people are. Since you are trying to make this workspace available to others who may have a serious need for it, it is an extra kindness to write your functions so that they will fit on normal size pieces of paper.

Document each program or similar group of programs. We will use as an example a hypothetical program for preparing and updating bibliographies; we already saw the DESCRIBE for this in Figure I5.1. There will be one or more functions for entering items into the bibliography, one or more for modifying already entered items, and one or more for printing. Each of these types of activity should have a separate documentation function. A good choice is to use names that end in INFO, such as PRINTINFO, ENTERINFO, CHANGEINFO.

What should one of these INFO programs contain? First of all, a general introduction to the type of programs it documents: "the functions described here are used in adding new items to your bibliography."

```
          DESCRIBE
THIS IS A COLLECTION OF PROGRAMS WHICH PERMITS YOU TO CREATE A BIBLIOGRAPHY
AND ASSOCIATE WITH EACH ITEM IN THE BIBLIOGRAPHY ZERO OR MORE KEYWORDS.  WHEN
YOU WISH TO PRINT THE BIBLIOGRAPHY YOU CAN EITHER PRINT THE WHOLE THING OR
GIVE A LIST OF KEYWORDS, AND ONLY THE ITEMS WHICH HAVE AT LEAST ONE OF THOSE
KEYWORDS ASSOCIATED WITH THEM WILL BE PRINTED.

MORE INFORMATION IS GIVEN IN THE -----INFO PROGRAMS WHICH GIVE MORE
DETAIL ON HOW TO USE THE PROGRAMS.  THESE ARE:

ENTERINFO          HOW TO ENTER ITEMS INTO THE BIBLIOGRAPHY
PRINTINFO          HOW TO PRINT BIBLIOGRAPHIES
UTILITYINFO        A FEW USEFUL FUNCTIONS NOT DISCUSSED ELSEWHERE
WORKSPACEINFO      HOW TO GET STARTED IN A CLEAR WORKSPACE OR CONTINUE
                     YOUR BIBLIOGRAPHY OVER MORE THAN ONE WORKSPACE
GLOBALINFO         A LIST OF THE GLOBAL VARIABLES WHICH MUST EXIST
PROGRAMMERINFO     SOME HINTS ON THE STRUCTURE OF THE PACKAGE, WHICH MAY
                     HELP YOU MODIFY THE PROGRAMS OR GET OUT OF UNFORSEEN JAMS.

OF COURSE,  ALL THESE PROGRAMS SHOULD BE ERASED BEFORE YOU START TO WORK
AS THEY TAKE UP SPACE BETTER USED ELSEWHERE(UNLESS YOU HAVE UNLIMITED
WORKSPACES).
```

FIGURE I5.1. A sample DESCRIBE.

Then a list of the programs being described, and finally a detailed description of each.

What is a detailed description? It covers several things. First, it tells what the effect of the program is. Second, it tells how to call it: if only the name is needed, say so; if it takes arguments, how many and what kind? What are the special cases? If the program requires vector arguments, will it accept scalars? What can happen if the wrong type of argument is given?

What does the program do if it is working correctly? What sorts of questions will it ask? What kinds of answers should be given? (Do *not ever* assume that your program is self-explanatory.) What sort of output does the program give?

Does it do clever things like give the user a chance to put in a new sheet of paper by stopping and waiting for a special signal, like a carriage return? Does it require a lot of "think time?" Can it ever run out of work space; if so how can that be prevented? How can the user's data be recovered in case something like this does happen?

Figure I5.2 shows a sample INFO from the bibliography package.

EXERCISES

I5-1. What do you know about the bibliography programs after reading the two figures? What more should you have been told?

I5-2. Note that Figure I5.2 references the program and INFO for entering items into the bibliography. This cross-referencing would be acceptable if you knew that the user had already looked at ENTERINFO. How do you know?

PROGRAMS THE USER DOESN'T SEE

So far, we have been describing the documentation for the most important programs, the ones that the user actually has to call directly. There are usually other programs as well: these should, in general, be handled in less detail, but they should be documented. You might have a function called FUNCTIONSINFO, which gives the name of *every* program in the workspace and a very brief description of what it does. Include the ones that the user may call directly, but separate them from the others.

Another thing that can be done with programs the user doesn't see is indicate in the documentation of the other programs which of these get called, but don't do this unless it is likely to provide useful information. If the workspace is best used by erasing some functions when others are being called, this kind of documentation is invaluable. If the programs are designed so that the user can safely make some small

INSTRUCTIONS FOR USING PROGRAM
PRINT

    PROGRAM PRINT IS USED FOR RETRIEVAL OF THE BIBLIOGRAPHY
IT LETS YOU PRINT ALL THE BIBLIOGRAPHY ENTRIES OR ONLY THOSE
TO WHICH CERTAIN KEYWORDS HAVE BEEN ADDED.
    THE PROGRAM WILL PRODUCE THE LIST OF ENTRIES THE WAY THAT
THEY WERE ENTERED. THE ENTRIES WILL BE SEPARATED BY BLANK LINES.
EACH PAGE IS NUMBERED. WHEN THE PROGRAM COMES TO THE BOTTOM OF A PAGE
THE TYPEBALL WIGGLES AND THEN PAUSES. PUT IN A NEW PAGE OR ROLL THE
PAPER UP A FEW LINES AND THEN HIT CARRIAGE RETURN;THIS PAUSE AND
WIGGLE ALSO OCCUR BEFORE THE FIRST PAGE IS PRINTED.

    THE PROGRAM FIRST ASKS FOR THE NUMBER OF LINES ON A PAGE. THIS
SHOULD BE APPROXIMATE, WITH A FEW LINES LEFT TO SPARE AT THE BOTTOM. IT
THEN FINDS OUT WHAT KEYWORDS ARE TO BE USED TO RETRIEVE INFORMATION. YOU
CAN RETRIEVE ON AS MANY KEYWORDS AS YOU LIKE(THE ENTRY MODE IS MUCH THE
SAME AS FOR ENTER) OR YOU CAN LIST ALL THE ENTRIES.

FIGURE I5.2. A sample INFO.

changes in them, such documentation is again important. It is less important if, say, the programs are going to be used by preschoolers to learn arithmetic. However, it will still be likely that someone, probably another programmer, will have to occasionally modify the programs, and certain documentation is required for that purpose, but of a different sort from what you would supply to a user.

OTHER CONSIDERATIONS

Documenting the functions is most of the battle, but not all of it. While you will surely have localized all possible variables, it is sometimes convenient to have a few global variables. If so, then document them. A GLOBALINFO function should list each global variable, what its default (starting) value is, where it gets values assigned to it, where it is used, what other values the user may want to give to it and what the effect will be of each.

Be sure and tell the user how to get started. A function called GETTINGSTARTEDINFO, or something similar but shorter, can collect all the facts needed to get the programs rolling. What initializations need to be done? What does the user need to do to erase all of this documentation if that is necessary to provide enough room to run the programs?

Sometimes you can expect that the user will have to create new workspaces with the same programs (as in our bibliography example, when the amount of data gets too big to fit all in one workspace). How does one carry over the essential programs and variables to a new workspace and leave alone things best left alone? The place for such information is a WORKSPACEINFO.

Of course, all of this is not being done just for the user. If you've never carefully documented a workspace before you'll be surprised at how much you'll learn about your own programs and how much better they will become. Furthermore, if you, or someone else, ever need to change the programs, the documentation will be invaluable. Since, now that the programs are fresh in your mind, you probably can remember a lot of the special features of the way you set things up that the user doesn't need, but another programmer might, write a PROGRAMMERINFO to collect the information which a programmer might need. What sort of data structures are you using? What unorthodox techniques did you use? These things will often be discussed, in comments, in specific programs, but it does no harm, and potentially much good, to collect them all together.

Sometimes, too, you write some programs which could be used in other contexts (like our IF, ERROR and WHEN). You might want to make them available by describing them separately as utility programs—in UTILITYINFO.

Having written all of this documentation, and more if necessary, read it. Check it carefully: don't just look for what you said, look for what you didn't say. Writing documentation is as important, and difficult, as writing the programs—since you are working in a natural language, though, it is easier to make mistakes and harder to debug them.

You may be concerned about the profusion of INFO names. They may seem forbidding here, but remember that your DESCRIBE lists each, with some information about what it tells (the name is not enough). Also, you shouldn't worry about the amount of space taken up by all of these functions. After all, the GETTINGSTARTEDINFO explains how to erase them before running the programs. And if they take up too much room for the other programs to fit you can have separate workspaces for your documentation functions and for your actual programs (with each one telling the user how to find the other, of course). If this seems clumsy, it is much better than what is often available.

Now, *don't* save all this in a public library. First, wait a week and look at the whole thing carefully. It's easy to make simple mistakes which can have major effects on the success of your workspace: some workspace have been put into public libraries with stop commands activated on their major programs or with large stacks of pending programs. Try to make sure that you aren't doing something similar. Then give the package to some other people and ask them to try it out.

Finally, don't save it yourself in a public library, even if your computer system allows you to do so. Send a copy of the documentation to the responsible person at the computer center. Ask for comments (there may, for example, be standards that you weren't aware of) and ask them to save it: there may be a special public library for programs like yours, and you'd probably prefer to have it there.

EXERCISES

I5-3. Figure I5.3 shows a sample GLOBALINFO. Does it tell everything you would want to know as a user? As a programmer?

I5-4. If all of this hasn't convinced you as to the need for careful documentation, try this: pick 10 workspaces at random from your public libraries, find out from their documentation what they are supposed to do and then try to use them.

I5-5. We could use variables instead of programs for our documentation: one advantage is that a user who wishes to interrupt the printing can hit the attention key, without ending up with a suspended function. To meet the objections presented earlier, we would need programs for editing character strings. Design a package of such editing functions.

GLOBALINFO
        GLOBAL VARIABLES

    THE FOLLOWING IS A LIST OF SOME VARIABLES WHICH MUST
BE GLOBAL TO ALL PROGRAMS.
THE ONES MARKED WITH * SHOULD EXIST BEFORE ANY PROGRAMS ARE RUN AND
MAY BE CHANGED BEFORE RUNNING ANY PROGRAMS IF THAT SEEMS CONVENIENT TO YOU.
    THE OTHERS ARE CREATED WITHIN SOME PROGRAM TO BE USED BY
SOME PROGRAM. THE CREATING PROGRAM NAME IS GIVEN.

ALLEND*   USED IN ENTER TO SIGNIFY 'EXIT FROM PROGRAM'.
                 MUST BE 1 CHARACTER.
BKSP   USED BY PRINTLINE TO MAKE TYPEBALL WIGGLE
CLASSEP*   USED BY ENTER TO SEPARATE KEYWORD NUMBERS FROM TEXT OF ENTRY:
                 MUST BE 1 CHARACTER.
CLISTΔ   CREATED BY CINITΔ-THIS IS THE LIST OF KEYWORDS
CLISTΔTAB   CREATED BY CINITΔ-THIS IS THE STRUCTURE OF CLISTΔ
ERROREND*   USED IN ENTER TO SIGNIFY 'STOP TAKING THIS ENTRY'
                 MUST BE 1 CHARACTER.
LINESDUN   CREATED IN PRINTLINE-NUMBER OF LINES PRINTED ON CURRENT PAGE
LINESEP*   USED BY ENTER TO SEPARATE LINES OF ENTRY. CANNOT APPEAR IN
                 ANY ENTRY. MUST BE 1 CHARACTER.
LISTΔ   CREATED BY INITΔ. THESE ARE THE BIBLIOGRAPHY ITEMS.
LISTΔTAB   CREATED BY INITΔ. THIS IS THE STRUCTURE OF LISTΔ
PAGENUM   CREATED BY PRINTLINE-THE NUMBER OF THE CURRENT PAGE.
PAGESIZE   CREATED BY PRINT-THE NUMBER OF LINES TO A PAGE.

OF COURSE, THE VARIABLES WHICH ARE SINGLE CHARACTERS AND ARE USED TO CODE
VARIOUS FUNCTIONS SHOULD BE DIFFERENT FROM EACH OTHER.

FIGURE I5.3. A GLOBALINFO.

9

Bills of Materials

An Example of Program Development

There was one who was famed for the number of things
    He forgot when he entered the ship:
His umbrella, his watch, all his jewels and rings,
    And the clothes he had bought for the trip.

He had forty-two boxes, all carefully packed,
    With his name painted clearly on each:
But, since he omitted to mention the fact,
    They were all left behind on the beach.

In this chapter we will discuss some of the recordkeeping which must go on in any manufacturing operation. Manufactured products are rarely conceived of as being created from scratch. The product is usually considered to be made up of *assemblies*, each of which is in turn made up of its own constituent assemblies (subassemblies), until we finally get to the point where all the assemblies are simple parts. This decomposition into assemblies is a matter of great practical value, as a given item may be a subassembly for various different assemblies, and a corporation will often keep inventories of assemblies as well as of simple parts: if the pump in your air conditioner breaks down during the summer, you expect the company to have another pump all ready to send you and are not willing to wait for them to make one.

A SIMPLE BILL OF MATERIALS

All the relationships between the various assemblies and parts are given by a *bill of materials*. A bill of materials may take many forms, but the basic concept is invariant: for each assembly it shows those other assemblies and parts which directly make it up. Figure 9.1 shows a simple bill of materials for a paper cutter. A paper cutter can be made from one arm assembly, one base, one guide and eight No. 2 screws. To make an arm assembly requires a handle, a blade and two more No. 2 screws.

For a large product, with many hundreds of assemblies, it is important to be able to easily find out how many of the various simple parts are needed to manufacture some assembly. For example, how many No. 2 screws are needed to make the paper cutter? There are eight needed on the first *level*, two more for the arm assembly and four more for the guide, a total of 14. How many No. 5 screws are needed? Each leg requires one, but there are four legs needed for each base so that a total of four is needed for each paper cutter. Just tracing through in this way to find the total requirements for some part can be nontrivial for a large product and this is the task we will tackle first.

It is reasonable to assume that the actual bill of materials has been made available to us in some form which we can easily use. One common representation of a bill of materials is an array. Suppose that there are s assemblies (counting the product itself as one) and t parts. The array will then have s columns and (s+t) rows. The entry at a given row and column tells how many of the parts or assemblies represented by that row are required for the assembly represented by that column. For example, Figure 9.2 shows such an array for the paper cutter, together with the correspondence between row and column numbers and the constituents of the paper cutter. The entry 1 in row 2 and column 1 indicates that one item 2 (an arm assembly) is required to make one item 1 (a paper cutter). Similarly, the 4 in row 5 and column 3 shows that four legs are required to make one base.

```
PAPER CUTTER
      ARM ASSEMBLY (1)
            HANDLE (1)
            BLADE (1)
            NO.2 SCREWS (2)
      BASE (1)
            CUTTING SURFACE (1)
            LEGS (4)
                  RUBBER TIPS (1)
                  NO.5 SCREWS (1)
      GUIDE (1)
            RULER (1)
            PAPER HOLDER (1)
            NO.2 SCREWS (4)
      NO.2 SCREWS (8)
```

FIGURE 9.1. A bill of materials.

1.	PAPER CUTTER	0	0	0	0	0
2.	ARM ASSEMBLY	1	0	0	0	0
3.	BASE	1	0	0	0	0
4.	GUIDE	1	0	0	0	0
5.	LEG	0	0	4	0	0
6.	HANDLE	0	1	0	0	0
7.	BLADE	0	1	0	0	0
8.	NO.2 SCREW	8	2	0	4	0
9.	CUTTING SURFACE	0	0	1	0	0
10.	RUBBER TIP	0	0	0	0	1
11.	NO.5 SCREW	0	0	0	0	1
12.	RULER	0	0	0	1	0
13.	PAPER HOLDER	0	0	0	1	0

FIGURE 9.2. A bill of materials array.

We can expect this array to have certain properties which will make our task somewhat easier. (Presumably some other programs will have the responsibility for putting the array together in the proper way—which does not mean that our program should not check to make sure that the properties it expects are present.) Certainly we would not expect any assembly to have itself as one of its subassemblies. By the same reasoning, if assembly A is used in assembly B, then assembly B should not be used in assembly A. This means that there is a way to number the assemblies so that the upper right-hand corner of the array, the main diagonal and the elements above it, consist of all zeros. We will assume (and check) that the array is presented to us in this *lower diagonal form*. Note that the array in Figure 9.2 is in lower diagonal form.

Another reasonable expectation is that no column will be entirely zeros, for this would indicate an assembly (as distinct from a simple part) with no subassemblies or parts. We cannot make the same assumption about the rows, however. In Figure 9.2 it is clear that the first row must be all zeros since it is not a subassembly of anything. Furthermore, since a company often manufactures many similar products, such as the deluxe paper cutter and the executive paper cutter, which have many parts in common with each other, it might be reasonable for all of these products to be part of the same array, and then each such product would be associated with an all zero row.

Figure 9.3 shows a structure chart for the basic task of computing the total number of each kind of part required to make a specific assembly, called UNIT, which will be an argument to the program.

We first check that the array, which will be a global variable called NEEDS, and the argument UNIT have the proper form. The variable NUMBERS is a vector which we initialize to be equal to the column of NEEDS which corresponds to UNIT; in this way each entry of NUMBERS represents the number of the corresponding part or assembly needed to make assembly UNIT. At first, NUMBERS just shows the direct constituents of UNIT, but we will *explode* each assembly into its constituents until we finally have only parts represented in NUMBERS.

By the assumption that the array is lower diagonal, we see that for an assembly numbered T the only assemblies which can be its constituents are those numbered higher than T. Thus, we can examine the elements of NUMBERS which represent assemblies (rather than simple parts) one by one. Suppose that in making our assembly UNIT we need n copies of some assembly A; we can find out what the subassemblies of A are and then add the appropriate number of each to the corresponding element of NUMBERS. For each subassembly of A, we find out how many are needed to make up one A from NEEDS and then multiply by n to find out how many are needed for UNIT.

As an example, we can explode the base of the paper cutter, assembly 3. Column 3 of the array is shown in Figure 9.4A. The base requires

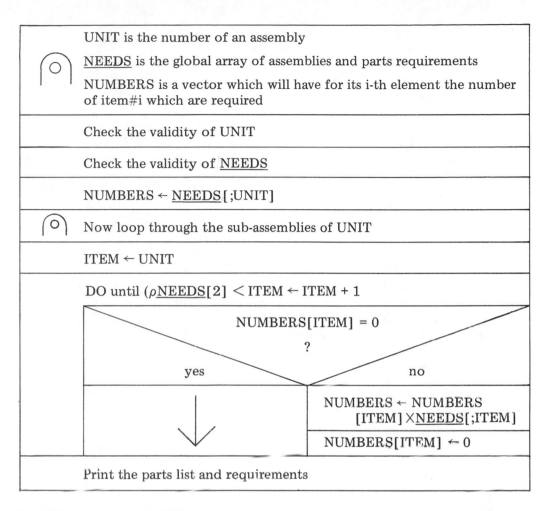

| UNIT is the number of an assembly |
| NEEDS is the global array of assemblies and parts requirements |
| NUMBERS is a vector which will have for its i-th element the number of item#i which are required |

Check the validity of UNIT

Check the validity of NEEDS

NUMBERS ← NEEDS[;UNIT]

Now loop through the sub-assemblies of UNIT

ITEM ← UNIT

DO until (ρNEEDS[2] < ITEM ← ITEM + 1

NUMBERS[ITEM] = 0 ?

yes   no

| | NUMBERS ← NUMBERS [ITEM] ×NEEDS[;ITEM] |
| | NUMBERS[ITEM] ← 0 |

Print the parts list and requirements

FIGURE 9.3. A design for TOTALS.

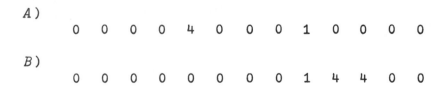

A)
      0   0   0   0   4   0   0   0   1   0   0   0   0

B)
      0   0   0   0   0   0   0   0   1   4   4   0   0

FIGURE 9.4. Exploding the base.

four of assembly 5 (the legs), so we add to this vector four times the fifth column, and then set the third element equal to 0 since that assembly has already been exploded. The result is Figure 9.4B. Since the first five elements of the vector (corresponding to assemblies) are now all 0 we have exploded the base into its ultimate constituents: one cutting surface, four rubber tips and four No. 5 screws. It is clear that, because of the structure of the array, once we explode an assembly (or ignore it because its entry in NUMBERS is 0) we never have to consider it again.

Figure 9.5 shows the program TOTALS which implements the structure chart. The first line is a call to a program CHECKUP which inspects the array NEEDS to be sure that it has the desired properties; CHECKUP is shown in Figure 9.6. The remainder of TOTALS is relatively straightforward, although the last two lines, which actually print the totals, may be a little complicated. The first sets up a two column array whose first column consists of part and assembly numbers and whose second column is the vector NUMBERS. Since only the elements of NUMBERS which correspond to simple parts are nonzero at this point, the last line prints only those rows which correspond to simple parts.

```
      ∇ TOTALS UNIT;NUMBERS;ITEM;SIZE;DISPLAY
[1]     CHECKUP
[2]     ⍝-----THIS CHECKS FOR VALIDITY OF THE ASSEMBLIES-AND-PARTS
[3]     ⍝------VERSUS ASSEMBLIES ARRAY, NEEDS
[4]     'TOTALS:ARGUMENT NOT SCALAR ' ERROR 1<⍴,UNIT
[5]     'TOTALS:ARGUMENT   NOT INTEGER' ERROR UNIT≠⌊UNIT
[6]     'TOTALS:ARGUMENT OUT OF BOUNDS ' ERROR(UNIT≤0)∨(UNIT>(⍴NEEDS)[2])
[7]     NUMBERS←NEEDS[;UNIT]
[8]     ITEM←UNIT
[9]   ΔITEM:→ENDΔITEM WHEN(⍴NEEDS)[2]<ITEM←ITEM+1
[10]    NUMBERS←NUMBERS+NEEDS[;ITEM]×NUMBERS[ITEM]
[11]    NUMBERS[ITEM]←0
[12]    →ΔITEM
[13]  ENDΔITEM:'THE PART NUMBERS AND QUANTITIES FOR ASSEMBLY ';UNIT;' ARE:'
[14]    SIZE←⍴NUMBERS
[15]    DISPLAY←(((SIZE,1)⍴⍳SIZE),((SIZE,1)⍴NUMBERS))
[16]    DISPLAY[(⍴NEEDS)[2]↓⍳SIZE;]
      ∇
```

FIGURE 9.5. The program.

```
      ∇ CHECKUP;SIZE;UPPER
[1]     ⍝-----THIS ROUTINE CHECKS THE ASSEMBLIES+PARTS ARRAY NEEDS
[2]     'NEEDS NOT PROPERLY SHAPED ' ERROR 2≠⍴⍴NEEDS
[3]     'NEEDS CONTAINS NEGATIVE NUMBERS ' ERROR∨/,0>NEEDS
[4]     'NEEDS NOT INTEGER ' ERROR∨/,NEEDS≠⌊NEEDS
[5]     'NEEDS CONTAINS ASSEMBLIES WITH NO CONSTITUENTS ' ERROR∨/0=+/[1] NEEDS
[6]     UPPER←(⍳SIZE)∘.≤⍳(SIZE←(⍴NEEDS)[2])
[7]     'NEEDS IS NOT LOWER DIAGONAL ' ERROR~∧/,0=NEEDS[⍳SIZE;]×UPPER
      ∇
```

FIGURE 9.6. Checking for errors.

Figure 9.7 shows the results of running the program for various assemblies in the paper cutter.

EXERCISES

9-1. Lines 7 and 8 of CHECKUP create an array which is upper diagonal and multiply this with part of <u>NEEDS</u>. If <u>NEEDS</u> is lower diagonal the result should be all zeros. Explain the details of this operation.

9-2. Rewrite TOTALS so that it does not assume that the array is lower diagonal.

9-3. Rewrite CHECKUP so that if the array is not lower diagonal the program tries to put it in that form and only reports an error if it cannot be made lower diagonal.

9-4. Rewrite CHECKUP so that if there are assemblies with no constituent parts they are deleted from <u>NEEDS</u>.

9-5. Rewrite TOTALS so that only nonzero parts requirements are printed.

9-6. Rewrite TOTALS so that the result is a total requirements chart: that is, it will show how many of each assembly are required as well as how many of each part.

9-7. It is possible to use a primitive operator to find the immediate constituent requirements of any assembly. Let NUMBERS be the vector whose length is the number of assemblies, which is all zeros except for a one in the position corresponding to the desired assembly. Then the expression in Figure 9.8 is a vector whose size is the number of rows of <u>NEEDS</u> and whose elements indicate the requirements for the corresponding assemblies and parts which are immediate constituents of the original assembly. Investigate the properties of this *inner product* operation and write a version of TOTALS which uses it. (*Hint*: what happens if more than one element of NUMBERS is nonzero?)

inner product

9-8. Write a program which creates the array <u>NEEDS</u> from information supplied by the user at the terminal.

9-9. Part of what is important about a report is the way it is presented. Often we would like to get our output printed on clean sheets of paper. Modify TOTALS so that if the input is not in error it prints a message telling the user to put in a clean sheet of paper and then waits until the user signals that it should begin. (*Hint*: use quote-quad input to make it wait and have the signal be a carriage return.)

```
      TOTALS  1
THE  PART  NUMBERS  AND  QUANTITIES  FOR  ASSEMBLY  1  ARE:
      6     1
      7     1
      8    14
      9     1
     10     4
     11     4
     12     1
     13     1


      TOTALS  3
THE  PART  NUMBERS  AND  QUANTITIES  FOR  ASSEMBLY  3  ARE:
      6     0
      7     0
      8     0
      9     1
     10     4
     11     4
     12     0
     13     0


      TOTALS  5
THE  PART  NUMBERS  AND  QUANTITIES  FOR  ASSEMBLY  5  ARE:
      6     0
      7     0
      8     0
      9     0
     10     1
     11     1
     12     0
     13     0
```

FIGURE 9.7. Running the program.

$NEEDS+.\times NUMBERS$

FIGURE 9.8. An inner product operation.

INVENTORIES

It is somewhat more realistic to suppose that the firm has on hand a large inventory of the parts and assemblies needed, and so will not necessarily need to purchase every single part needed to produce the next batch of paper cutters. It is relatively straightforward to modify the program TOTALS in Figure 9.5 to take advantage of the existence of an inventory.

We can assume that the inventory is given by a vector INVENTORY whose size is the same as the number of rows of NEEDS. In the program TOTALS, whenever we calculate the number of parts or subassemblies needed to make a given assembly (ITEM) on line 10 we would first subtract the number of assemblies of that type which are already in the inventory. Thus, we would only be calculating the parts requirements for assemblies which actually need to be produced. Since the loop variable ITEM only takes on values associated with assemblies, we would still not have taken account of the fact that there may be a large number of unassembled simple parts in the INVENTORY as well. So, when the loop terminates we should subtract from the vector, NUMBERS, of parts requirements the parts inventory. Of course, in neither of these subtractions do we want to end up with a negative number, which might happen if the inventory is larger than the requirement. In each case, therefore, we will use the *maximum* operator to ensure that the results of the subtractions are never smaller than 0.

maximum

Figure 9.9 shows the revised program. The subtractions take place in lines 11 and 15. It is likely that, under the assumption of a large inventory, most of the parts needed to produce some assembly will be on hand, and so most of the requirements listed will be 0. Thus, in lines 17–23 we only print the nonzero parts requirements: a special message is printed in line 23 if no parts at all are needed to produce the assembly. Naturally, we also modify CHECKUP to investigate the new datum, INVENTORY. Figure 9.10 shows a version of CHECKUP which ensures that INVENTORY is a nonnegative integer vector of the proper length.

```
      ∇ TOTALS UNIT;NUMBERS;ITEM;SIZE;NON∆ZERO
[1]     CHECKUP
[2]     ⍝-----THIS CHECKS FOR VALIDITY OF THE ASSEMBLIES-AND-PARTS
[3]     ⍝------VERSUS ASSEMBLIES ARRAY, NEEDS
[4]     ⍝------AND FOR A VALID INVENTORY ARRAY INVENTORY
[5]     'TOTALS:ARGUMENT NOT SCALAR ' ERROR 1<ρ,UNIT
[6]     'TOTALS:ARGUMENT  NOT INTEGER' ERROR UNIT≠⌊UNIT
[7]     'TOTALS:ARGUMENT OUT OF BOUNDS ' ERROR(UNIT≤0)∨(UNIT>(ρNEEDS)[2])
[8]     NUMBERS←NEEDS[;UNIT]
[9]     ITEM←UNIT
[10] ∆ITEM:→END∆ITEM WHEN(ρNEEDS)[2]<ITEM←ITEM+1
[11]    NUMBERS←NUMBERS+NEEDS[;ITEM]×(0⌈NUMBERS[ITEM]-INVENTORY[ITEM])
[12]    ⍝-----SUBTRACTING ASSEMBLIES ON HAND FROM NEEDS
[13]    NUMBERS[ITEM]←0
[14]    →∆ITEM
[15] END∆ITEM:NUMBERS←0⌈NUMBERS-INVENTORY
[16]    ⍝-----SUBTRACTING PARTS ON HAND
[17]    →NONE IF∧/NUMBERS=0
[18]    'THE PARTS REQUIRED FOR ASSEMBLY ';UNIT;' ARE:'
[19]    NON∆ZERO←(NUMBERS≠0)/⍳ρNUMBERS
[20]    SIZE←ρ,NON∆ZERO
[21]    ((SIZE,1)ρNON∆ZERO),((SIZE,1)ρNUMBERS[NON∆ZERO])
[22]    →0
[23] NONE:'NO PARTS NOT IN THE INVENTORY ARE REQUIRED FOR ASSEMBLY ';UNIT
      ∇
```

FIGURE 9.9. The revised program.

```
      ∇ CHECKUP;SIZE;UPPER
[1]     ⍝-----THIS ROUTINE CHECKS THE ASSEMBLIES+PARTS ARRAY NEEDS
[2]     ⍝------AND THE INVENTORY VECTOR INVENTORY
[3]     'NEEDS NOT PROPERLY SHAPED ' ERROR 2≠ρρNEEDS
[4]     'NEEDS CONTAINS NEGATIVE NUMBERS ' ERROR∨/,0>NEEDS
[5]     'NEEDS NOT INTEGER ' ERROR∨/,NEEDS≠⌊NEEDS
[6]     'NEEDS CONTAINS ASSEMBLIES WITH NO CONSTITUENTS ' ERROR∨/0=+/[1] NEEDS
[7]     UPPER←(⍳SIZE)∘.≤⍳(SIZE←(ρNEEDS)[2])
[8]     'NEEDS IS NOT LOWER DIAGONAL ' ERROR~∧/,0=NEEDS[⍳SIZE;]×UPPER
[9]     'INVENTORY NOT A VECTOR ' ERROR 1≠ρρINVENTORY
[10]    'INVENTORY NOT NONNEGATIVE INTEGERS ' ERROR∨/INVENTORY≠⌊|INVENTORY
[11]    'INVENTORY DOES NOT CONFORM WITH NEEDS ' ERROR(ρINVENTORY)≠(ρNEEDS)[1]
      ∇
```

FIGURE 9.10. The revised error checker.

The program TOTALS is now 23 lines long. While this is not an excessive size, it is long enough that it becomes a little hard for us to grasp the entire program at once. It seems that as programs get to be close to 25 lines long they reach the maximum size that we can deal with easily **rule-of-25** (this is known as the "rule-of-25"). So, even though TOTALS is not quite that big, we should look at it carefully to see if there is some action that really does not belong.

The program has three basic actions: exploding assemblies, calculating parts requirements, and printing the results. These seem to fit well together. A fourth important action, checking the data for validity, does seem to be a different sort of thing, and so its details have been buried in the routine CHECKUP. But what about checking the validity of the argument to TOTALS? Isn't that more like what goes on in CHECKUP than the rest of the actions in TOTALS? Indeed it is, and it is quite easy to bury that, too, in CHECKUP: the revised programs appear in Figures 9.11 and 9.12.

```
      ∇ TOTALS UNIT;NUMBERS;ITEM;SIZE;NONΔZERO
[1]     CHECKUP
[2]     ₳-----THIS CHECKS FOR VALIDITY OF THE ASSEMBLIES-AND-PARTS
[3]     ₳------VERSUS ASSEMBLIES ARRAY, NEEDS
[4]     ₳------AND FOR A VALID INVENTORY ARRAY INVENTORY
[5]     ₳------AND THAT THE ARGUMENT UNIT IS VALID
[6]     NUMBERS←NEEDS[;UNIT]
[7]     ITEM←UNIT
[8]   ΔITEM:→ENDΔITEM WHEN(ρNEEDS)[2]<ITEM←ITEM+1
[9]     NUMBERS←NUMBERS+NEEDS[;ITEM]×(0⌈NUMBERS[ITEM]-INVENTORY[ITEM])
[10]    ₳-----SUBTRACTING ASSEMBLIES ON HAND FROM NEEDS
[11]    NUMBERS[ITEM]←0
[12]    →ΔITEM
[13] ENDΔITEM:NUMBERS←0⌈NUMBERS-INVENTORY
[14]    ₳-----SUBTRACTING PARTS ON HAND
[15]    →NONE IF∧/NUMBERS=0
[16]    'THE PARTS REQUIRED FOR ASSEMBLY ';UNIT;' ARE:'
[17]    NONΔZERO←(NUMBERS≠0)/ιρNUMBERS
[18]    SIZE←ρ,NONΔZERO
[19]    ((SIZE,1)ρNONΔZERO),((SIZE,1)ρNUMBERS[NONΔZERO])
[20]    →0
[21] NONE:'NO PARTS NOT IN THE INVENTORY ARE REQUIRED FOR ASSEMBLY ';UNIT
      ∇
```

FIGURE 9.11. Further revisions to the program.

```
      ∇ CHECKUP;SIZE;UPPER
[1]     ₳-----THIS ROUTINE CHECKS THE ASSEMBLIES+PARTS ARRAY NEEDS
[2]     ₳------AND THE INVENTORY VECTOR INVENTORY
[3]     ₳------AND THE ARGUMENT, UNIT, TO TOTALS
[4]     'NEEDS NOT PROPERLY SHAPED ' ERROR 2≠ρρNEEDS
[5]     'NEEDS CONTAINS NEGATIVE NUMBERS ' ERROR∨/,0>NEEDS
[6]     'NEEDS NOT INTEGER ' ERROR∨/NEEDS≠⌊NEEDS
[7]     'NEEDS CONTAINS ASSEMBLIES WITH NO CONSTITUENTS ' ERROR∨/0=+/[1] NEEDS
[8]     UPPER←(ιSIZE)∘.≤ι(SIZE←(ρNEEDS)[2])
[9]     'NEEDS IS NOT LOWER DIAGONAL ' ERROR~∧/,0=NEEDS[ιSIZE;]×UPPER
[10]    'INVENTORY NOT A VECTOR ' ERROR 1≠ρρINVENTORY
[11]    'INVENTORY NOT NONNEGATIVE INTEGERS ' ERROR∨/INVENTORY≠⌊|INVENTORY
[12]    'INVENTORY DOES NOT CONFORM WITH NEEDS ' ERROR(ρINVENTORY)≠(ρNEEDS)[1]
[13]    'TOTALS ARGUMENT NOT SCALAR ' ERROR 1<ρ,UNIT
[14]    'TOTALS ARGUMENT NOT INTEGER ' ERROR UNIT≠⌊UNIT
[15]    'TOTALS ARGUMENT OUT OF BOUNDS ' ERROR(UNIT≤0)∨(UNIT>(ρNEEDS)[2])
      ∇
```

FIGURE 9.12. Further revisions to the error checker.

Some sample output is shown in Figure 9.13.

EXERCISES

9–10. If we need 1749 paper cutters we have no effective way to get the parts requirements. Running TOTALS would only tell us the requirements for one paper cutter. Multiplying that by 1749 might not be enough, as the inventory would change each time we make a paper cutter and we might run out of something half-way through. Modify the program TOTALS so that the user can request the parts requirements for any number of some assembly. Don't forget to alter the print statements to reflect the number of assemblies being produced, or to check any additional arguments or input in CHECKUP.

9–11. By combining some statements we would shorten TOTALS considerably. In fact, by combining many statements on one line, we can often decrease the size of a program way below 25 lines. Explain why such clever manipulations do not avoid the problems which the rule-of-25 is designed to eliminate. (*Hint*: there may be an APL programmer nearby who writes programs that way. Try to read one of them.)

AN EFFICIENT DATA STRUCTURE

We have been doing very well writing programs for our little 5-by-13 bill of materials array, but many products are considerably larger. Other test cases will verify for you that the program will certainly work on larger arrays, but the program itself is not the only limitation. It is not at all difficult to imagine a product with so many assemblies and sub-assemblies that the resulting array will not fit into one workspace. There are various techniques for circumventing this problem. All of them are likely to require programs which take longer to run; in fact, the trade off between time and space is probably the most common one in programming. The increase in running time shouldn't bother us as long as the resulting program does the job which the one we have now can't.

One way to fix the program is suggested if we look back at the array NEEDS in Figure 9.2. Of the 65 elements in the array, only 14 are nonzero. An array in which most of the elements are zero is called *sparse*. It is clearly a tremendous waste of space to store a large sparse array. Don't be misled into thinking that the zeros give us no information; they are informative, but in a negative way. We would have the same information if we just listed those places in the array which are not zero.

```
      INVENTORY ← 0 0 0 0 1 0 0 2 0 0 1 0 1
      TOTALS 1
THE PARTS REQUIRED FOR ASSEMBLY 1 ARE:
    6    1
    7    1
    8   12
    9    1
   10    3
   11    2
   12    1


      TOTALS 5
THE PARTS REQUIRED FOR ASSEMBLY 5 ARE:
   10    1


      INVENTORY ← 2+INVENTORY
      INVENTORY
2   2   2   2   3   2   2   4   2   2   3   2   3
      TOTALS 1
THE PARTS REQUIRED FOR ASSEMBLY 1 ARE:
   8    4


      TOTALS 5


NO PARTS NOT IN THE INVENTORY ARE REQUIRED FOR ASSEMBLY 5
```

FIGURE 9.13. Comparing needs with inventory.

We could do this with a three column array: in each row the first entry would be the number of a row of NEEDS, the second entry would be a column number and the third entry would be the value in the given row and column of NEEDS. The space taken up by this array, which we might call XNEEDS, is three times the number of nonzero elements of NEEDS. It is reasonable to assume that a bill of materials array would be at least so sparse that no more than one-third of its elements are nonzero.

Figure 9.14 shows the array NEEDS and two possible versions of XNEEDS. It is easy to check that each of these faithfully represents NEEDS. In one the rows are ordered, while in the other they seem to be random. Should we require that the array XNEEDS always be in some specified order, as we did with NEEDS?

Actually, we would be wiser to make no such assumptions about XNEEDS. Suppose that the company decides to make some additions to the product, such as using the No. 2 screws throughout. It is easy to just change the row of XNEEDS that reads 11 5 1 to read 8 5 1. If we do not require that XNEEDS be in a particular order, then we do not have to go through a (possibly expensive) sorting process after we make this change. As we will see, making any assumptions about the order will just lead us up a blind alley anyway, as we do not need to make such assumptions. We will, however, keep our basic assumptions about NEEDS, which XNEEDS represents.

Looking at TOTALS in Figure 9.11 to see what changes the use of XNEEDS forces upon us we see that, aside from the comments, the only appearances of NEEDS in the program are on lines 6, 8 and 9. On line 8 we need to know the number of columns of NEEDS and on line 6 we are implicitly asking for the number of rows. We will use a global variable XSHAPE to represent these two quantities. It will be a vector of size 2: the first element will be the number of rows of NEEDS and the second will be the number of columns.

The references made to NEEDS on lines 6 and 9 are requests for specific columns. Thus, it is clear that we need to write a function which, given any column number of NEEDS, can produce that column by looking at XNEEDS. Such a program is COLUMN, given in Figure 9.15. After checking the validity of the argument, we let ROWS have for its value the vector of the numbers of those rows of XNEEDS whose second element is equal to the argument, INDEX. Each of these rows represents an element in column number INDEX. Thus, after initializing the return value RESULT to be all zeros, with length equal to the length of a column of NEEDS, those elements of RESULT which represent rows of NEEDS having nonzero entries in column INDEX are set to be those corresponding nonzero entries. Notice that COLUMN makes no assumptions about the way that the rows of XNEEDS might be arranged.

```
0 0 0 0 0
1 0 0 0 0
1 0 0 0 0
1 0 0 0 0
0 0 4 0 0
0 1 0 0 0
0 1 0 0 0
8 2 0 4 0
0 0 1 0 0
0 0 0 0 1
0 0 0 0 1
0 0 0 1 0
0 0 0 1 0
```

```
 2 1 1        12 4 1
 3 1 1         5 3 4
 4 1 1         8 1 8
 5 3 4         7 2 1
 6 2 1         8 2 2
 7 2 1         8 4 4
 8 1 8         4 1 1
 8 2 2         9 3 1
 8 4 4         2 1 1
 9 3 1        13 4 1
10 5 1         3 1 1
11 5 1        10 5 1
12 4 1         6 2 1
13 4 1        11 5 1
```

FIGURE 9.14. Three versions of the array.

```
    ∇ RESULT←COLUMN INDEX;ROWS
[1]   ⍝-----PRODUCES REQUESTED COLUMN OF BILL-OF-MATERIALS ARRAY
[2]   'COLUMN:ARGUMENT NOT SCALAR ' ERROR 1<ρ,INDEX
[3]   'COLUMN:ARGUMENT NOT INTEGER ' ERROR INDEX≠⌊INDEX
[4]   'COLUMN:ARGUMENT OUT OF BOUNDS ' ERROR(INDEX<1)∨INDEX>XSHAPE[2]
[5]   ROWS←(XNEEDS[;2]=INDEX)/⍳(ρXNEEDS)[1]
[6]   RESULT←XSHAPE[1]ρ0
[7]   RESULT[XNEEDS[ROWS;1]]←XNEEDS[ROWS;3]
    ∇
```

FIGURE 9.15. Reconstructing one column.

A revised version of TOTALS which uses XNEEDS and COLUMN is shown in Figure 9.16. Notice that we have changed the comments to reflect the current status of the program. We have not finished our corrections yet, however, as we must also modify CHECKUP.

In Figure 9.12 CHECKUP looks for five different types of errors in NEEDS. The first is now irrelevant since we will no longer be indexing into NEEDS. The second and third will now be performed on XNEEDS. We would also like to retain the fourth and fifth checks. To see if there are any assemblies without constituents we can examine the columns one at a time, using COLUMN, to see if any column is all zero. Similarly, the last check can be effected by looking to see if any element of column i is a positive integer smaller than i.

Of course, some additional checks on XNEEDS will also be necessary. The elements in the first two columns should be meaningful row and column indices—that is, within the bounds specified by XSHAPE. Since we will be using XSHAPE, we will want to check it, too. Figure 9.17 shows the resulting program.

EXERCISES

9–12. Compare the running time of the newest version of TOTALS with that of one of the earlier ones. Try to determine what the difference in running times would be if the array NEEDS were as large as you could get into your workspace. How long does the latest version of TOTALS take with an array XNEEDS which is as large as you can get into your workspace? How long would a previous version take with the corresponding NEEDS?

9–13. Prepare detailed documentation for the program package consisting of CHECKUP, TOTALS and COLUMN. Explain what global variables are necessary, what they represent and what form they should take. Explain how to use the programs, what the output means, what error messages might occur and what action to take in each case.

9–14. Repeat Exercises 9–3 and 9–4, using XNEEDS instead of NEEDS.

STRUCTURING SPARSE CHARACTER DATA

One of the important tasks of a computer programmer is to translate the output of the computer and to put it in the form desired by the programmer's "customers." For example, the output of TOTALS would almost certainly *not* be acceptable in an industrial organization.

```
      ∇ TOTALS UNIT;NUMBERS;ITEM;SIZE;NON∆ZERO
[1]     CHECKUP
[2]     ⍝-----THIS CHECKS FOR VALIDITY OF THE ASSEMBLIES-AND-PARTS
[3]     ⍝------VERSUS ASSEMBLIES ARRAY, XNEEDS
[4]     ⍝------(WHICH REPRESENTS THE ORIGINAL ARRAY NEEDS)
[5]     ⍝------AND FOR A VALID INVENTORY ARRAY INVENTORY
[6]     ⍝------AND THAT THE ARGUMENT UNIT IS VALID
[7]     NUMBERS←COLUMN UNIT
[8]     ⍝-----PRODUCING COLUMN NUMBER UNIT OF NEEDS
[9]     ITEM←UNIT
[10]  ∆ITEM:→END∆ITEM WHEN XSHAPE[2]<ITEM←ITEM+1
[11]    →∆ITEM IF NUMBERS[ITEM]=0
[12]    NUMBERS←NUMBERS+(COLUMN ITEM)×(0⌈NUMBERS[ITEM]-INVENTORY[ITEM])
[13]    ⍝-----SUBTRACTING ASSEMBLIES ON HAND FROM NEEDS
[14]    NUMBERS[ITEM]←0
[15]    →∆ITEM
[16]  END∆ITEM:NUMBERS←0⌈NUMBERS-INVENTORY
[17]    ⍝-----SUBTRACTING PARTS ON HAND
[18]    →NONE IF∧/NUMBERS=0
[19]    'THE PARTS REQUIRED FOR ASSEMBLY ';UNIT;' ARE:'
[20]    NON∆ZERO←(NUMBERS≠0)/⍳⍴NUMBERS
[21]    SIZE←⍴,NON∆ZERO
[22]    ((SIZE,1)⍴NON∆ZERO),((SIZE,1)⍴NUMBERS[NON∆ZERO])
[23]    →0
[24]  NONE:'NO PARTS NOT IN THE INVENTORY ARE REQUIRED FOR ASSEMBLY ';UNIT
      ∇
```

FIGURE 9.16. Using the new data structure.

```
      ∇ CHECKUP;ASSEMBLY
[1]     ⍝-----THIS ROUTINE CHECKS THAT XNEEDS REPRESENTS A
[2]     ⍝------PROPERLY FORMED ASSEMBLIES+PARTS ARRAY NEEDS
[3]     ⍝------(WHICH INVOLVES CHECKING THE VECTOR XSHAPE);
[4]     ⍝------IT ALSO CHECKS THE INVENTORY VECTOR,INVENTORY
[5]     ⍝-----AND THE ARGUMENT, UNIT, TO TOTALS
[6]     'XSHAPE NOT A VECTOR ' ERROR 1≠⍴⍴XSHAPE
[7]     'XSHAPE NOT SIZE 2 ' ERROR 2≠⍴XSHAPE
[8]     'XSHAPE NOT POSITIVE INTEGERS ' ERROR∨/(XSHAPE≤0)∨(XSHAPE≠⌊XSHAPE)
[9]     'XNEEDS NOT AN ARRAY ' ERROR 2≠⍴⍴XNEEDS
[10]    'XNEEDS DOES NOT HAVE EXACTLY 3 COLUMNS ' ERROR 3≠(⍴XNEEDS)[2]
[11]    'XNEEDS NOT NONNEGATIVE ' ERROR∨/XNEEDS<0
[12]    'XNEEDS NOT NONNEGATIVE INTEGERS ' ERROR∨/,XNEEDS≠⌊XNEEDS
[13]    'XNEEDS HAS COLUMN OR ROW INDEX EQUAL TO 0 ' ERROR∨/,0=XNEEDS[; 1 2]
[14]    'XNEEDS HAS ROW INDEX TOO LARGE ' ERROR∨/XNEEDS[;1]>XSHAPE[1]
[15]    'XNEEDS HAS COLUMN INDEX TO LARGE ' ERROR∨/XNEEDS[;2]>XSHAPE[2]
[16]    ASSEMBLY←0
[17]  ∆ASSEMBLY:→END∆ASSEMBLY WHEN XSHAPE[2]<ASSEMBLY←ASSEMBLY+1
[18]    'XNEEDS HAS ASSEMBLY WITH NO CONSTITUENTS ' ERROR∧/0=COLUMN ASSEMBLY
[19]    'XNEEDS NOT LOWER DIAGONAL ' ERROR∨/(⍳ASSEMBLY)∈(0≠COLUMN ASSEMBLY)/⍳XSHAPE[1]
[20]    →∆ASSEMBLY
[21]  END∆ASSEMBLY:'INVENTORY NOT A VECTOR ' ERROR 1≠⍴⍴INVENTORY
[22]    'INVENTORY DOES NOT CONFORM WITH XNEEDS ' ERROR XSHAPE[1]≠⍴INVENTORY
[23]    'INVENTORY NOT NONNEGATIVE INTEGERS ' ERROR∨/INVENTORY≠⌊|INVENTORY
[24]    'TOTALS ARGUMENT NOT SCALAR ' ERROR 1<⍴,UNIT
[25]    'TOTALS ARGUMENT NOT INTEGER ' ERROR UNIT≠⌊UNIT
[26]    'TOTALS ARGUMENT OUT OF BOUNDS ' ERROR(UNIT≤0)∨(UNIT>XSHAPE[2])
      ∇
```

FIGURE 9.17. Checking the new data structure.

Only the programming staff is likely to know which is part number seven. What we really want is a listing that tells how many blades need to be ordered. Probably both the name and part number for each item should be given, while TOTALS now gives neither.

A simple solution to this problem is evident. We could create two arrays. The ith row of the first would hold the name of the part which TOTALS now identifies as i, and the ith row of the second could hold the part number. Then, when TOTALS is printing the requirements for the ith part it could also print the ith rows of the two arrays. We could keep one array with two planes or even just use a one plane array: of course we cannot mix numbers and characters in an array, but since we don't compute with the part numbers we can treat them as character strings. To keep all the information in a two-dimensional array, we would keep part numbers and names together in one string; to do this we would separate them by some special symbol, yielding things like 'No. 5 Screw!332905'. It is simple, using the *index* operator to separate the name from the number before printing.

There is a larger problem, however, with which neither of these possibilities deals. The array, no matter how many planes it has, is going to be rather sparse. Looking at the names in Figure 9.2 we can see that from a third to a half of the array would very likely consist of blanks whose only purpose was padding some rows so that they would be the same length as other rows. While this is a different form of sparseness from what we saw before, involving blanks rather than zeros, it is just as wasteful of space when large arrays are involved. Notice though that this array is structured in a way that the other one wasn't. In the other array a nonzero element could occur almost anyplace, while here the nonblank elements (including the blanks between words in a name) come bunched together in clusters.

We can take advantage of this clustering by keeping two structures. One is a vector of the character strings we are interested in (for simplicity, we will just keep the part names and ignore the stock numbers), stored one right after the other. The other structure will be a numeric array which will indicate where in the vector a specific word is. This is comparable to separating the third column of <u>XNEEDS</u> and treating it as a separate vector. In this case, though, we can get away with storing less information than before. We don't need to store row and column information for each character in a name: it suffices to keep only the location in the vector of the first character in a name, and then the length of the name. Figure 9.18 shows how this might work in a simple case.

As the array indicates, the second name begins in position 7 of the array and has six characters, so that it must be NORMAN. By taking advantage of the structure of the original array in this way, we need to store only the number of significant elements plus twice the number of names, rather than a much larger total of three times the number of nonzero elements as before.

GLORIANORMANBILLY JEANBOBBY

```
 1     6
 7     6
13    1 0
23     5
```

FIGURE 9.18. Representing a character array.

This method of storage requires both an array $\underline{PLACES}$ and a vector $\underline{NAMES}$. The program in Figure 9.19 will yield as its result the Nth name from the list $\underline{NAMES}$. The actual look-up operation takes just one line, line 6. Since we want to select $\underline{PLACES}[N;2]$ successive elements from $\underline{NAMES}$, we start with the vector 1, 2, ..., $\underline{PLACES}[N;2]$ and then add to all of its elements the quantity $^-1 + \underline{PLACES}[N;1]$. This causes us to select the correct number of successive elements ($\underline{PLACES}[N;2]$) from the correct position ($\underline{PLACES}[N;1]$).

```
      ∇ Z←FIND N
[1]    ⍝-----RETURNS N-TH NAME FROM LIST NAMES
[2]    'FIND: ARGUMENT NOT SCALAR ' ERROR 1<ρ,N
[3]    'FIND: ARGUMENT NOT POSITIVE ' ERROR N≤0
[4]    'FIND:ARGUMENT NOT INTEGER ' ERROR N≠⌊N
[5]    'FIND:ARGUMENT OUT OF BOUNDS' ERROR(ρPLACES)[1]<N
[6]    Z←NAMES[¯1+PLACES[N;1]+⍳PLACES[N;2]]
      ∇



      FIND 1
PAPER CUTTER

      FIND 7
BLADE
```

FIGURE 9.19. Accessing the stored character array.

Finally, Figure 9.20 shows a revised TOTALS which incorporates the improved output formatting. In fact, except for the message which says that no parts at all are required, all of the printing has been moved to a separate program, PRINTOUT, shown in Figure 9.21.

In PRINTOUT we find, as we did before, the numbers of those parts which are actually required, and then enter a loop to print their names and requirements. To have the output appear in neat columns, we would want the numbers always to appear starting in the same column, regardless of the length of the name. Thus, in line 7 we calculate the number of spaces from the beginning of the line to the column of numbers by adding five to the length of the largest name. Then when we print the name and number in line 13 we ensure that the name is followed by the right number of blanks: when the left-hand argument of the operator *take* is larger than the length of the right-hand argument, the latter is padded with blanks.

```
      ∇ TOTALS UNIT;NUMBERS;ITEM
[1]     CHECKUP
[2]     ⍝-----THIS CHECKS FOR VALIDITY OF THE ASSEMBLIES-AND-PARTS
[3]     ⍝------VERSUS ASSEMBLIES ARRAY, XNEEDS
[4]     ⍝------(WHICH REPRESENTS THE ORIGINAL ARRAY NEEDS)
[5]     ⍝------AND FOR A VALID INVENTORY ARRAY INVENTORY
[6]     ⍝------AND THAT THE ARGUMENT UNIT IS VALID
[7]     NUMBERS←COLUMN UNIT
[8]     ⍝-----PRODUCING COLUMN NUMBER UNIT OF NEEDS
[9]     ITEM←UNIT
[10] ΔITEM:→ENDΔITEM WHEN XSHAPE[2]<ITEM←ITEM+1
[11]    →ΔITEM IF NUMBERS[ITEM]=0
[12]    NUMBERS←NUMBERS+(COLUMN ITEM)×(0⌈NUMBERS[ITEM]-INVENTORY[ITEM])
[13]    ⍝-----SUBTRACTING ASSEMBLIES ON HAND FROM NEEDS
[14]    NUMBERS[ITEM]←0
[15]    →ΔITEM
[16] ENDΔITEM:NUMBERS←0⌈NUMBERS-INVENTORY
[17]    ⍝-----SUBTRACTING PARTS ON HAND
[18]    →NONE IF∧/NUMBERS=0
[19]    NUMBERS PRINTOUT UNIT
[20]    →0
[21] NONE:'NO PARTS REQUIRED FOR ',FIND UNIT
      ∇
```

FIGURE 9.20. Final revisions to the program.

```
      ∇ NUMBERS PRINTOUT UNIT;PARTS;NAME;BLANKS
[1]     ⍝-----NUMBERS IS VECTOR OF REQUIREMENTS
[2]     ⍝------FOR ASSEMBLY NUMBERED UNIT
[3]     ⍝------VALIDITY OF ARGUMENTS ASSURED BY
[4]     ⍝------THE CALLING PROGRAM
[5]     'THE PARTS REQUIRED FOR ',(FIND UNIT),' ARE:'
[6]     PARTS←(NUMBERS≠0)/⍳ρNUMBERS
[7]     BLANKS←5+⌈/,PLACES[PARTS;2]
[8]     ⍝-----GIVES THE NUMBER OF SPACES BETWEEN
[9]     ⍝------NAMES AND NUMBERS
[10]    PARTS←0,PARTS
[11] ΔPARTS:→ENDΔPARTS WHEN 0=ρPARTS←1↓PARTS
[12]    NAME←FIND 1↑PARTS
[13]    BLANKS↑NAME;NUMBERS[1↑PARTS]
[14]    →ΔPARTS
[15] ENDΔPARTS:→0
      ∇
```

FIGURE 9.21. The output program.

The output from this latest version of the program is shown in Figure 9.22.

EXERCISES

9-15. Update CHECKUP to reflect the new data structures.

take   9-16. What does *take* do when the right-hand argument is numeric and has length less than the left-hand argument?

9-17. Would the calculation in FIND be made simpler if it was done in 0-origin indexing?

9-18. If space is important, we don't really need both columns of PLACES. Show that either column by itself would give us all the information we need.

9-19. A different way to handle the names is to place them in a vector, separated by some special symbol which is guaranteed not to appear in any name. To find the Nth name we have only to search for the locations of the (N—1)st and Nth occurrences of the special symbol. Use this method in place of the one given in the text: compare space requirements and running times.

9-20. The format of Figure 9.22 would be improved if all the low order digits of the various numbers appeared in the same column. Do this. (*Hint*: read Chapter 8.)

9-21. Include with each name a part number, separating the two by a special symbol. PRINTOUT should put the name and part number in different columns.

9-22. Revise the documentation you did in the previous section.

9-23. The problem of handling character strings of various lengths is sufficiently important that it deserves the creation of a package of utility programs to deal with it. There should be programs for adding an item, dropping an item, and finding the location of an item which is already in the list, as well as a version of FIND to retrieve items from the list. A program to list all the items would also be useful. Note that each modification of the list requires a corresponding modification in PLACES. After the package is completed and tested, prepare documentation on it and offer it to your public library.

```
     INVENTORY ← 0 0 1 0 0 0 0 2 0 0 0 1 0

     TOTALS 1
THE PARTS REQUIRED FOR PAPER CUTTER ARE:
HANDLE              1
BLADE               1
NO.2 SCREW          12
PAPER HOLDER        1

TOTALS 5
THE PARTS REQUIRED FOR LEG ARE:
RUBBER TIP       1
NO.5 SCREW       1
```

FIGURE 9.22. Using the program.

RECURSION

We already have all the building blocks for another useful report-generating program. An *indented bill of materials* is a report in the form of the two shown in Figure 9.23. It is an explosion of some assembly, with all subassemblies of the same level indented the same amount. In the first example the assembly being exploded is the paper cutter, which is listed as a first level assembly. Its direct constituents are second level assemblies and so on.

We used a similar bill of materials in Figure 9.1 to create the array <u>NEEDS</u> in the first place, but as the various models and subassemblies are changed in production the original bills of materials may become out of date. Thus, a program which can explode any assembly in this way can be a valuable tool.

Because the explosion required is similar to ones we have already done we will write the program in a different but equally natural way. Let us consider what the program which produces Figure 9.23 must do: different programs for the same general task may sometimes result from different ways of dividing the problem into small, manageable pieces. Suppose we say that "exploding a simple part" consists of printing its name. What then will it mean to explode an assembly, all of whose constituents are simple parts? This cannot mean simply printing the names of the constituents, as it would in the approach we used for TOTALS, as that would leave us without the name of the assembly itself. Rather, it must mean printing the name of the assembly and then exploding the constituents. The result of the two interpretations would surely be the same if we chose to do a little fiddling, but the latter is preferable as it uses the concept, which has already been defined, of exploding a part.

Now we have a well-defined notion of explosion:

To explode a part we print its name.

To explode an assembly we print its name and then explode it constituents.

This covers even the case where the constituents are not all simple parts, for if one happens to be an assembly we just apply the second part of the definition to it. Imagine that we had a program called EXPLODE to explode a part or assembly. The definition that we have would mean that EXPLODE had to call itself! For a part, EXPLODE would just print the part name. For an assembly, EXPLODE would print the assembly name and then EXPLODE each of the constituents.

It might seem at first that having a program call itself would yield a monster which would never stop growing. This could happen, but there is no reason for it to happen in this case since the process of having EXPLODE call itself within a call to itself within a call to itself... must

```
1. PAPER CUTTER
   2. ARM ASSEMBLY
      3. HANDLE
      3. BLADE
      3. NO. 2 SCREW
   2. BASE
      3. LEG
         4. RUBBER TIP
         4. NO. 5 SCREW
      3. CUTTING SURFACE
   2. GUIDE
      3. NO. 2 SCREW
      3. RULER
      3. PAPER HOLDER
   2. NO. 2 SCREW


1. ARM ASSEMBLY
   2. HANDLE
   2. BLADE
   2. NO. 2 SCREW
```

FIGURE 9.23. Indented bills of materials.

terminate when we reach a part, for then the calling process stops and backs up. For example, in Figure 9.23 when we explode the paper cutter we then explode the arm assembly which entails exploding the handle. The handle is a simple part so its name is printed and then we "back up" to the next constituent of the arm assembly and explode it. When we get to the No. 2 screw, and explode it, we again back up to the arm assembly. But this has no more constituents so we back up to the paper cutter and explode its next constituent, the base.

Another problem which could come up when a program calls itself is that some variable might be given one value in the calling version and a different value in the called version. When the called version finishes execution and control backs up to the calling version, which value does the variable have? Actually, there is no problem *if* the variable was local. For then it is no different from the situation where a different program was called. APL saves the value of the variable in the calling program, and restores it when control returns from the called program.

When a program calls itself, we say that it is *recursive*. There is nothing special that we have to do to make a program recursive in APL, except that we must make sure that there is a point at which the calls stop: in this case they stop when we reach a simple part, and we know that we must reach a simple part because of the properties of XNEEDS which are verified in CHECKUP.

Figure 9.24 shows a recursive program named INDENT which will produce the indented bill of materials report for an assembly. INDENT takes two arguments: LEVEL is the level number to be assigned to the part or assembly currently being exploded and UNIT is the number of that part or assembly. The name will be indented $3\times$LEVEL spaces and preceded by the level number. Line 5 is the control which makes the recursion terminate: if the item is a part, exit. Otherwise, in line 7 we find the constituents of the item and then, in the loop from lines 8 to 13, each constituent is exploded, one level deeper. It may be useful for you to try a hand simulation of the program, keeping track of all the variables.

Notice that the main loop in the program is different from others we have seen. Instead of adding to a variable and halting when the variable reaches a certain value, this loop control statement removes an element from a vector each time, stopping when the vector becomes empty.

The program INDENT does not contain any check on the validity of its arguments or of the global variables. We would not want to check the global variables each time through the program, so long as they are checked at least once and not subsequently changed. It is not necessary to check the arguments each time since the program will produce correct arguments in the call at line 10 if it is given correct arguments to start with. It is therefore logical to create a program to do the first call to INDENT, checking the variables and starting the ball rolling.

```
     ∇ LEVEL INDENT UNIT;NEWΔUNIT;CONSTITUENTS
[1]    ⍝-----RECURSIVE PROGRAM TO PRINT
[2]    ⍝------INDENTED BILL OF MATERIALS. CALLED
[3]    ⍝------FIRST BY STARTΔINDENT
[4]    ((3×LEVEL)ρ' ');LEVEL;'. ';FIND UNIT
[5]    →0 IF UNIT>XSHAPE[2]
[6]    ⍝------SO AS NOT TO EXPLODE SIMPLE PARTS
[7]    CONSTITUENTS←0,(XNEEDS[;2]=UNIT)/XNEEDS[;1]
[8]   ΔCONSTITUENTS:→ENDΔCONSTITUENTS WHEN 0=ρCONSTITUENTS←1↓CONSTITUENTS
[9]    NEWΔUNIT←1↑CONSTITUENTS
[10]   (LEVEL+1) INDENT NEWΔUNIT
[11]   ⍝-----EXPLODING NEWΔUNIT ONE LEVEL FURTHER INDENTED
[12]   →ΔCONSTITUENTS
[13] ENDΔCONSTITUENTS:→0
     ∇
```

FIGURE 9.24. Producing the indented bill.

STARTΔINDENT in Figure 9.25 is such a program. Its single argument is the major assembly being exploded. After calling CHECKUP, it then starts the process going in line 4 by calling INDENT, specifying level 1. Once INDENT gets control it begins to explode assemblies and doesn't return to STARTΔINDENT until it is done.

EXERCISES

9-24. Revise CHECKUP so that it will be suitable for the job it needs to do in STARTΔINDENT. In particular, make sure that the messages reflect that the program is being called by STARTΔ-INDENT, and not by TOTALS.

9-25. Revise STARTΔINDENT so that it prints the day on which the report is being generated.

9-26. Revise INDENT so that it also performs the function of TOTALS, giving the requirements for each assembly as well as its name.

9-27. What errors are likely to occur when using recursive programs? Can you use ERROR to shield against them?

9-28. Could TOTALS itself have been written recursively? If so, compare the running times of the two versions. If not, why not?

9-29. Could INDENT have been written nonrecursively? If so, compare the running times of the two versions. If not, why not?

9-30. Write a comprehensive reporting package using the building blocks we have already developed. The user should be able to ask for any number of different pieces of information, such as: the actual number of parts required, the number required when the inventory is empty or has some given value, indented bills of materials with or without parts requirements, etc.

9-31. How would you do Exercise 9-30 if you had to complete it as quickly as possible? How would you do it if you had to take up as little workspace as possible?

9-32. Except for recursive programs, a collection of programs is very much like a manufactured item. Use the program INDENT to prepare an indented bill of materials showing which programs in this chapter are called by which others (but exclude INDENT). INDENT is a special case since CHECKUP would reject XNEEDS if it showed INDENT as a constituent of INDENT. Redesign the system of programs so that we can include INDENT in the bill of materials (often called a *hierarchy chart*). We need only show INDENT as a constituent of itself once to establish that it is recursive, so the chart should show it only twice, and not as a constituent of itself which in turn is a constituent of itself which. . .

```
     ∇ START∆INDENT UNIT
[1]    ⍝-----PRODUCES INDENTED BILL OF MATERIALS
[2]    ⍝------BY CALLING INDENT
[3]    CHECKUP UNIT
[4]    1 INDENT UNIT
     ∇
```

FIGURE 9.25. Starting the recursion.

9-33. The scientist Leonard of Pisa, also called Fibonacci, studied the the breeding of rabbits in the thirteenth century. As an approximation he made the following simplifying assumptions: (a) rabbits never die; (b) one pair of rabbits (of opposite sex) produces as offspring a single pair consisting of a male and a female; (c) starting from the time that they are one month old, a pair of rabbits can produce a new pair at the end of every month. The result of the study is that if you start with a single newborn pair of rabbits, at the end of both the first and second months that is all you have. But then, after the third month you will have two pair, then three, then five, then eight, and so on. If f_n is the number of pairs of rabbits after n months, then $f_1 = f_2 = 1$, and for $n > 2$, $f_n = f_{n-1} + f_{n-2}$. Write both recursive and nonrecursive programs for finding the value of f_n and compare both their running times and the amount of workspace they require. (*Note*: when a recursive program is running it requires much more room than otherwise, because of all the versions of the program that APL must remember. One way to evaluate the amount of room required is to print out the amount of space remaining each time you enter the program. Another is to see just how big a vector you can leave sitting in the workspace when the program is running.)

DEPTH ERROR

9-34. What is DEPTH ERROR? Write a program which generates one. Devise a means of protecting against them.

9-35. With a very large bill of materials, having many levels, it might be necessary to indent more than the actual width of the page. Can you correct for this in some way inside the program? Can you correct it by changing the specifications (i.e., the definition of an indented bill of materials)? This is the final problem of the chapter; is it also the final problem in the program? How do you know?

10

Epilogue

"It is this, it is this that oppresses my soul,
    When I think of my uncle's last words:
And my heart is like nothing so much as a bowl
    Brimming over with quivering curds!

"It is this, it is this—" "We have had that before!"
    The Bellman indignantly said.
And the Baker replied, "Let me say it once more.
    It is this, it is this that I dread!

"I engage with the Snark—every night after dark—
    In a dreamy delirious fight:
I serve it with greens in those shadowy scenes
    And I use it for striking a light;

"But if ever I meet with a Boojum, that day,
    In a moment (of this I am sure),
I shall softly and silently vanish away—
    And the notion I cannot endure!"

There is still more to programming than we have been able to cover. In this last chapter we try to present some directions for further study. We have concentrated mostly on programming itself, and will continue to do so. There is, however, a great deal to be learned about the things that get programmed as well. For almost any task or algorithm that you want to program there have been many people who studied and wrote about problems which were similar enough to be helpful to you. A good example of this is sorting. The bubble sort algorithm which we looked at in Chapter 6 is relatively easy to program and is therefore efficient of programmer time. However, it requires many comparisons and is inefficient of machine time. In many applications it is important to sort large amounts of data quickly and many algorithms have been devised which are faster than the bubble sort. There are many sources which discuss and compare algorithms of various types: the most complete is probably the seven volume series *The Art of Computer Programming* by Donald E. Knuth (Addison-Wesley) an excellent, although difficult, study of many different types of algorithms, including techniques for programming them.

APL

APL is an extremely powerful language. This power stems from a number of factors: the fact that it is terminal-oriented, the simplicity of the system commands, the fact that it can be used in calculator mode and the variety of its operators. We have deliberately underemphasized the operators, for this reason: anything which can be done with a combination of operators can also be done as a program with decisions and repetitions. As you learn more about APL you will be more and more able to replace many lines of program with single APL expressions, but there will always be cases where the operators themselves will not suffice and you will have to fall back on making explicit choices and on looping.

Now that you can write programs though, if you intend to make much use of APL you should develop more facility with the operators. The experimental approach in Chapter 3 will still prove to be a useful one: try to make up tasks for yourself to do using certain operators, and then try to do them. This is the equivalent of the typical assignment in a language course, "make up a sentence using each of these words." It may prove to be just as painful at first, but really will result in an expanded working vocabulary.

Another good way to learn the language is to read in it. Find examples of APL programs and try to understand what they do. If you use a source like the public libraries there will be many programs of varying quality. If you read them closely you will certainly find a number of bad practices (such as branching to absolute line numbers) and should not be surprised, during your careful reading, to find that many of the programs will fail to work properly in certain situations. However, in most of these cases the errors will probably not be in the use of operators (which you are trying to learn) but in tying the program logic together (which you already know how to do). These errors should not deter you and may in fact, prove to be instructive in themselves. Reading programs will prove to be one of the best ways there is to learn programming.

It can be very useful to have a "pocket dictionary" when learning new operators. There is probably a reference manual which goes along with your system, and if you don't already have a copy you should get one. However, the reference manual may not be even approximately pocket size; in this case, you will probably find the *APL/360 Reference Manual* by Sandra Pakin (Chicago: Science Research Associates, Inc., 1972) to be a valuable reference, even if your system if not exactly like APL/360 (one of the APL systems supplied by IBM).

OTHER LANGUAGES

Since APL is very much different from most of the other commonly available programming languages it seems fair to devote a few minutes to them. Most of the other languages are based on an "English-like" format. A program is built up of statements which are similar to English in having "nouns" and "verbs." This analogy should not be pushed too far, but it is useful in comparison with APL. APL also has "nouns" and "verbs," but does not have the same concept of a statement. In APL you can put together as many "verbs" and "nouns" (operators and data structures) as you can fit on one line, or fewer if you so desire. The other languages have, for the most part, rather fixed formats: there are statement forms in which you can insert variable names or expressions. One typical example of this is the statement

DO I = 1 TO 10;

This is a statement which forms the control for a loop, and says that the statements which make up the loop will be performed ten times, with the variable I getting the values 1,2,...,10 in succession. The words DO and TO and the equal sign are fixed in place; any variable name can appear where the I is, and any variable name, number or expression can replace the 1 or the 10.

Instead of the wealth of operators that APL gives us, these other languages provide *control structures*. There are specific statement forms for looping and for decisions. They have the advantage of making it easier to learn all about the language, and of restricting the number of substantially different ways that things can be done. In fact, the forms we used for process boxes in our structure charts were in part motivated by the statement forms of some of these languages.

The three most common languages in the United States (especially in university computing environments) are probably FORTRAN, COBOL and PL/I. Each of these comes in many slightly different dialects. There are also some languages, like Algol, which are more popular in other countries. If you have the chance to learn a new language, and if you have a choice as to which one, we recommend PL/I. PL/I is, in its own way, a rich and complex language; probably you will never learn more than a fraction of what it offers, but having learned that you will have tremendous computing power available to you and you should find it easy to learn any of the other languages at some future time.

One dialect of PL/I that we recommend if you can find it is PL/C. This is a student-oriented version which omits some of the more complicated features but which provides special aids for finding and detecting bugs. Even if PL/C is not available to you, you will probably find either of these two books helpful as you learn PL/I (possibly in connection with a "straight PL/I" book if you aren't working on PL/C):

R. Conway and D. Gries, *An Introduction to Programming: A Structured Approach Using PL/I and PL/C* (Cambridge, Mass.: Winthrop Publishers, 1973).

G. Weinberg, N. Yasukawa, R. Marcus, *Structured Programming in PL/C: An Abecedarian* (New York: John Wiley and Sons, 1973).

STRUCTURED PROGRAMMING

Perhaps, in closing, we should mention something about the mysterious phrase "structured programming," which appears in the title, but nowhere else. At the time this book is being written there is still some controversy about exactly what structured programming is. But there is no disagreement about the fact that it is valuable.

We prefer to think of it as an attitude, rather than a collection of techniques: according to one of the leaders in the field, structured programming is common sense programming. Programming is different from most other human endeavors in that we can never really escape the fine details. Most things that we do which, like programming, involve building large structures from small ones allow us at some point to leave the details of the small structures behind forever. This may be because of the nature of the tasks or because we know how to do them better. But with programming it seems that we cannot simply progress from the small to the large. It is very common for a programmer to return to a program that was written a month (or a day) previously and to find it a mystery: "Let's see, what does that variable represent? And how did I get to this part of the program? And when does this loop terminate? Wow! I must have been half asleep when I wrote this—I don't remember anything."

Programmers have often tended to program as though, once they wrote down a piece of code, they would be done with it. This, however, is simply not the way it has usually worked out. When engineers build a bridge they can usually build a stanchion and then, with confidence, decide that it is done and will support the necessary loads, and then forget it. Programmers have no books of tables or formulae to tell them when a routine is done and will do what it is supposed to do. Even worse, the programmer's customer (who may be the programmer) has a tendency to change the requirements in drastic ways—not unlike deciding that a half-finished bridge should be made over into a tunnel.

Structured programming is the general name which is being used for all the techniques which programmers are compiling to make programming easier and, at the same time, more reliable. One large part of structured programming is writing programs from structure charts: not everyone uses these charts, but most programmers are now using the basic constructs—sequence, looping, and choice—to build their programs. Another important principle which is associated with structured programming is that we should write small programs, using subroutines as needed, rather than very large programs.

We have tried to suggest that about 25 lines is a reasonable length for an APL program. It may (we hope) seem obvious to you, but the fact that as programs get larger the effects of errors can propagate further and further from their source and be harder and harder to find, is still a revelation to some programmers. Programs which get very large have other undesirable effects as well. When you make a change in a program you should certainly get a new listing to refer to and to protect you against loss due to system failure. It is reasonable to list a 15–25 line program many times in one session at the terminal, but a 100 line program is likely to never be listed at all, so that the more work that you put into it, the less the actual program corresponds to your last listing.

A measure of the newness of the whole programming business is that there is still controversy over whether to use names (for variables and labels and programs) that are meaningful or meaningless. One side argues that meaningless names, such as XXX or XBGY, make programs impossibly difficult to read; the other points out that calling a variable LASTBLANK may make it clear that it was intended to represent the last blank, or its location, but that this does not mean that it actually *does* represent the last blank; calling a variable ZERO does not mean that its value must be 0. In fact, an entire draft of this book was written in which the variable names were all meaningless; on retrospect we found it wiser to use names that were not only meaningful, but also relevant to the problem (CURRENT instead of INDEX as the name for a loop index in Chapter 6, for example), and to strive to use names that did not mislead the reader of the program.

Basically, structured programming comprises both a number of common sense principles, many of which were not common sense until someone's flash of insight pointed them out to us, and also new techniques which are just beginning to be articulated to help insure the reliability of programs.

In this book we have not tried to teach you *about* structured programming. We have settled for presenting examples of well-structured programs. We did not tell you what not to do, because the reasons for not doing it are not always clear until one has had experience with programming, and to do so would have taken us far off our track. It can be very useful to see examples of practices which can cause trouble, and of alternatives which avoid it: an excellent (and inexpensive!) collection of bad and good programming examples is *The Elements of Programming Style* by Brian W. Kernighan and P. J. Plauger (New York: McGraw-Hill, 1974).

If all of structured programming were to be summarized in one word, it might well be *design*. While one can, of course, design poorly, or design well but then not follow that design, one of the main problems in programming has always been confusing the algorithm with the program. In APL, for example, we have had to create special forms because the language did not provide us with built in analogues of the repetition and choice process blocks of the structure chart. But by proceeding *from* the structure chart (the design) *to* the program we were able to create programs which clearly represented the algorithms; simply separating the phase of struggling with the idiosyncrasies of APL from the phase of struggling with the idiosyncrasies of the problem made our task significantly easier.

Therefore, *design*. It will help reduce the complexity of the programming process, so that you can write correct programs with less total effort. It also serves as a good description of the program: once you have written a correct program you may need to be concerned about other factors, such as making it run faster or squeezing it into less workspace. Or, it may be necessary to make changes to the program after it is written. In any of these activities, a good design serves as a good road map, helping you see what places need to be changed and what other places will be affected. In architecture or engineering the first step is always the careful preparation of a design, usually based on previous design sketches. Programming is an equally complex and important intellectual activity, and deserves the same sort of careful systematic approach.

Appendix One

Error Messages

The error messages on the following pages are grouped according to their most probable cause. The list below is an alphabetized cross reference to their order in the following pages.

ERRORS ASSOCIATED WITH SYSTEM COMMANDS

Signing On

1 *ALREADY SIGNED ON* — Someone is using this terminal. If it isn't you, and you need the terminal, try to find the user. If that is impossible, sign off with *)CONTINUE HOLD*.

2 *INCORRECT SIGN ON* — You probably made a mistake in the form of the command, although if you just turned the terminal on the computer may have rejected a perfectly correct sign on. Try again.

3 *NUMBER IN USE* — Someone else is using this number. The operator can find out who really owns the number and where the other user is.

4 *NUMBER NOT IN SYSTEM* — Either the number really isn't in the system or the number has a lock on it and the wrong lock was used.

5 *NUMBER LOCKED OUT* — Someone with the power to do so has told the computer not to accept this number. Find out who, and why.

Load or Copy

6 *OBJECT NOT FOUND* — The indicated workspace does not contain the particular object requested.

7 *WS NOT FOUND* — The workspace requested could not be found.

8 *WS LOCKED* — The requested workspace has a lock which was not given correctly.

9 *WS FULL* — The active workspace was filled by the material being copied before the copy could be completed. *Note*: A partially copied function may put the workspace into definition mode.

Save

10 *NOT SAVED, WS QUOTA USED UP*   You have already saved as many different workspaces as you are allowed. You can put this one into CONTINUE or try to incorporate it into one of your other workspaces, until you can get your quota increased.

11 *NOT SAVED, THIS IS* WSID   The active workspace has a name which precludes its being saved. It might be unnamed, or you might have loaded a public library workspace into it, so that it has a name which cannot appear in your library, or you might have used the form of the SAVE command where you gave the name of the workspace explicitly and the name you gave didn't match the actual name.

12 *IMPROPER LIBRARY REFERENCE*   Attempt to save a workspace whose name indicates that it came from a public library or the library of another user. Use WSID command to change the name.

Other Activities

13 *NOT WITH OPEN DEFINITION*   You are in definition mode and tried to do something which can't be done then. Close definition mode and try again.

14 *IMPROPER LIBRARY REFERENCE*   You tried to SAVE, DROP or LIB for some library belonging to another user or the public libraries.

15 *MESSAGE LOST*   You were sending a message, but signaled attention before the message could be delivered. Try again and wait for the signal SENT.

16	*SI DAMAGE*	A function which is pending has been erased or copied. Clear the state indicator.
17	*NOT ERASED*: NAMES	The items listed could not be erased; probably, they are functions which are either pending or in definition mode.
18	*NOT GROUPED, NAME IN USE*	The name you tried to use was not legal as a group name because it was already being used for a function or variable.

ERRORS ASSOCIATED WITH USING APL

Grammatical

19	*SYNTAX*	Incorrectly formed expression: likely possibility is that a name is being used with too many or too few arguments.
20	*VALUE*	A value has not been assigned to a variable or is not being returned from a function invocation.
21	*DOMAIN*	An operator is being used with invalid arguments.
22	*INDEX*	Attempt to find nonexistent element of a vector or array.
23	*LENGTH*	Attempt to combine arrays or vectors which are not conformable.
24	*RANK*	Something about the structure of a data item precludes its being used in this context.

Functions

| 25 | *DEFN* | Improper attempt to define or edit a function (name may already be in use, improper number of arguments, function is pending) or use of del in unexpected context. *Note*: Once a function has been created, to enter definition mode give only the name after the del, not all of line 0. |

26	*DEPTH*	Too many levels of a function calling a function calling a function. . . Try to clear state indicator.
27	*SI DAMAGE*	A function which is pending has had its header line or a line with a label on it changed, or has been erased or copied. Can also occur when a function which is pending but not at the top of the SI list is changed in any way.

Other Errors

28	*CHARACTER*	Improper overstruck character.
29	*SYMBOL TABLE FULL*	There are too many different names in this workspace. The problem can be corrected with the SYMBOLS command.
30	*SYSTEM*	An error that APL couldn't handle. Some mysterious numbers will be printed and the workspace will be cleared. Bring all of this to the computer center APL staff.
31	*NONSE*	Short for nonsense. APL's catchall when it knows something is wrong, but doesn't know what.

Appendix Two

System Commands

The various commands are grouped by function. The list below is an alphabetical cross reference to their order in the following pages.

Items in brackets are optional. When a range is shown, as)*DIGITS* 1–16, any integer in the indicated range may be used: DIGITS may be set to any of the values 1, 2, ..., 16.

GETTING ON AND OFF

1	)NUMBER[:LOCK]	Sign on.
2	)*CONTINUE*	Ends the session and stores the active workspace in CONTINUE.
3	)*CONTINUE HOLD*	Same as CONTINUE, but holds the phone connection.
4	)*OFF*[:LOCK]	Ends the session. If lock is given, it replaces previous lock.
5	)*OFF HOLD* [:LOCK]	Same as OFF, but holds the phone connection.

GETTING THINGS IN AND OUT OF A WORKSPACE

6	)*COPY* WSID[:LOCK]	Copies all objects from workspace WSID to your active workspace.
7	)*COPY* WSID[:LOCK] NAME	Copies object NAME from workspace WSID to your active workspace.
8	)*ERASE* NAME(S)	Erases all named objects from your active workspace.
9	)*PCOPY* WSID[:LOCK]	Same as COPY, but will not copy from WSID an object with the same name as an object already in your active workspace.
10	)*PCOPY* WSID[:LOCK] NAME	Asks that object NAME be copied from workspace WSID if there is no object in your active workspace also named NAME.

MOVING WORKSPACES

11	)*DROP* WSID	Deletes the saved workspace WSID. Has no effect on active workspace.

12	)*LOAD* WSID[:LOCK]	Replaces the active workspace by a copy of the stored workspace WSID.
13	)*SAVE*	Active workspace replaces stored workspace with same name.
14	)*SAVE* WSID[:LOCK]	Saves the active workspace under the name WSID.

AFFECTING THE CONTENTS OF A WORKSPACE

15	)*CLEAR*	Replaces active workspace with clear workspace.
16	)*DIGITS* 1–16	Sets the number of digits which APL will display when it prints numbers.
17	)*GROUP* NAME LIST	All the objects in LIST are grouped under the name NAME.
18	)*GROUP* NAME	Removes the group association from the objects which formed group NAME.
19	)*ORIGIN* 0–1	Sets the index ORIGIN to the value given.
20	)*SYMBOL* NUMBER	Sets the size of the symbol table: this has a direct effect on the total number of different names which you can have in your workspace.
21	)*WIDTH* 30–130	Sets the width of the maximum length line which APL will print.
22	)*WSID* NAME	Gives a name to the active workspace.

FINDING OUT ABOUT THE CONTENTS OF A WORKSPACE

23	)*FNS* [LETTER]	Lists all the program (function) names in the active workspace in alphabetical order [beginning with those whose first letter is LETTER].
24	)*GRP* NAME	Lists objects belonging to group NAME.

25	)*GRPS* [LETTER]	Lists names of all groups [beginning with those whose first letter is LETTER].
26	)*SI*	Displays the state indicator, the list of pending functions.
27	)*SIV*	Same as)SI, but for each function listed shows the names of all its local variables.
28	)*VARS* [LETTER]	Lists all the variables in the active workspace [beginning with those whose first letter is LETTER].
29	)*WSID*	Gives the name of the active workspace.

MISCELLANEOUS

30	)*LIB*	Lists names of all stored workspaces.
31	)*LIB* NUMBER	Lists names of all stored workspaces in designated public library.
32	)*MSG* PORT TEXT	Sends the message TEXT to port (terminal) indicated: your keyboard locks up until response comes.
33	)*MSGN* PORT TEXT	Same as MSG except that your keyboard does not lock.
34	)*OPR* TEXT	Like MSG except that message is sent to APL operator.
35	)*OPRN* TEXT	Like MSGN except that message is sent to APL operator.
36	)*PORTS*	Lists port (terminal) numbers and some identification of user signed on at each (this may be first three letters of last name, for example).

Appendix Three

Dictionary of Operators

This is a fairly, but not absolutely, complete dictionary of the operators: like a dictionary it cross-references other entries and uses examples when they are clearer than definitions. Some of the operators can be extremely complex: in such cases the full abilities are not discussed completely, only hinted at. Two important terms are redefined below, as are the three operators on operators: reduction, inner product, and outer product. The headings under the name of each operator give a summary of the operators' important characteristics. First, whether the operator is scalar or mixed. Second, whether it is dyadic or monadic. Third, what types of arguments it allows, such as numeric, character, integer, or any: an entry such as "integer/any" indicates that the left argument must be integer, but the right argument is unrestricted.

ORIGIN All indexing operations, including subscripting and use of the operator iota, deal with integers; the indices always begin at the origin and increase in steps of 1. The origin can be set to be 1 or 0 (the default value is 1) and its value affects the results of a number of operators, as indicated in the definitions.

COORDINATES Any data structure with dimension greater than 1 has many coordinates—as many as its dimension. A matrix has two coordinates: the rows and the columns. More specifically, the components of the first coordinate are the rows and the components of the last coordinate are the columns. In higher dimensional arrays, the last coordinate still references columns, but the first coordinate will not be the rows. A number of operation on arrays normally are defined in terms of their action on the last coordinate, but may be modified by insertion of $\lfloor K \rfloor$ after the operator sign to act on the Kth coordinate instead.

COMBINATIONS OF PRIMITIVE OPERATORS

Let F and G represent two primitive operators.

REDUCTION If V is a vector, (F/V) has the same value as $V[1] FV[2] FV[3] F...FV[\rho V]$. For V a higher dimensional array, action is along the last coordinate (i.e., on entire columns) unless specified otherwise.

INNER PRODUCT For A and B vectors, AF·GB is F/AGB. When the arguments have higher dimension, elements of the result are formed by combining components of each argument: for example, if A and B are both dimension 2, an element of the result is the inner product of a row of A with a column of B.

OUTER PRODUCT A∘. FB is formed by applying F to each component of A on the left and each component of B on the right. Its dimension is always the sum of the dimensions of A and B. For example, if F is multiplication, the results gives each component of A multiplied with each component of B; when A and B are vectors, "component" means element, but as the dimensions grow a component is one of the entities determined by a coordinate (as the last coordinate determines the columns).

SCALAR OPERATORS

+

ADDITION, SUM
Scalar, dyadic, numeric
    Does just what you think.

+

IDENTITY
Scalar, monadic, numeric
    Has no effect on its argument.

-

SUBTRACTION
Scalar, dyadic, numeric
    No surprises.

-

NEGATION
Scalar, monadic, numeric
    Examples:

```
          - 5
  ‾5
          - ‾3
  3
```

×

MULTIPLICATION
Scalar, dyadic, numeric
    Does multiplication.

×

SIGNUM
Scalar, monadic, numeric
    Yields ‾1, 0 or 1 depending
    on whether the argument is
    negative, zero or positive.

÷

DIVISION
Scalar, dyadic, numeric
    A÷B is A divided by B.
    (0÷0) is 1.
    Any other division by 0
    is an error.

÷

RECIPROCAL
Scalar, monadic, numeric
    (÷B) is the same as (1÷B).
    The argument cannot be 0.

⌊   (D)

MINIMUM
Scalar, dyadic, numeric
    Yields the smaller of
    its arguments:

```
     3⌊5
  3
       4⌊4
  4
```

⌊   (D)

FLOOR
Scalar, monadic, numeric
    Yields the largest integer
    which is less than or equal
    to the argument:

```
     ⌊6.3
  6
       ⌊‾2.7
  ‾3
```

⌈   (*S*)

MAXIMUM
Scalar, dyadic, numeric
    Yields the larger of its
    arguments:
        3⌈5
  5
        4⌈4
  4

⌈   (*S*)

CEILING
Scalar, monadic, numeric
    Yields the smallest integer
    which is greater than or
    equal to the argument:
        ⌈6.3
  7
        ⌈⁻2.3
  ⁻2

| (*M*)

MODULUS, RESIDUE
Scalar, dyadic, numeric
    (A|B) is the smallest num-
    ber r between 0 and A–1
    such that (B–r) is an integer
    multiple of A. If A is 0, B
    must be nonnegative, and
    the result is B:
        3|5
  2
        2.6|6.6
  1.4

| (*M*)

ABSOLUTE VALUE
Scalar, monadic, numeric
    (|B) is the same as (B⌈–B):
        |3.3
  3.3
        |⁻4
  4

!   (.   *K*)

COMBINATION, CHOOSE
Scalar, dyadic, numeric
    (A!B) is the number
    of combinations of B
    things taken A at a time,
    when A and B are integers.
    In all cases, the same as:
    (!B)÷((!A)×!(B–A))

!   (.   *K*)

FACTORIAL
Scalar, monadic, numeric
    (!B) is B×(B–1)×...×2×1
    if B is a positive integer, 1
    when B is 0, and an error if
    B is a negative integer. For
    any other values of B the
    result is the value of a
    mathematical function
    called the gamma function.

Note: Dyadic *?* is a mixed operator.

?   (Q)

ROLL, RANDOM
Scalar, monadic, numeric
> For a positive integer B, the result of (*?* B) is a randomly selected element of the vector ιB:
> > *?* 5

3
> > *?* 5

2

~   (T)

NOT, TILDE
Scalar, monadic, logical
> Logical negation:
> > ~0

1
> > ~1

0

*   (P)

EXPONENTIATION
Scalar, dyadic, numeric
> Just what you think of by exponentiation:
> > 3 * 2

9
> > 2 * 3

8

Except
> > 0 * 0

1

And, for (A * B) to be defined: If A is 0, B is nonnegative; if A is negative, B must be the quotient of an integer and an odd integer.

*   (P)

EXPONENTIAL
Scalar, monadic, numeric
> (* B) is the same as (e * B) where e is the mathematical constant whose value is approximately 2.7182818285.

⊛ (O,P)

LOGARITHM
Scalar, dyadic, positive
  (A⊛B) is the logarithm of B
  to the base A, equal to
  ((⊛B)÷A). A and B are both
  positive and A cannot be 1
  unless B is also 1.

⊛ (O,P)

NATURAL LOGARITHM
Scalar, monadic, positive
  (⊛B) is the logarithm of
  B to the base e, where e
  is approximately
  2.7182818285. B must be
  positive.

○ (O)

CIRCULAR
Scalar, dyadic, integer/numeric
  (A○B) is one of 15 functions of B, as determined
  by A. For certain non-
  positive values of A there
  are restrictions on B, as
  shown:

○ (O)

PI TIMES
Scalar, monadic, numeric
  Multiplies its argument
  by Pi, approximately
  3.14159265.

FUNCTION	A	A	FUNCTION	NOTES
		0	$(1-B*2)*.5$	$B\leq 1$
sine	1	‾1	arc sine	$1\geq |B$
cosine	2	‾2	arc cosine	$1\geq |B$
tangent	3	‾3	arc tangent	
$(1+B*2)*.5$	4	‾4	$(‾1+B*2)*.5$	$1\leq |B$
sinh	5	‾5	arc sinh	
cosh	6	‾6	arc cosh	$B\geq 1$
tanh	7	‾7	arc tanh	$1> |B$

Note: The functions ending in h (sinh, arc tanh, etc.) are the hyper-
bolic trigonometric functions and their inverses.

>   (7)

GREATER THAN
Scalar, dyadic, numeric
  (A>B) is 1 if A is greater
  than B, 0 otherwise.

≥   (6)

GREATER THAN OR EQUAL TO
Scalar, dyadic, numeric
>   (A ≥B) is 1 if A is greater than
>   or equal to B, 0 otherwise.

≤   (4)

LESS THAN OR EQUAL TO
Scalar, dyadic, numeric
>   (A ≤B) is 1 if A is less than or
>   equal to B, 0 otherwise.

<   (3)

LESS THAN
Scalar, dyadic, numeric
>   (A<B) is 1 if A is less than B,
>   0 otherwise.

=   (5)

EQUAL TO
Scalar, dyadic, any
>   (A=B) is 1 if A equals B, 0
>   otherwise.

≠   (8)

NOT EQUAL TO
Scalar, dyadic, any
>   (A≠B) is 1 if A is not equal
>   to B, and 0 if A is equal to B.

∧   (0)

AND
Scalar, dyadic, logical
>   (A∧B) is defined by the table:

		A	
		0	1
B	0	0	0
	1	0	1

∨   (9)

OR
Scalar, dyadic, logical
 (A∨B) is defined by the table:

		A	
		0	1
B	0	0	1
	1	1	1

⍲   (0 , T)

NAND
Scalar, dyadic, logical
 (A⍲B) is defined by the table:

		A	
		0	1
B	0	1	1
	1	1	0

⍱   (9 , T)

NOR
Scalar, dyadic, logical
 (A⍱B) is defined by the table:

		A	
		0	1
B	0	1	0
	1	0	0

MIXED OPERATORS

ρ   (R)

RESHAPE
Mixed, dyadic, integer/any
 (AρB) is a structure with size
 A made up of the elements
 of B; A is a vector (possibly
 empty) of nonnegative
 integers.

ρ   (R)

SIZE, SHAPE
Mixed, monadic, any
 Yields the vector giving
 the size of its argument.

ι (I) ι (I)

INDEX   **INDEX GENERATOR**

Mixed, dyadic, any/any   Mixed, monadic, integer

(AιB) has size (ρB). A must   (ιB) is a vector of B suc-

be a vector. Each element   cessive integers, starting

of the result is the location   with the origin:

of the first occurrence in   ι3 [1 origin]

A of the corresponding   1 2 3

element of B. "Non-   ι5 [0 origin]

occurrence" is indicated by   0 1 2 3 4

the value 1+(ρA):

          (9 17 15)ι(2,3)ρ9 17 11 15 6 28

1   2   4

3   4   4

Note: In 0 origin the result
would have been:

0   1   3

2   3   3

φ   (O,M)

ROTATION

Mixed, dyadic, integer/any

(AφB) is like B except that the elements (for B a vector) or columns (for B an array) are rotated A "steps": to the left if A is positive, to the right if A is negative. If B is an array, A may be a scalar or may have dimension one less than B. If A is not a scalar its different elements indicate how to rotate the columns *within* a given row:

```
      3φ1 2 3 4 5 6 7
4 5 6 7 1 2 3
      ¯3φ'CORNPOP'
POPCORN
      (2 ¯3)φ(2,4)ρ'PSLI'
LIPS
SLIP
```

Note: We can also specify Aφ[K]B to rotate along the Kth coordinate; see *coordinates*.

φ   (O,M)

REVERSAL

Mixed, monadic, any

(φB) has the same shape as B. The elements (for B a vector) or columns (for B an array) are reversed:

```
      φ'KRANS'
SNARK
      φ(2,3)ρ1 2 3 4 5 6
3 2 1
6 5 4
```

Note: Can specify φ[K]B to reverse along the Kth coordinate; see *coordinates*.

↑   (*Y*)

TAKE
Mixed, dyadic, integer/any
>   (A↑B) specifies a structure
>   which is made up of some
>   elements of B. If A is a scalar,
>   B is a vector; if A is a vector
>   its size must be equal to the
>   dimension of B. Each element
>   of A corresponds to a coordi-
>   nate of B and specifies the
>   number of components of B
>   to be taken from the front
>   (A> 0) or back (A≤ 0). Should
>   there not be sufficient com-
>   ponents in a coordinate of B,
>   zeros (for B numeric) or
>   blanks (for B character) are
>   added:

```
        3↑1 2 3 4 5 6
1 2 3
       ‾2↑'123456'
56
        7↑1 2 3 4 5 6
1 2 3 4 5 6 0
       ‾7↑'123456'
b123456
        (2 3)↑(3,4)ρι12
1 2 3
5 6 7
        (‾2 ‾2)↑(3,4)ρι12
   7   8
11 12
```

↓   (*U*)

DROP
Mixed, dyadic, integer/any
>   Similar to take except that
>   the left argument specifies a
>   number of components to be
>   dropped:

```
        3↓1 2 3 4 5 6
4 5 6
       ‾2↓1 2 3 4 5 6
1 2 3 4
```

,

CONCATENATION, LAMINATION
Mixed, dyadic, any/any

(A,B) is formed by "attaching" B to A. If neither A nor B has dimension greater than 1 the result is a vector where the elements of A precede those of B. In general, the form (A,[K]B) specifies that A and B are to be joined along the Kth coordinate. For A and B to be conformable their dimensions must not differ by more than one, unless one is a scalar. If the dimensions are not equal, the one with the smaller dimension is restructured to be like the other, with a unit Kth coordinate. K can also be non-integer. The result is then a structure whose dimension is one greater than the larger of the dimensions of the arguments. The extra dimension is the ($\lceil$K)th. It has two possible indices—the first gives A and the second gives B:

,

RAVEL
Mixed, monadic, any

Produces a vector with the same elements as the argument.

CONCATENATION (continued)

```
            (1 2 3),(4 5 6)
1 2 3 4 5 6
            5,(2,2)ρι4
5 1 2
5 3 4
            5,[1](2,2)ρι4
5 5
1 2
3 4
            ((2,3)ρ'BIGBOY'),(2,3)ρ'TOPCAT'
BIGTOP
BOYCAT
            ((2,3)ρ'BIGBOY'),[.5]ρ'TOPCAT'
BIG
BOY

TOP
CAT
```

⍉ $(O,/)$

DYADIC TRANSPOSE
Mixed, dyadic, integer/any
   (A⍉B) can function in two
   different ways. A may
   specify a permutation of
   coordinates of B:
       2 1 ⍉(2,2)ρ'*HBOO*'
HO
BO

Or A may specify that a
structure of dimension lower
than B is to be formed. Coordinates of the result are
formed from elements of B
for which certain specified
coordinate indices are equal
(such coordinates are specified
by having the corresponding
elements of A be equal):
      1 1⍉(3,3)ρι9
1 5 9

Note: In either case the size
of A must be equal to the
dimension of B.

⍉ $(O,/)$

MONADIC TRANSPOSE
Mixed, monadic, any
   For a matrix B, (⍉B)
   interchanges rows and
   columns of B:
      ⍉(2,4)ρι8
1 5
2 6
3 7
4 8

For an array of dimension
greater than 2, the last two
coordinates are transposed.

/

COMPRESS

Mixed, dyadic, logical/any

(A/B) selects from B those
components that correspond
to unit elements of A:

        0 1 1 0 1 0 0/'CAPULET'
APL

With array right arguments
compression usually acts to
select whole columns:

        1 0 0/(3,3)ρι9
1
4
7

However, different coordinates
can be specified; see *coordinates*.

        1 0 0/[1](3,3)ρι9
1 2 3

\

EXPAND

Mixed, dyadic, logical/any

The right argument is expanded
by inserting zeros (for numeric
data) or blanks (for character
data) in places corresponding
to zeros on the left:

        1 0 1 1 1\'OSAY'
O SAY

        0 0 1 0\5
0 0 5 0

        1 0 1 1\(2,3)ρι6
1 0 2 3
4 0 5 6

Expansion along other coordinates than the last can be
specified; see *coordinates*.

$$\top \qquad (N)$$

ENCODE

Mixed, dyadic, numeric/numeric
(A$\top$B) represents the right
argument in a form defined
by the left argument. For
example, to express 25
inches as feet and inches,
write:

```
      3  12T25
2  1
```

If there were more than three
feet (= one yard, the only
reason for putting a three on
the left) in the right hand
argument that information
would have been lost:

```
      3  12T38
0  2
         2  3  12T38
1  0  2
```

For arguments of higher
dimension than vectors the
result is an array in which
coordinates are encodings of
components of B according to
components of A. The dimension of the result is always
the sum of the dimensions of
the arguments.

⊥   (B)

DECODE

Mixed, dyadic, numeric/numeric

This is effectively the inverse operator to encode:

        3 12⊥2 1
    25
        1 3 12⊥1 0 2
    38

Of course, decode cannot restore information which might have been lost by encode:

        3 12⊥(3 12⊤38)
    2

The arguments are conformable if one is a scalar or if the last coordinate (number of columns) on the left is equal to the first coordinate on the right.

?   (Q)

RANDOM

Mixed, dyadic, integer

(A?B) is a vector of A elements chosen at random from the integers (ιB); A must be less than or equal to B.

        4?6
    2 5 1 3
        4?4
    1 4 3 2

⍋   (H , M)

GRADE UP

Mixed, monadic, numeric

Gives the order in which the elements of the argument should be taken to put them in ascending order:

        ⍋4 5 1 2 1
    3 5 4 1 2

⍒   (G , M)

GRADE DOWN

Mixed, monadic, numeric

Gives the order in which the elements of the argument should be taken to put them in descending order:

        ⍒4 5 1 2 1
    2 1 5 3 4

∈   (E)

MEMBERSHIP
Mixed, dyadic, any/any
The size of (A∈B) is the
same as that of A: an
element has value 1 if the
corresponding element of
A appears someplace in
B; otherwise, it has value 0.

⊞   (L,÷)

MATRIX DIVISION
Mixed, dyadic, numeric/numeric

⊟   (L,÷)

MATRIX INVERSE
Mixed, monadic, numeric

The monadic form performs the mathematical operation
of inverting a matrix; the dyadic form solves systems of
linear equations defined by the arguments. Detailed discussion is somewhat outside the scope of this book.

I   (B,N)

I-BEAM
The I-beam, as an operator which deals with system functions,
is the most likely to be completely different on different
systems: some systems do not even have the I-beam, but do
have other ways of accomplishing the same functions. You
should treat the list here with skepticism: find out what your
system uses for similar system commands. Just for the sake of
pointing out the variety of the I-beam, we describe two of the
dyadic I-beams which have been made available to users on
certain systems.

Monadic:
I19   The amount of time the keyboard has been unlocked
      during the current session (60ths of a second).
20   Time of day (60ths of a second).
21   CPU time since sign on (60ths of a second).
22   Remaining unused workspace (in bytes: a byte is
      the amount of room taken by a character; integers
      take up four bytes, logical numbers (0,1) take up
      one-eighth byte and other numbers take up eight
      bytes).
23   Number of users currently signed on.
24   Amount of time since you signed on (60ths of a second).
25   The date.

26   The number of the program line now being run (if there is a program running).

27   The vector of the line numbers of all the pending functions.

28   A code denoting the type of terminal you are using.

29   Your sign-on number.

5IN   Causes a time delay of N 300ths of a second.

14IC   Causes the character vector C to be printed. (1) This will cause C to be printed even if it is longer than the WIDTH, a useful feature when you want to print lines with many backspacings and overprintings; (2) After the line is printed, the carriage does not return and the 14 I-beam returns as a value the empty vector.

6I0,N   Sets ORIGIN to N.

1,N   Sets seed to N.

2,N   Sets DIGITS to N.

3,N   Sets WIDTH to N.

4,N   Sets fuzz to N.

Appendix Four

Utility Functions

This appendix contains the three utility functions, IF; ERROR and WHEN. If they are not already available on your system you should enter them into your workspace.

```
     ∇ Z←LABEL IF CONDITION
[1]    'IF:CONDITION RANK' ERROR 1≠ρ,CONDITION
[2]    'IF:LABEL RANK' ERROR 1≠ρ,LABEL
[3]    'IF:DOMAIN' ERROR~CONDITION∈ 0 1
[4]    Z←CONDITION/LABEL
     ∇
```

```
     ∇ TEXT ERROR CONDITION
[1]    →(1≠∨/,CONDITION×CONDITION=1)/0
[2]    TEXT;'  ERROR'
[3]    →
     ∇
```

```
     ∇ Z←LABEL WHEN CONDITION
[1]    'WHEN:CONDITION RANK' ERROR 1≠ρ,CONDITION
[2]    'WHEN:LABEL RANK' ERROR 1≠ρ,LABEL
[3]    'WHEN:DOMAIN' ERROR~CONDITION∈ 0 1
[4]    Z←CONDITION/LABEL
     ∇
```

Index

Note: Page numbers in the left-hand column refer to text pages. Page numbers in the right-hand column refer to pages with figures.